WOMEN'S STUDIES QUARTERLY

VOLUME 47 NUMBERS 1 & 2 SPRING/SUMMER 2019

An educational project of the Feminist Press at the City University of New York, the College of Staten Island, City University of New York, and LaGuardia Community College, City University of New York, with support from the Center for the Study of Women and Society at the Graduate Center, City University of New York

WSQ: Women's Studies Quarterly, a peer-reviewed, theme-based journal, is published in the summer and winter by the Feminist Press at the City University of New York.

COVER ART

The Ghost by Simi Kang

WEBSITE

feministpress.org/wsq

EDITORIAL CORRESPONDENCE

WSQ: Women's Studies Quarterly, The Feminist Press at the City University of New York, The Graduate Center, 365 Fifth Avenue, Suite 5406, New York, NY 10016; wsqeditorial@gmail.com.

PRINT SUBSCRIPTIONS

Subscribers in the United States: Individuals—$60 for 1 year; $150 for 3 years. Institutions—$85 for 1 year; $225 for 3 years. Subscribers outside the United States: Add $40 per year for delivery. To subscribe or change an address, contact *WSQ* Customer Service, The Feminist Press at the City University of New York, The Graduate Center, 365 Fifth Avenue, Suite 5406, New York, NY 10016; 212-817-7915; info@feministpress.org.

FORTHCOMING ISSUES

Together, Ujju Aggarwal, The New School, Linta Varghese, Borough of Manhattan Community College, City University of New York, and Rupal Oza, Hunter College, City University of New York, consulting editor

Inheritance, Maria Rice Bellamy, College of Staten Island, City University of New York, and Karen Weingarten, Queens College, City University of New York

RIGHTS & PERMISSIONS

Fred Courtright, The Permissions Company, 570-839-7477; permdude@eclipse.net.

SUBMISSION INFORMATION

For the most up-to-date guidelines, calls for papers, and information concerning forthcoming issues, write to wsqeditorial@gmail.com or visit feministpress.org/wsq.

ADVERTISING

For information on display-ad sizes, rates, exchanges, and schedules, please write to *WSQ* Marketing, The Feminist Press at the City University of New York, The Graduate Center, 365 Fifth Avenue, Suite 5406, New York, NY 10016; 212-817-7918; sales@feministpress.org.

ELECTRONIC ACCESS AND SUBSCRIPTIONS

Access to electronic databases containing backlist issues of *WSQ* may be purchased through JSTOR at www.jstor.org. Access to electronic databases containing current issues of *WSQ* may be purchased through Project MUSE at muse.jhu.edu, muse@muse.jhu.edu; and ProQuest at www.il.proquest.com, info@il.proquest.com. Individual electronic subscriptions for *WSQ* may also be purchased through Project MUSE.

ISSN: 0732-1562 ISBN: 978-1-936932-58-0 $25.00

Contents

PART V. **POETIC WORKS**

Editor's Note

In Cristina García's novel *Monkey Hunting* (2003), the protagonist Chen Pan migrates from rural China to Cuba in 1857 via a slave ship. Pan initially works as an indentured servant on a sugarcane plantation, but later escapes. After opening a small business, he buys and marries an enslaved *mulata* and begins a family. The novel is an intergenerational story that follows Pan's granddaughter, who lives under Mao Zedong's Cultural Revolution, and his great-great-grandson, who migrates with his father to the United States and later serves in the Vietnam War. Similarly, Mira Nair's 1991 film *Mississippi Masala* is a cross-generational tale chronicling a Ugandan Indian family's forced migration to England and then to the United States. While the father, Jay, longs for his home in Uganda, his daughter Mina makes peace with their life in the United States and falls in love with an African American man. Both *Monkey Hunting* and *Mississippi Masala* offer nuanced stories of Asian diasporas in terms of migration, displacement, cultural hybridity, and interethnic relations.

These fictional narratives echo many of the themes explored in this issue. Movement to, from, and across Asia is not new. Asian diasporic communities can be found all over the globe, including Africa, the Americas, Europe, and Australia. As depicted in García's and Nair's cultural texts, Asian migration is often marked by multiple migrations over the course of a few generations. This constant movement can ferment feelings of nostalgia and loss, but migration can also be the catalyst for new forms of kinship; creative, hybrid forms of expression; and the reinvention of urban, suburban, and rural spaces. This issue of *WSQ* taps into the varied

WSQ: Women's Studies Quarterly 47: 1 & 2 (Spring/Summer 2019)

experiences of Asian diasporas around the globe through an intersectional optic that views gender and sexuality as central to the process of migration.

The label "Asian" encompasses a heterogeneous group of people with varied histories of colonization (both as the colonizer and the colonized), spoken and written languages, and cultural practices. The "push" and "pull" factors for migration also differ among Asian groups— while some migrate for more economic opportunities, others leave for political refuge. U.S. policy also shapes Asian migration. For example, the 1882 Chinese Exclusion Act in the United States and the 1923 Chinese Immigrant Act in Canada both restricted immigration from China until the 1940s. During World War II, Japanese internment in the United States cast East Asians not only as second-class citizens but also as enemies. These policies and practices cemented the image of Asians as the perpetual foreign Other in the popular imagination. As a result of the passage of the Immigration and Nationality Act of 1965, Asian migration to the United States soared to the thousands, but Orientalist discourses continued to circulate in the United States and Europe. U.S. military intervention in countries like Cambodia, Granada, the Philippines, and Vietnam also greatly influenced Asian migratory routes and patterns to the United States and other parts of the world. As such, militarization and colonialism remain a central part of the Asian diasporic experience.

While some Asian groups are considered model minorities in Europe and the United States, this framing is uneven. For example, Cambodians are one of the poorest communities in the United States. Additionally, while Asian migrants might be valued for certain kinds of gendered labor (e.g., Indian men in the technology industry or Asian-Pacific women in domestic work), they are not always welcomed into mainstream society. In addition to facing centuries-old Orientalism, contemporary Asian diasporas exist in countries that are increasingly hostile to immigrants, particularly in Europe and the United States. Ironically, Asian consumer products and practices—like Korean skin care, matcha tea, and yoga—are routinely co-opted for U.S. consumption, but Asian migrants are not necessarily welcomed. For example, Chinatowns exist globally, but some merely exist for the consumption of non-Asians with few Chinese people actually living in those areas (McDonogh and Wong 2012).

This issue reaffirms *WSQ*'s commitment to transnational feminisms. Over the last ten years, *WSQ* has published a number of pieces that examine the gendered and queer experiences of immigrants across the world. However, *Asian Diasporas* is the first issue to focus exclusively on issues of migration on a global scale. Beyond *WSQ*, it is rare that diasporas are studied outside of an Africanist or Jewish framework. The academic and creative works in this issue carefully weave together multiple narratives and ways of understanding gendered Asian diasporas. Most of the pieces in this issue theorize what Angharad Valdivia (2004) calls the "pains of hybridity," in an attempt to make sense of experiences of loss, discrimination, belonging, community, and affirmation. As we currently experience a global humanitarian crisis for refugees, this issue urges us to revisit the root causes of migration and how diasporas process grief, memory, and kinship in new spaces.

This issue was a transnational endeavor that required communication between authors and the editorial team across the country and abroad. On behalf of Natalie Havlin and myself in our roles as *WSQ* general editors, I thank guest editors Lili Shi and Yadira Perez Hazel for their vision and patience in coordinating many authors and editors across various time zones and places. We thank *WSQ*'s creative editors Rosalie Morales Kearns and Patricia Smith for editing the prose and for curating the poetry, respectively. We are especially grateful to *WSQ*'s editorial assistant Elena Cohen for shepherding the logistics of the issue from beginning to end. Thank you to *WSQ*'s social media coordinator, Kirsten Cornielson, for promoting *Asian Diasporas* online. We also appreciate the tremendous support *WSQ* receives from the Feminist Press, especially from Jamia Wilson, Lauren Rosemary Hook, Nick Whitney, Jisu Kim, Drew Stevens, Hannah Goodwin, and Lucia Brown. Dana-Ain Davis and Eileen Liang at the Center for the Study of Women and Society at the CUNY Graduate Center are also instrumental in developing and promoting each *WSQ* issue. We also extend our gratitude to the *WSQ* Editorial Board for providing early feedback about the significance and direction of the issue.

Finally, we would like to recognize the generosity of the Office of the Provost at the CUNY Graduate Center, the Office of the Dean of Humanities and Social Sciences at the College of Staten Island, and the Office of the Provost at LaGuardia Community College. The support of multiple campuses demonstrates CUNY's commitment to supporting research in women's, gender, and sexuality studies across New York City, the nation, and the world.

We dedicate this issue to the memory of *WSQ*'s beloved board member, Meena Alexander (1951–2018).

Jillian M. Báez
Assistant Professor of Communications
Department of Media Culture
College of Staten Island
City University of New York

Works Cited

García, Cristina. 2003. *Monkey Hunting.* New York: Random House.

McDonogh, Gary, and Cindy Wong. 2011. "Beside Downtown: Chinatowns and Global Downtowns." In *Global Downtowns,* edited by Gary McDonogh and Marina Peterson, 273–97. Philadelphia: University of Pennsylvania Press.

Mississippi Masala. 1991. Directed by Mira Nair. New York: Cinecom Pictures.

Valdivia, Angharad N. 2004. "Latinas as Radical Hybrid: Transnationally Gendered Traces in Mainstream Media." *Global Media Journal* 3, no. 4: 1–21.

Introduction: Locating Feminism in Asian Diasporas

Lili Shi[1] and Yadira Perez Hazel[2]

Let us begin by telling the story behind our cover art, how we think diasporic life is captured in a ghost position that orients our special issue, and how our repositioning of the ghost artwork acts metaphorically as our feminist agentive move to invite specific ways of reading and looking.

Why Asian diasporas? Why ghosts? How does the ghostliness of diaspora play into the ways we interrogate the nation and transnationalism, critique imperialism and empire, and reimagine the diasporic past, present, and future? And simultaneously, how does the ghostliness of diaspora engage feminism, gender, and sexuality? And beyond popular discourses of oppression and violence, how does a ghostly diasporic position hold feminist temporal and spatial possibilities for agency and resistance?

An amazingly creative project published in *Asian American Literary Review*, guest edited by Mimi Khúc in 2016, *Open in Emergency: A Special Issue on Asian American Mental Health* presents a deck of Asian American tarot cards, "featuring original art and text revealing the hidden contours of Asian American lives" (*Asian American Literary Review* 2016). In this deck, *The Ghost* tarot card captures an important affective and discursive trope of Asian diasporic existence as a ghostliness that we chose to visually represent our special issue. As widely studied across academic disciplines, the ghost has been an important allegorical emblem in Asian diasporas' experiences and histories (e.g., Cheng 2001; Cho 2008; Gordon 2008; Mimura 2009; Langford 2013). As one of our pieces (Liu, this issue) articulates, the "ghostly position" represents the uniquely racialized subjectivity that Asian diasporas occupy, with "loss of origin and perpetual ghostly emptiness of racial otherness." Our collection of works in this special issue

WSQ: Women's Studies Quarterly 47: 1 & 2 (Spring/Summer 2019)

inherits the diasporic ghostliness, yet with an explicitly feminist analytics. We engage Braziel and Mannur's proclamation that diaspora, as an important category of critical analysis, is always "inseparable, epistemologically or historically, from inquiries of race, gender, class, and sexuality" (2003, 5). We propose a feminist diasporic position, the feminist ghostliness, to examine Braziel and Mannur's underpinning, one that invites disruptive temporal and spatial possibilities of viewing travel, time, space, and belonging in resistance to normative nationalist and masculinist understandings of such in moments of transnationality and postcoloniality.

On our cover, we turned the vertical card sideways, placing it horizontally to capture the poetics of this issue: the disruption of spatial and geographical politics, and the subversion of the oppositional, up-and-down hierarchy between past and present, here and there, memory and present, dream and reality. Such subverted spatial politics refuse to prioritize any specific diasporic points of lineage or transgression, but compel the

The Ghost is and is not a card in the major arcana. Sometimes misinterpreted as a demon, a haint, or Death, the Ghost is your Ancestor and your shadow. The Ghost is me. Hungry, I am your history. I smuggled myself across the Pacific, searching for my husband and hoping for welcome. Instead, the sea swallowed me. Women burned money for me, offered me oranges and biscuits, bribed me to stay away. They didn't understand that the border between past and present, like all borders, is illusory. Their prayers came to me as joss smoke, which I gathered into the guise of a body. Now you glimpse me out of the corner of your eye and I look like the echo to a memory, a woman in a book you once read, a dust speck of a way of life now long gone. Don't you know I am always walking among you? I made you a person of this land. I make you a person of this land. Dear children, you who would forsake me, erase me; dear children born of my cravings who would call me just a story; you children of the future who would proclaim the past over and irrelevant, I demand you answer me one question: how have the forces of history brought you to this moment? ✻ Shawna Yang Ryan

FIG. 1. *The Ghost*, by Simi Kang, text by Shawna Yang Ryan, first published in *Open in Emergency: A Special Issue on Asian American Mental Health* (*AALR* volume 7, issue 2, Fall/Winter 2016), guest edited by Mimi Khúc.

readers to look at them holistically, side by side (e.g., hanging bodies are now floating, trees now grow sideways), preventing things from "falling through" in the endless continuation of diasporic historicity and futurity, a feminist agentic interruption of *looking at the ghost*. In so doing, we honor and ask the question from the tarot card's text: "How have the forces of history [and, we add, future] brought you to this moment?"

Transnational Feminist Diasporas as Rejection to Nationalism

The idea of this special issue evolves from Lili Shi's experience in summer 2016. A group of faculty at the City University of New York led by Soniya Munshi, Caroline Hong, Linta Varghese, and Jennifer Hayashida initiated a year-long program called "Building Asian American Studies" (BAAS) across CUNY classrooms. As participants trained in different disciplines, we discussed "Asia," "America," and "diaspora" in the contexts of world events and movements such as Brexit, the inauguration of Trump, world refugee crises, and other global concerns. We became increasingly anxious over the popular discourses that embolden the problematic binary and antagonistic thinking of national vs. alien, citizen vs. noncitizen, home vs. displaced, belonging vs. nonbelonging, and authentic vs. tainted/hybrid. With inspiration and support from the BAAS community, Lili Shi as a new board member of *WSQ* proposed this special issue on *Asian Diasporas* in fall 2017, with coeditorship with Yadira Perez Hazel at the University of Melbourne. Transcontinentally, we asked how a women's studies journal from the West operating in such seemingly dark political times could productively invite a conversation of feminism that engages scattered communities, persons, experiences, memories, and identities that go beyond the epistemologies and hegemony of the Global North. The overriding influence and power of "nation," "nation-states," and Western epistemologies privilege particular ways of knowing and knowledge production that, we as coeditors feel, fail to address the complexity, contradictions, and dynamism of Asian diasporas in a context of increased white supremacy and white ethnonational populism (Thangaraj et al. 2018; Lenneis and Agergaard 2018). In due course, we, the two editors, produce this issue to problematize the nation-centered and therefore masculinist and tyrannical imaginations of travel, community, geography, and belonging (see Manalansan 2003; George 2005; Thangaraj 2015; Gopinath 2018). We aim to do this by recentering diaspora, particularly Asian diasporas, as entry points of comparative times and spaces—an always already intersectional underpinning for investigating feminism in transgeographical and transhistorical contexts—and to protest against popular nationalist discourses.

We do not propose the conception of *diaspora* as an antithesis of nation, because that would perpetuate binary thinking. Nor do we see it merely as an unavoidable secondary trope of inquiry entangled with nation imposed by global conditions. Rather, we see it as a site of feminist inquiry in its own right. On one hand, it is a site where various gender politics interplay with transnational geopolitics and scattered hegemonies (see Grewal and Kaplan 1994; Campt and Thomas 2008); on the other, it is a site of protest and contestation of such hegemonies, including various global patriarchies or first-world White feminisms (Puar 2017). As the artist Favianna Rodriguez proclaims in her artwork featured in *WSQ*'s *Beauty* issue in spring 2018, migration and immigration are feminist issues. We echo strongly with that sentiment, and further propose that *diaspora* does the work of disrupting the cohesive nature of the nation(s) while interjecting longer transhistorical, transnational connections between Asian communities across the world.

With such orientation that destabilizes the link between identity, territory, and nation, this issue speaks to the work of Gayatri Gopinath (2018) to imagine conviviality, desires, socialities, and protest that invoke dynamic conceptions of region. By centering region, we also move beyond the masculinist colonial cartography of the world, beyond a traditional geographical notion of Asia, and instead conceptualize Asia as comparative time and space (Schlund-Vials, this issue). Thus, we then ask: What stories do we hear about diaspora when we foreground gender? What specificities of geography, history, and transnationality do we learn? What role does gender play in the transgression of the national and the diasporic? How do the studies of feminism and studies of Asian diasporas shed light on each other? What unique struggles do Asian diasporas encounter as a historically feminized group in colonialist discourse? In what light should we study Asian diasporas beyond the Global North's imaginaries of "Asia" and its related gender identities, localities, populations, and bodies? What does a feminist investigation of Asian diasporas tell us about white ethnonational populism and race?

These are the central questions that we have raised for this issue. As a point of departure, we valorize "Asian diasporas" as gendering spaces and times that intertwine stories of race, transnationalism, citizenship, and postcoloniality. We contend that "Asia" is not only a geographic term, but also a comparative one that institutes collapsing notions of time, space, and racial formations (Lowe 2015). "Asia" is the collective sum of heterogeneous racial, regional, transhistorical, and transnational politics that transcends bodies and identities of "Asia" across the Global South and North as well as global mediascapes (Hoang 2015). If "Asia" is in flux, polyvalent, and with multiple referents, this special issue embraces an expansive notion of diaspora, one that is beyond the mere causal result of travel and migration that reifies the binary of home and settlement that subsequently "privileges the mobility of masculine subjects" (Campt and Thomas 2008, 2). We propose Asian diasporas as scattered communities, identities, imaginaries, connectivities, and relationships that are beyond U.S. Black/White racial logics, while influenced and transformed by global struggles of nation, intimate relations to empire, and postcoloniality.

Some early critiques of diaspora study claim that diaspora is "theoretically studied, while methodologically indistinct and ahistorical" that "celebrate transnational mobility and the hybridity" (Robbins 1995). Deeply grounded in the rigor and mission of transnational and intersectional feminist analytics as well as the comparative racialization framework, this issue embarks upon several theoretical rejections. First, we reject essentialist notions of geography, race, ethnicity, nation, and identity. And therefore, second, we reject the binary oppositions between home/displacement, national/diasporic, national/international, Asia/West, origin/dispersed, authentic/hybrid. Third, we reject views that see diaspora as merely individuals' adventures of mobility. Instead, we contend that diasporic inquiries are always political, conditioned by global flows of capital, bodies, and desire. Fourth, we reject linear and monolithic notions of diaspora.

With these rejections, this special issue—our feminist ghostliness of Asian diasporas—also embarks on the following moments of departure. One, it spotlights diasporas as unsettled temporal, geographical, and human spaces created through relationships. As spaces of relationality, this issue interrogates the power of globalization to analyze (dis)connections in the historical and contemporary mapping of the Asian diasporas as they are imagined, constructed, and operationalized in political and popular discourse and academic scholarship. The works in this special issue invite, even possibly demand, that we reconsider the larger question of what are the physical and experiential borders of Asian diasporas with a collection of histories and critical reinvestigation of histories from those marginalized. We consider stories and histories that were ghosted by national and grand discourses that privileged the masculine, the imperial and capitalist, yet played central roles in the making of families and communities around the world.

Two, diaspora, Asian, gender, and sexuality are meant to be seen as agentive spaces to engage, expand, unsettle, and complicate academic inquiries. As such, these concepts were created to do "work" of building, constructing, exploring, identifying, and largely connecting the terrains of Asia, transnationalism, feminism, and diasporic Asianness, where (g)local power continuously acts through relationships to generate spectrums of experiences and identities.

Three, this special issue is a first in this feminist journal to create a space for reorienting the inquiry of gender and sexuality through the integration of ethnic and racial diasporic lives and discourses highlighting the multiple ways in which seemingly similar biological and cultural blocs create a continuously transforming nexus of meanings and experiences.

Diasporic Materialities and Media

We structured this special issue in several thematic parts, featuring diasporic materialities and media, diasporic geographies, diasporic critiques, and essays revisiting Aihwa Ong's classic works. In Part I, "Diasporic Materialities and Media," the three academic pieces center Asian feminist diasporic lives through subjects' multimedia and multisensory engagement with traditional artifacts and media. Through manipulations with artifacts—photocopies (Fraser), frescoes (Gunasena), and traditional music (Pillai)—that embody national and heteropatriarchal power, these studies tell agentive stories of the poetics of diaspora in subverting the mundane materiality of life, proposing materiality and mediascapes as important gendering sites of diaspora formation and feminist subjectivity negotiation.

In "Diasporic Object Lessons: Material Identity and the Korean Diaspora in the Work of Theresa Hak Kyung Cha," Alison Fraser interrogates the feminist agentic material poetics of Korean diaspora in Cha's work. By delineating Cha's artistic appropriation of low-status photocopying into bookbinding and art, Fraser makes the argument that Cha embraces the mechanical possibilities of this American duplication system while simultaneously subverting it. She proposes that Cha uses photocopies to bind cross-genre books and arts to destabilize assumptions of unimportant women's work and to resist American bureaucratic norms of citizenship. In doing so, Cha reclaims and repossesses *paperwork* as a symbol to legitimize and legalize Korean diaspora's existence by carrying and reproducing diasporic memories and stories in this "modest site of self-possession."

Similarly engaged with inquiries on materiality, Natassja B. Gunasena in her "'Something Like Kali and Durga Must've Rocked': Sri Lankan Femininity and the Poetics of Diaspora" interprets the diasporic poetics of frescoes of Sri Lanka's famous Sigiriya fortress, along with other texts and ethnographic data. Gunasena contextualizes the material poetics of the frescoes—being culturally authentic and traditional, yet which visually remain as naked and seductive female Buddhist goddesses, as transnational and commodified icons of Sri Lankan femininity that protects the nationalist patriarchy. Gunasena argues that the frescoes perform "the dual (paradoxical) function of representing the Lankan nationalist feminine against former colonial powers while also emanating the seductive appeal of exoticism that Sri Lanka offers Western tourists like many other Global South nations." Through examining another two "texts" located at various "threshold" moments in the Lankan nationalist schema—queer poetry and lived personal trajectories—Gunasena creatively delineates that Sri Lankan "homes" exist in various times and places, challenging us to transgress the national and the diasporic.

In "A Question of Voice: Indo-Caribbean American Feminism through Music in New York City," another piece that centralizes diasporic medium—through music and bodily performance—Rupa Pillai discusses the tensions and contradictions of Indo-Caribbeanness in Kathak (the traditional Indian music and dance) performers' diasporic feminist subjectivity. She argues that due to the unique historicity of "twice migration," the Indo-Caribbean women performers as "double diaspora" in the transnational music scape of Indian music in New York City are forced to centralize the *bhadramahila* or "respectable (Hindu) woman" in their performance to claim authenticity and belonging to the Indian American diaspora and to be associated with Indian Americans' model minority status in the U.S. racial landscape. In this account, multiple nationalisms and capitalist heteropatriarchies are at play, conditioning diasporic Kathak music far from being a liberating medium, but as a site of disciplining hegemonies.

Echoing with such theses of diasporic media and materialities, our two creative essays, "American Movies" by Grace M. Cho and "Facebook Mama" by Sokunthary Svay, tell stories of Asian diasporic women as active agents experiencing identities, kinships, trauma, and (non)belonging across diasporic time and space in the postwar global techno-mediascape, from Hollywood to Facebook. These two creative pieces present the sensual and affective accounts of the paradoxical functions of diasporic materialities and media as being both limiting and liberating, as presenting spaces of belonging and nonbelonging. Overall, Part I explores the material and temporal possibilities for feminist agency in Asian diasporas, as well as the labor and woes associated with such.

Diasporic Geographies

The three essays in this section valorize feminist geographies in Asian diasporas. As proposed earlier in this introduction, we see Asia as a comparative notion of time-space, and we abide by M. Jacqui Alexander's notion of "different geographies of feminism," which primarily interrogate "multiple operations of power" that are gendered and sexualized and simultaneously raced and classed "yet not practiced within the hermetically sealed or epistemically partial border of the nation-state" (2005, 268, 4). The essays in this section explore these notions in different ways.

Specifically, in a special invited piece from Cathy J. Schlund-Vials, "Diaspora Revisited: Toward a Transnational Feminist Critique," Schlund-Vials creatively conducts a paired manipulation of interpretive poetics of Monica Sok's poem "Yearning" (2016) and Audre Lorde's "Grenada Revisited: An Interim Report" (1984) to underscore the above transgeographical and transhistorical notions of feminist geography from Cambodia to Grenada. Schlund-Vials tactically highlights the feminist recollective labor that Sok and Lorde engender against nationalist and masculinist notions of geography and war. She does so by connecting the two poets' shared feminist memory-work on diasporic displacement and (non)belonging—across time and spatial borders—to U.S. militarization as an indirect consequence of "Asia-oriented" Cold War policy. In such attempts, Schlund-Vials maps Asian diasporic geographies by relating transnational feminist subjectivities in shared geopolitical conditions and poetics of (non)belonging, rejecting traditional notions of borders, nation, and time, and creating possibilities to rethink transnational feminism.

Sonja Thomas's "Cowboys and Indians: Indian Priests in Rural

Montana" challenges the dominating bicoastal geographic outlook of diasporic Asianness in the United States. Through her in-depth ethnographic research, Thomas utilizes a comparative racialization framework to expand the complexity within Asian diasporas. She contextualizes the racialization and gendering of Indian Catholic priests within unique global labor organizing and migration for faith-based communities. By engaging Asian settler colonialism and queer ruralism in her discussion, she delineates an engendering of Asian diasporic geography beyond the two coasts and beyond the U.S. racial binary of Black/White.

Another piece in this section is Diane Wong's "Shop Talk and Everyday Sites of Resistance to Gentrification in Manhattan's Chinatown." By unearthing ethnographic richness of ordinary space in the neighborhood and tracking women's everyday communication therein, Wong proposes a feminist microgeography of resistance in Chinatown against the city's capitalist and masculinist spatial violence of gentrification. She pays special attention to mundane "shop talk" and uncovers its social and political function as the foundation for feminist intergenerational grassroots action that mobilizes women in the neighborhood. She charts the diasporic Chinese women's space of consciousness and activism around "shop talk" and argues that diasporic feminist political space often exists beyond the elite level and the electoral realm, in ordinary spaces that involve intergenerational discourses of collective memory, resistance, dissent, movement, and hope for the future. This section thus subverts traditional masculinist notions of space, geography, time, and border-marking. Through the subversive transnational and translocal ways of engaging space, these articles together beg for a feminist notion of geography, a spatial/temporal logic that prioritizes shared geopolitical conditions, affect, (non)belonging, and connectivity that mobilize feminist diasporic consciousness.

Diasporic Critiques

This section gathers essays from various disciplines, especially literary criticism, that capture, highlight, or critique specific tropes of Asian diasporic discourses. Against the clichéd yet overwhelmingly popular model minority and perpetual-foreigner discourses, the essays of this section turn the reader's attention to the absent (Cassinelli), the nameless (Baksh), the unintelligible (Yeung) and alternatively, the melancholic (Liu), and the difficult and unfeeling Asian diasporas (Lee). These academic essays, along with Yeung's short story, treat gender, not only as a diasporic identity or experience under national patriarchy and racial violence, but also as an imaginative and discursive space of subversion and resistance against assimilation, against "uplift," against "being a good Asian," against the punitive neoliberal state, and in due course as an entry point of diasporic futurity (Liu).

Peggy Lee's "Turning Diaspora to Dirt: Addiction and Illness in Asian American Critique" locates the "Asian addict" in global capitalism beyond the binary conceptualization of rebel/model minority in the Asian American critical framework, and the U.S. Black/White racialization discourse. Through a reading of Nami Mun's 2008 novel *Miles from Nowhere*, where "dirt" configures as a central allegory, Lee theorizes "diasporic dirt" as a framework to challenge the rehabilitative impulse within identitarian and masculinist politics and narratives of diasporic "uplift" often valorized in Asian Americanist critique. Engaged with a feminist interrogation on diasporic women writers' texts, Lee highlights the unstable and unpredictable locations of diaspora signified by "dirt."

Anita Baksh's "'Write Us into Existence': An Interview with Sokunthary Svay" addresses the marginalized and nonexistent discourses of the lived experiences of the Khmer diaspora. The writer Sokunthary Svay, whose short story "Facebook Mama" is also featured in this special issue, protests the dominating "survivor memoirs" discourse and monolithic public knowledge about her diasporic community. She announces, "I don't want to keep talking about the Khmer Rouge. How can we imagine ourselves outside of that?" This interview highlights the writer's thoughts on absent Asianness within the hegemonic discourses and imaginaries of "Asia."

In "Narrating Against Assimilation and the Empire: Diasporic Mourning and Queer Asian Melancholia," Wen Liu denounces traditional understandings of "Asia" and "queer" as simplistic concepts of identity that promise belonging. Alternatively, through her narrative studies with queer Asian American activists involved in anti-imperialist organizing, she complicates "Asia" as a geopolitical and embodied space, and "queer" as a necessarily agentic verb. As space with an imaginative capacity, *Asia* compels diaspora to navigate affect realms of "belonging and burden, pride and shame, resilience and distress." And racialized queerness, as a verb and narrative structure, can act as an agentive strategy in engaging diasporic melancholia to escape and counter colonial patriarchy and racial violence.

To this end, Liu explores how narratives of queer grief in the framework of racial melancholia act as forms of protest against the splitting of Asian and American identity in the U.S. Empire, and in turn invites transgression, contestation, and extension of boundaries in the in-between time-space of diaspora.

Diasporic critique carries out in Cassinelli's essay as his alternative reading that centers queerness in Nora Okja Keller's 1997 novel *Comfort Women*. As many literary scholars highlight, the mother-daughter narrative—in which the daughter inherits trauma from her mother—is a common trope in novels of Asian diasporas; however, Cassinelli recontextualizes the novel's diasporic political intimacies through gender and sexuality in relation with and as responses to conditions of militarization and colonialism. He argues that tracing back the multiplicity of sexualities in Korean diaspora constitutes another genealogy of feminist critique. As such, gender and sexuality in these essays were not treated merely as tools to analyze or spaces to explore diasporic lives. Instead, gender and sexuality are seen as the very entryway, the access point, the center of inquiry that promises agency to subvert and resist, so that diaspora lives can be better seen, better articulated, and better lived, and so that the ghost is conditioned to be free.

Classics Revisited

In this section, emerging scholars engage with pivotal scholarship within the field of Asian diasporic studies. We selected Aihwa Ong's scholarship for its influence on understanding transnational citizenship and various Asian diasporic subjectivities. Ong's work reorients the supposed "Orient" by effectively pushing the fields of Asian American and Asian studies and diasporas studies to contend with the imperialistic and capitalist underpinnings of nation building and the nation's treatment of migrants. The three essays chosen for this section exhibit how Ong's works illuminate, contest, and valorize discussions of Asian diasporic subjectivity and gendered Asianness in different texts: in lived migratory experiences as Iranian New Zealanders (Rangi), in the current Burmese Rohingya Muslim refugee crisis as an effect of the totalizing U.S. humanitarian-rescue discourse (Hue), and in the diasporic tension of Asianness and belonging reshuffled in the cinematic context of *Crazy Rich Asians* (Chen).

Books in Review

We also included in our special issue a book review by Gordon Alley-Young on two books featuring transnational migratory and arranged marriages in Asian diasporas: Marian Aguiar's *Arranging Marriage: Conjugal Agency in the South Asian Diaspora* and Sari K. Ishii's *Marriage Migration in Asia: Emerging Minorities at the Frontiers of Nation-States*. Continuing the theme of agency, Alley-Young centers his review on how the two books complicate and unearth feminine agency in stereotypically oppressive spaces of marriage and citizenship within Asian diasporas.

Alerts and Provocations

Our Alerts and Provocations section of this special issue is dedicated to the memory of Meena Alexander, whose poetry and scholarship are deeply engaged with the expressions and conditions of the feminist Asian diasporas. Meena is also a longtime *WSQ* board member and peer reviewer, whose insights and mentorship have benefited generations in our *WSQ* community.

Limitations of This Issue

This special issue not only explores issues of gender and sexuality in Asian diasporas but centers them as entry points to explore feminist agency, geography, and diasporic belonging. It is, however, in no way a complete or comprehensive presentation of various methodologies and topics that engage feminism with Asian diasporas. It has its gaps and woes. When our CFP was published, we were overjoyed to receive many submissions from junior scholars and graduate students around the world. We were sad to reject those who enthusiastically presented the undervisited, some even unknown, Asian diasporic communities in the global scape, yet whose writing and research were not consistent with North American academic standards—an ultimate dilemma and challenge for feminist scholarship to engage voices from the Global South and North in postcoloniality. We also wish we had more page space to include a more diverse array of researches of Asian diasporas, methodologically and topic-wise. To name a few, we missed topics on masculinities, disability, aging, labor, and class. There were five more wonderful new books on Asian diasporas that we planned to review but could not. Two junior Asian diasporic scholars who agreed to the reviews encountered major life challenges during the process and could not commit at the end. The precarious conditions they had to face as junior international women scholars of color are constant reminders of the violence within capitalism's neoliberal order, even in academia. As we have discussed earlier, we hope our special issue does its job of building and expanding, and opens up pathways for future special issues in other journals and edited volumes, across global and local spaces, on gendered and gendering Asian diasporas.

Conclusion

In conclusion, by centralizing gender, and proposing a symbolic and agentive feminist ghost position, the essays collected in this special issue together chart a methodologically diverse and politically vivacious time-space of Asian diasporas. The key theses that emerge from these wonderful essays are twofold. One, valorizing the agentic rather than the oppressed or oppressive subjectivities and locations of diaspora is a productive orientation for feminist intellectual labor. Reterritorialization demands much more work and creativity than criticism and announcing deterritorialization. And two, focusing on the in-between, far-beyond, and rerouted gaps and transgressions of the national and the diasporic—of their "scattered hegemonies" rather than border-binding geographies and identities of home and displacement—is especially productive feminist labor in order to interrogate and protest against the endogamous discourses of patriarchy and nation, in search for feminist "diasporic points of becoming" (Liu, this issue).

Acknowledgments

This special issue of *WSQ* was indeed a transnational and transdiasporic feminist collaboration. We thank our general editors Jillian M. Báez and Natalie Havlin for introducing us (Lili and Yadira) and making this issue possible across oceans and time zones. We also thank their unwavering support and detailed guiding knowledge throughout the production process, during which we both coped with major life events, or rather, diasporic milestones: Lili gave birth to a baby boy and Yadira applied for Australian residency and was appointed to a new research position. Our special thanks goes to our editorial assistant Elena Cohen for her careful attention and responsiveness. We also thank our creative editors Rosalie Morales Kearns for editing the prose and fiction, and Patrícia Smith for curating the poetry. To the Feminist Press team, many thanks for your technical and editorial efforts, as well as your continuous work in providing a platform for which to amplify feminist perspectives from diverse walks of life. We are immensely grateful for Mimi Khúc and Lawrence-Minh Bùi Davis for letting us use the *The Ghost* tarot card from *AALR's Asian American Tarot: A Mental Health Project*. We thank Simi Kang, the image's artist, and Shawna Yang Ryan, the writer of the text for the card.

Lili thanks her colleagues at the City University of New York, especially the organizers and fellows at the Building Asian American Studies summer institute at CUNY who planted the original idea of this issue and for hosting Lili's intellectual tribe in her diasporic life. Lili thanks Gordon Alley-Young, the chair of her home department of Communications and Performing Arts at Kingsborough CUNY for being the best feminist mentor and chair, granting her a desired teaching schedule for this issue to happen, and for contributing for this issue. She thanks Maureen Minielli and Catherine Ma, from her home institution, for being the best feminist allies, listeners and problem-solvers. Lili also thanks her colleagues at her writing circle, Stan Thangaraj and Sarah Muir at City College, and Jan Padios of University of Maryland at College Park, who offered various support at multiple stages of this issue and also for being Lili's role models as exemplary feminist scholars.

Yadira would like to thank Jillian M. Báez for seeing the collaborative possibilities between Lili Shi and her, connecting them in a way that made the process of negotiating great distances and time zones a generative and fulfilling process. She would like to also thank the Indigenous Settler Relations collaboration at Melbourne University for pushing her to think deeper about the nexus points between communities who move and those who get moved or are forced to accept settlements. It is from this space that Yadira interrogates and does the work of exploring the possibilities that exist in diasporas. Yadira would like to thank her virtual writing group, Dr. Claudia Sofía Garriga-López, and Dr. Paula Sanders, who cultivate a safe, communal space for writing, growth, and healing. Finally, Yadira would like to thank Lili Shi for the intellectual foresight, effort, and skill she put forward at every step of cultivating this special issue. Not only has her family grown by one (son-shine) during the duration of this special issue, her efforts have widened the field by connecting emerging and established feminist scholars of color and the fields of diaspora, Asian, and gender studies are much stronger for it.

Lili Shi is associate professor of communication studies at Kingsborough Community College of the City University of New York. Her research focuses on transnationalism and diaspora in Brooklyn Chinatowns, particularly maternal identities in lived experiences of transnational birthing. Dr. Shi teaches culture and communication with a critical focus on gender, language, identity, and space. She was born and raised in southwest China as an ethnic Yi descendant of Yunnan Province. She is a transnational and diasporic feminist scholar, teacher, and mother. She can be reached at lili.shi@kbcc.cuny.edu.

Yadira Perez Hazel is a cultural anthropologist and honorary fellow at the School of Social and Political Science at the University of Melbourne. Dr. Perez Hazel completed a PhD in cultural anthropology at the University of Virginia and BA with honors from Cornell University. She has taught at CUNY Borough of Manhattan Community College and Hunter College in the United States; Waikato University and Auckland University in New Zealand; and the University of Melbourne in Australia. She has published on issues of national and racial identity, Asian diasporas in the Caribbean, migration, and belonging. She also continues to work with nonprofits and arts institutions on developing and conducting effective community-based research. She can be reached at yperez@unimelb.edu.au.

Notes

1. First author, cocurator of special issue articles and primary writer of introduction.
2. Second author, cocurator of special issue articles and contributor of introduction.

Works Cited

Alexander, M. Jacqui. 2005. *Pedagogies of Crossing: Meditations on Feminism, Sexual Politics, Memory, and the Sacred.* Durham, NC: Duke University Press.

Asian American Literary Review. 2016. "Asian American Tarot: A Mental Health Project." Kickstarter campaign. July 19. https://www.kickstarter.com/projects/1750978990/asian-american-tarot-a-mental-health-project.

Braziel, Jana E., and Anita Mannur, eds. 2003. *Theorizing Diaspora: A Reader.* Hoboken, NJ: Wiley-Blackwell.

Campt, Tina, and Debra Thomas. 2008. "Gendering Diaspora: Transnational Feminism, Diaspora and Its Hegemonies." *Feminist Review* 90: 1–8.

Cheng, Anne Anlin. 2001. *The Melancholy of Race: Psychoanalysis, Assimilation, and Hidden Grief.* New York: Oxford University Press.

Cho, Grace M. 2008. *Haunting the Korean Diaspora: Shame, Secrecy, and the Forgotten War.* Minneapolis: University of Minnesota Press.

George, Sheba. 2005. *When Women Come First: Gender and Class in Transnational Migration.* Berkeley: University of California Press.

Gopinath, Gayatri. 2018. *Unruly Visions: The Aesthetic Practices of Queer Diaspora.* Durham, NC: Duke University Press.

Gordon, Avery F. 2008. *Ghostly Matters: Haunting and the Sociological Imagination.* Minneapolis: University of Minnesota Press.

Grewal, Inderpal, and Caren Kaplan, eds. 1994. *Scattered Hegemonies: Postmodernity and Transnational Feminist Practices.* Minneapolis: University of Minnesota Press.

Hoang, Kimberly K. 2015. *Dealing in Desire: Asian Ascendancy, Western Decline, and the Hidden Currencies of Global Sex Work.* Berkeley: University of California Press.

Khúc, Mimi, ed. 2016. *Open in Emergency: A Special Issue on Asian American Mental Health. Asian American Literary Review* 7, no. 2 (Fall/Winter).

Langford, Jean M. 2013. *Consoling Ghosts: Stories of Medicine and Mourning from Southeast Asians in Exile.* Minneapolis: University of Minnesota Press.

Lenneis, Verena, and Sine Agergaard. 2018. "Enacting and Resisting the Politics of Belonging through Leisure. The Debate about Gender-Segregated Swimming Sessions Targeting Muslim Women in Denmark." *Leisure Studies* 37, no. 6: 706–20.

Lowe, Lisa. 2015. *The Intimacies of Four Continents.* Durham, NC: Duke University Press.

Manalansan IV, Martin F. 2003. *Global Divas: Filipino Gay Men in the Diaspora.* Durham, NC: Duke University Press.

Mimura, Glen M. 2009. *Ghostlife of Third Cinema: Asian American Film and Video.* Minneapolis: University of Minnesota Press.

Puar, Jasbir K. 2017. *Terrorist Assemblages: Homonationalism in Queer Times.* Durham, NC: Duke University Press.

Robbins, Bruce. 1995. "Some Versions of U.S. Internationalism." *Social Text* 45: 97–123.

Thangaraj, Stanley. 2015. *Desi Hoop Dreams: Pickup Basketball and the Making of Asian American Masculinity*. New York: NYU Press.

Thangaraj, Stanley, Aarti Ratna, Daniel Burdsey, and Erica Rand. 2018. "Leisure and the Racing of National Populism." *Leisure Studies* 37, no. 6: 648–61.

PART I. **DIASPORIC MATERIALITIES AND MEDIA**

Diasporic Object Lessons: Material Identity and the Korean Diaspora in the Work of Theresa Hak Kyung Cha

Alison Fraser

Abstract: Within a context where Korean identity is continually suppressed, the minutiae of material life—family photographs, diary entries, letters, official government documents—gain significance where they might otherwise be overlooked. Poet and visual artist Theresa Hak Kyung Cha regathers these materials to redefine boundaries in the diaspora. Against a backdrop of exile and separation from Korea, her mother tongue, and extended family, Cha interrogates the role materiality plays in shaping identity, memory, and the past and future, by using mundane cultural artifacts and (re)production techniques, especially photocopying (or xerography), to create documents that subvert or expand their original function. In the two-tonal medium of xerography, Cha literally challenges black-and-white notions about Korean identity, creating sites of self-possession from which she contends with exile, history, and materiality.
Keywords: Asian diaspora, identity formation, material culture, poetics, artist's books

Within a context where Korean identity is continually suppressed, the minutiae of material life—family photographs, diary entries, letters, official government documents—gain significance where they might otherwise be overlooked. Poet and visual artist Theresa Hak Kyung Cha regathers these materials to redefine boundaries in the diaspora, particularly the ownership of identity within the nonlinear movements of time and place. Born six years after the Japanese occupation of Korea had ended—a period during which use of the Korean language was forbidden—Cha immigrated with her family to the United States in 1962 (in the final years of the restrictive Johnson-Reed Immigration Act) where she assimilated to and resisted American life. Against this backdrop of exile and separation from

WSQ: Women's Studies Quarterly 47: 1 & 2 (Spring/Summer 2019)

her homeland, mother tongue, and extended family, Cha interrogates the role materiality plays in shaping identity, memory, and the past and future, by using mundane cultural artifacts and (re)production techniques, especially photocopying (or xerography), to create documents that subvert or expand their original function. In the two-tonal medium of xerography, Cha literally confronts black-and-white notions about Korean identity, creating sites of self-possession from which she contends with exile, history, and materiality.

Cha's experimentation with records, documents, and xerography, and her inclination toward book objects that cross genres and resist definition, demonstrate how the poet resists a linear conception of the Asian diaspora and reclaims the process of identity formation from centralized government-sanctioned processes. Trained as a visual artist and oriented to a transpacific perspective, Cha works the archive of history by imaging the book in multiple layers, confronting and reinscribing narratives of the diaspora. The resulting work releases historical documents from the archive. Designing books as artifacts highlights and augments the missing or abbreviated historical record of marginalized diasporic groups, while xerography provides a tool to challenge both the traditional literary marketplace and official methods of identity formation by putting into her hands the power to circulate her work and shape new identities for her family. Throughout the mid-1970s until just before the publication of *Dictée*, Cha created seven artist's books from photocopies or by photocopying—a third of the twenty-one artist's books extant in her collection at the University of California Berkeley Art Museum and Pacific Film Archive[1]—in addition to a major intermedia piece, *Chronology*.[2] These works provide an unexamined perspective on Cha's poetics and experience of citizenship and transnationalism that show how in the diaspora, the medium is not only the message but the reclamation of identity. Cha's work contains a multitude of registers that "undermin[e] any single paradigm of reading" (Yu 2009, 107). In its range of material possibilities, the text reflects the Asian American experience of a multiplicitous and sometimes contradictory identity.

Cha's work responds to the intersection of immigration law, office communication and automation, and women's labor issues, and a brief history of each of these areas helps contextualize her subversive approach. Immigration policy and office communication were and are deeply interrelated systems of control. In the aftermath of World War I, they came together in the Johnson-Reed Immigration Act (1924–1965), which emphasized "territoriality, border control, and documents" (Ngai 2004, 10). This new policy, reliant on carefully kept records, was harsh and exclusionary, and "demanded a system of visa controls to track the allocation of quotas and border surveillance to ensure that only persons with the proper documents entered the country" (2004, 17). Alongside the legal aspects of naturalization, including the requirement for original documents, which could be copied ad infinitum and retained by the state, were the ideological undercurrents of what Lisa Lowe calls "the terrain of national culture," which immerses the new immigrant "in the repertoire of American memories, events, and narratives and comes to articulate itself in the domain of language, social hierarchy, law, and, ultimately, political representation" (1996, 2). Highly regulated narratives around this terrain of national culture, coupled with systematic exclusion and duplication of state-sanctioned documents that create the subject's political identity as a U.S. citizen, develops an environment of hostility where the subject's previous memories, narratives, histories, and languages are supplanted.

Contemporaneous with this shift in naturalization practices, a related system of control was evolving in American offices. The informal system of oral communication was rapidly replaced with a complex, prescribed system of written documents in new genres readily accessible for copying, storage, and retrieval, so that "by 1920 the major elements of the modern communication system and its role as a tool of managerial control had been established" (Yates 1989, xv). Into this new workplace of increased managerial control entered women, appearing in force in the workplace during the Second World War: alongside "Rosie the Riveter" stood "Mimeo Minnie" (Meredith 1955, 299), the general office worker. After the war, women were systematically excluded from so-called male occupations and were employed predominantly in the female-dominated field of clerical work, which was particularly vulnerable to the automation of office work.[3] The increase in office place automation originated, as contemporary observers noted, from the same place from which early twentieth-century bureaucratic processes arose, "not only from a concern with increased efficiency, but also from employers' desire to expand their *control* over office employees" (Wharton and Burris 1983, 113). When women were not displaced by automation machines, including photocopiers, which were introduced to the commercial marketplace in 1959, they were the ones performing the low-skilled, low-paid work of running them.

Copies thus play a role in immigration, naturalization, and defining the place of women in the workplace, and the material significance of copies derives from these seemingly discrete but deeply interrelated institutions, particularly as it is fixed to various state apparatuses. Xerography has another political implication, one embraced by Cha: it both confronts the idea of the original or unique item, and puts the power of duplication and distribution (and therefore publication) into the hands of the individual, effectively presenting the opportunity to the general public to take roles previously held by editors and publishers, to the ire of those in traditional seats of power.[4] "Xerography is bringing a reign of terror into the world of publishing," wrote Marshall McLuhan with dismay, "because it means that every reader can become both author and publisher" (1966, 202). Publisher William Jovanovich (of Harcourt Brace Jovanovich) joined McLuhan's condemnation with the caustic evaluation that "the act of copying is indiscriminate, unselective, [and] uncompetitive. It is not a medium of art" (1971, 255). This "total revolution" necessarily posed a threat to new and old reproduction practices (McLuhan 1966, 202). What scholars and publishers like McLuhan and Jovanovich feared most was xerography's leveling power. Xerography offers the possibility of the "democratic multiple," to use Johanna Drucker's (2004, 69) phrase, because it is cheap to produce a book on a Xerox machine and easy to make many copies for distribution.

In creating identity as a Korean American in the diaspora, Cha exploits the possibilities presented by xerography as an aesthetic choice while subverting the hegemonic power structure of state documents that transforms immigrants into citizens and of traditional publication outlets through the feminized office (re)production machine of the photocopier. The photocopy's ubiquity and fungibility contributes to its dismissal as a political or artistic artifact, but, as Lisa Gitelman argues, an "interest in photocopies *as* photocopies was . . . complex and depended on xerography as an unacknowledged form of cultural production, a form of making, remaking and self-making that was framed in part by the always emergent bureaucratic norms of statecraft and citizenship" (2014, 88–89). The materiality of Cha's photocopied artist's books embraces these multiple sites of identity formation; as Joseph Jonghyun Jeon notes, "Thinking things in avant-garde Asian American poetry allows for discursive connections among otherwise disparate contexts" (2012, xxiii). In articulating a Korean American identity in these terms, Cha embraces what Christopher Lee has called the "idealized critical subject," who is able "to reveal suppressed or neglected histories and experiences of domination, knowledge that in turn becomes the basis of political contestation" (2012, 11). In doing so, the critical subject balances identities and subjectivities that may contradict or conflict. Nevertheless, our impulse is to reinscribe these divisions, and in Cha's critical reception, critics have tended to view her as either an avant-garde poet or an Asian American writer; consequently, both views have lost the full import of her message.

In her subversive and feminist act of social production in *Dictée* and her artist's books, Cha challenges the black-and-white dimensions of Korean identity as it is constructed in the United States. The frontispiece photocopy for *Dictée,* for instance, is dark and grainy, an effect of being photocopied again and again. Originally a photograph from a book, the image shows Korean graffiti found outside a Japanese labor camp that reads hauntingly, "Mother, I want to see you. I am hungry. I want to go home" (fig. 1). While xeroxes are assumed to be identical replications of an original, Cha manipulates them to confront their status as copies displaced from the original, connecting xerography to the diaspora through a shared process of distancing generations.

Fig. 1. Frontispiece of *Dictée.* Third Woman Press (1995). Image courtesy of the Poetry Collection of the University Libraries, University at Buffalo, the State University of New York.

Other critics have observed the significance of the material quality of this image. Michael Stone-Richards observes that this "first leaf . . . shows, not a photograph, but a *photocopy*, that is, an image of diminished light which is a photomechanical copy in relation to a prior image. . . . [I]t can be inferred from the image-quality and *texture* that it is the result of several copies of copies" (2009, 152). Juliana Spahr notes parenthetically that it "looks badly photocopied and several generations from the original," and the poor quality of the image "and obvious distance from the original suggests an impure product, an image that is several removes even from Cha" (2001, 150, 151). I argue that is the point to Cha's use of photocopies—that they are "several generations from the original." The idea of displacement is a recurrent, powerful theme in her work, and Cha's material poetics align with the diaspora. Both Cha and the materials that make up her work are "several generations from the original"—for her, from Korea and the Korean language, and for her work, from the piece of work (either the wall of the labor camp or the original photograph) from which it originated. The use of xerography in Cha's artist's books indicates her desire for ownership over the process of displacement as well as a desire to see or possess the original document.

For Cha, xerography was a distinctly American medium and an ideal stage of resistance against which to construct her diasporic projects, by embracing the mechanical possibilities of an American duplication system while simultaneously subverting them. In a xeroxed work *Transcription from a Friend's Memory Word for Word* (1977b), which alternates photocopied text and photographs, she interrogates reproduction while simultaneously using (re)production techniques in its composition. Cha's understanding of the past unfolds nonlinearly through many disparate players and over far-flung locations. Moving from her friend's memory in 1977 Berkeley backward to Cha's arrival in Hawai'i on August 31, 1962, the xeroxed book jumps time, geography, and multiple individuals' personal memories to create "a documentation" of the past.[5] Reflecting on her arrival to the United States, Cha reveals her childhood assumptions about her new country and specifically the "Gold Mountain," a nickname for San Francisco (where Cha eventually settled) given by Chinese immigrants:

> As a child, one imagined this "Gold Mountain"
> as having no two treasures alike.
> Instead, repetition became an inevitable

vocabulary member
Inexhaustible duplicates   self-regeneration
as necessity
This absolute wealth tyranny of objects
As force   force of the machinery (1977b, 5)

In Cha's first impression of America, repetition, not the English language, "became an inevitable / vocabulary member," and the constant reproduction of duplicates to create self-identity were a "necessity." This inorganic process seems at once terrifying and dystopian—"tyranny of objects / As force force of the machinery"—but also exciting and filled with new possibility. In a move that combines form and content, the composition of this book was made possible by the epitome of "Inexhaustible duplicates," the Xerox machine. Cha corrals the "force of the machinery" in her report of the past, bending it to work for her and outside of the system it was meant to impose.

In *Transcription,* Cha's earliest comments on reproduction and documentation reveal the tension between an identity authorized through official government channels and the desire to possess this identity for oneself. The political dimensions of xerography extend beyond its ability to circumnavigate traditional publishing outlets to its impact on official paperwork like that filled out by immigrants like Cha and her family. Gitelman theorizes that xeroxing documents can become a political act when a document is copied so many times that it cannot be suppressed, and argues that the Xerox offers for the first time a "modest site of self-possession" (2014, 17), granting an individual the ability to create and manipulate official documents. Indeed, the simple act of filing photocopied documents, Gitelman contends, has become "a means of self-possession" (2014, 93). Although the photocopy is by nature a secondary record, rather than a primary, originary record afforded intrinsic value, textual scholar Thomas Tanselle argues that "[e]ven a private xerographic copy can be a primary record if a person who used it becomes a subject of historical inquiry—or, of course, if one's topic is the history of reproductions" (1998, 100), as is the case in Cha's work. Cha's photocopied artist's books are drawn to creating these "modest sites of self-possession," though the documents she xeroxes are photographs rather than forms or paperwork, and by appropriating the machine so closely identified with women's work—the photocopier—Cha also insists on a self-possession of female identity. While both the photograph and the traditional use of photocopiers presuppose a hierarchy of agency (the photographer over the photographed, the boss over the secretary), in her xerography Cha subverts these frames.

While xeroxes attempt to create a standardized portrayal of a person or event, Cha demonstrates how they often instead highlight discrepancies in the record, particularly to citizens of the diaspora. Cha draws our attention to documents framed by "bureaucratic norms of . . . citizenship" (Gitelman 2014, 89) in a scene from *Dictée*:

> I have the documents. Documents, proof, evidence, photograph, signature. One day you raise the right hand and you are American. . . . Somewhere someone has taken my identity and replaced it with their photograph. The other one. Their signature their seals. Their own image. . . . But the papers give you away. Every ten feet. They ask you identity. (1995, 56)

This section details the malicious undercurrent of documentation: a person, perhaps Cha's mother (though her identity is left open), is stopped again and again by officials who demand to know her business and doubt that the person in the photograph is her. These officials do not "ask your identity" or "ask for your identity," but "ask you identity," suggesting through a lack of the possessive "your" that this new government identity is not hers. Rather than cement her identity, her interactions with government authorities mediated through her official paperwork begin to erode it: "They say you look other than you say. As if you didn't know who you were. You say who you are but you begin to doubt" (Cha 1995, 57). As her mother becomes a U.S. citizen, Cha charts the process in the material details (and the photocopies she still retains), emphasizing the fact that these papers at once confirm her identification with Americans and separate her from them: "identity" has been taken "and replaced . . . with their photograph," and yet "the papers give you away." These papers "give [her] away" in the sense of revealing identity but also in relinquishing her former identity or even personhood: she gives herself away to gain a documented identity.

Against this photographic anxiety, Cha creates "modest site of self-possession" in the xeroxed book *Father/Mother* (1977a) by photocopying photographs of her mother and father; these duplicate copies of her parents' physical identities insist on their individuality and on her own self-identity. This self-possession of family history has special historic significance in Korea, as F. A. McKenzie's *The Tragedy of Korea* (1908)—cited by Cha in *Dictée*—documents. After the destruction of their village in northeast Korea by the Japanese, the villagers reveal to McKenzie that they are much more concerned about the destruction of their family papers than their homes: "We are rebuilding our houses . . . but of what use is it for us to do so? I was a man of family. My fathers and fathers' fathers had their record. Our family papers are destroyed. Henceforth we are a people without a name, disgraced and outcast" (1908, 188). From this experience and others like it, McKenzie concludes that the "family record means everything to [Koreans]. When it is destroyed, the family is wiped out. It no longer exists, even though there are many members of it still living" (1908, 188). In the xeroxed book, Cha reclaims two photographs of her parents, making eight color xeroxes that alternate between a photo of her father and one of her mother. These photocopies also alternate between blue and red, rather than the standard black and white of photocopies, suggesting possible readings involving the incorporation of two of the three primary colors, the colors of the American flag, or emergency codes ("code red," "code blue"), and above all foreclosing on the acceptability of a black-and-white construction of Korean identity. The book is bound between covers made of a manila envelope, which suggests communication between two separate points. These images are thought to have been taken prior to the Cha's exile from Korea, before they arrived in the United States (1977a). Although the work contains only one source photograph of each of her parents, Cha manipulates the photocopying process to change the images, creating subtle differences in light and texture from page to page. The pages of *Father/Mother* become increasingly longer as the book proceeds, creating the impression of file folder tabs that make each individual page accessible at once (figs. 2A and 2B). In *Father/Mother,* Cha confronts the anxiety she expresses in *Dictée,* that "somewhere someone has taken my identity and replaced it with their photograph," and claims for these photographs their rightful identities, emphasized through repetition (1995).

Cha's interest in likeness and duplication through xerography stems in part from the demands of diasporic assimilation—both the ideological need to fit in with a new culture and the bureaucratic need to possess paperwork that legitimizes and legalizes one's existence. The process of becoming documented is a fundamental identity shift, as Cha recounts in *Dictée*:

Fig. 2A (right). Theresa Hak Kyung Cha: *Father/Mother* (detail), 1977; artist's book; 6.5 x 9.5 in.; University of California, Berkeley Art Museum and Pacific Film Archive; gift of the Theresa Hak Kyung Cha Memorial Foundation.

Fig. 2B (opposite). Theresa Hak Kyung Cha: *Father/Mother* (detail), 1977; artist's book; 6.5 x 9.5 in.; University of California, Berkeley Art Museum and Pacific Film Archive; gift of the Theresa Hak Kyung Cha Memorial Foundation.

> Every ten feet they demand to know who and what you are, who is represented. The eyes gather towards the appropriate proof. Towards the face then again to the papers, when did you leave the country why did you leave this country why are you returning to the country.
>
> You see the color the hue the same you see the shape the form the same you see the unchangeable and the unchanged the same you smell filtered edited through progress and westernization the same you see the numerals and innumerables bonding overlaid the same, speech, the same. (1995, 57)

Even those checking the paperwork are disembodied, described only as "the eyes." Insisting almost desperately—six times in one paragraph—that despite all this, everything is still "the same," Cha reveals the loss of agency implicit in this transformation. Although Cha claims that in this process "you see the color the hue the same"—or in other words, your perception of the world does not change—the alternating, unnatural colors applied to her parents' portraits in *Father/Mother* suggest otherwise, demonstrating that a person changes in being documented across borders. Each portrait of her father and mother is ostensibly the same, but through Cha's manipulation of xerography, she insists that stasis is not available.

Stasis in the diaspora is rejected again in *presence/absence* (1975),

which, like *Father/Mother,* also confronts the tension that is created from Cha's attempt at photocopied self-possession; though *presence/absence* insists on the presence of the family unit, it equally insists on its absence through a corruption of the xeroxes, suggesting by extension that something is lost in the process of duplication. Bound as a book between black covers, the thirty-six pages are black-and-white photocopies of one photocopy of a photograph of Cha and her siblings.[6] Unlike *Father/Mother,* where the photocopied photographs remain in the same position on the page, though the ink color and lighting change, in *presence/absence* the photograph moves farther and farther to the left and into the gutter—therefore not copying the image in its entirety, which is the opposite of the goal of photocopying—until the image completely disappears (fig. 3B). As the book progresses and the family portrait slides more and more into the book's gutter, the blank space left in its absence is filled with residue from the photocopying process. Unlike the photocopies of her parents in *Father/Mother,* the photocopied portrait of Cha's family is almost completely washed out, leaving the viewer, in the end, with their absence (fig. 3A).

presence/absence provides a commentary on Cha's attempt at reconstituting the family unit as it was in Korea, ultimately concluding that it is a failed task; at the same time, she offers the family a new identity. The sense of displacement that Cha expresses throughout her work is not defused,

Fig. 3A. Theresa Hak Kyung Cha: *presence/absence* (detail), 1975; artist's book; 11.25 x 8.75 in.; University of California, Berkeley Art Museum and Pacific Film Archive; Theresa Hak Kyung Cha Fund Purchase.

in large part due to the faded portrait but also to its displacement on the page, and its replacement with moiré (large-scale interference) patterns. In order to achieve this grainy effect, two patterns must converge which are not identical but similar and are displaced from one another. While this is an undesirable mistake in office photocopying, for Cha this process replicates in material form the idea that the family (which is composed of individuals who while not identical are similar) has become displaced from each other.[7] In *presence/absence*, the reprehensible error of the secretary becomes an opportunity for poetic expression and political commentary. Cha manipulates the photocopying process by increasing the image density far above standard, creating shadows and a "dirty" quality to the pages, which are deliberately not crisp. The effect is a textual quality of the photocopy that suggests the swirls of a fingerprint, the standard identifier. These patterns grow more distinct as the photocopied photograph wanes in intensity until it has almost disappeared. Likely the image of Cha's family was made from a photocopy several times removed from the original: the figures appear in outline only, looking more like crude drawings than a photographic reproduction, and further emphasize Cha's feeling of displacement, since the image is not accessible even to her (fig. 3B).

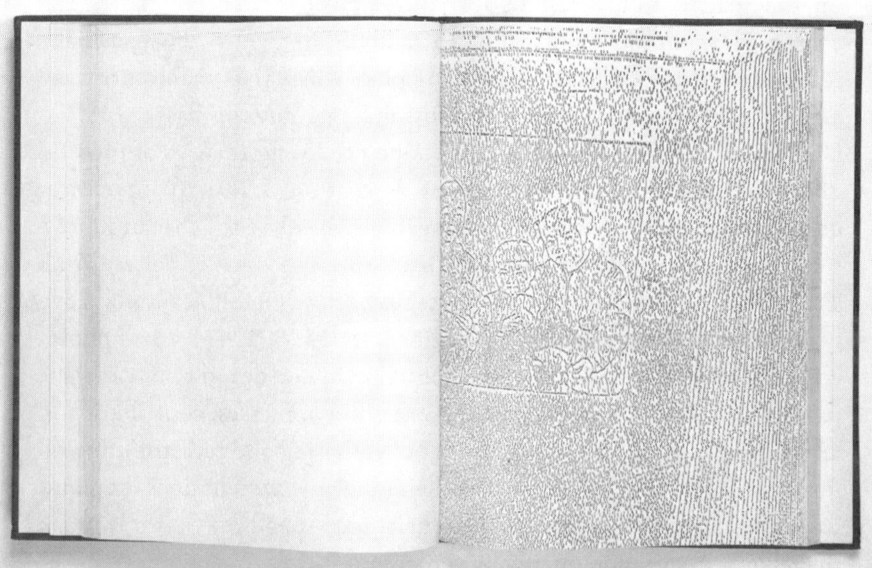

Fig. 3B. Theresa Hak Kyung Cha: *presence/absence* (detail), 1975; artist's book; 11.25 x 8.75 in.; University of California, Berkeley Art Museum and Pacific Film Archive; Theresa Hak Kyung Cha Fund Purchase.

Although each page taken individually offers a reading that separates Cha from her family, the xeroxed book is designed to recreate the nonlinear movements of those in the diaspora. The pages of *presence/absence* are individually static but collectively dynamic; a person flipping through the pages quickly would create a flip-book, showing the family portrait slowly emerging from the center of the book's binding. With the reader setting it into action, the pages of the book, which act like film stills, transform in movement[8]; the image of Cha and her siblings emerges from the book's gutter and advances across the page, ending in the center. In this way, the reader approaches the book from the back, forward, echoing Cha's description of returning to Korea in "Exilée":

> Backwards, from backwards from the back way back. to This. This
> phantom image/non-images
> almost non-images without images each ante-
> moment no more no more a moment
> a moment no duration no time. phantom no visible
> no name no duration no memory no reflection no echo (1980, 143)

Flipping backward through a book with "almost non-images," faded and corrupted by photocopying, with "no name[s]" to identify the figures, the reader struggles like Cha to get back to a place where the "phantom image/non-images" were once solid and colorful. Regarding this passage of "Exilée," Lawrence Rinder argues, "Any hope of closing the gap of physical distance is washed away in a flood of abnegation" (2001, 16). *presence/absence,* on the other hand, offers hope if one is willing to move in a direction contrary to assumed wisdom. Discussing the voice of *Dictée,* Trinh T. Minh-ha observes that it "slowly repeats, slowly modifies itself, slowly disintegrates, and then, slowly begins anew" (2001, 47). Cha's photocopies achieve the same effect visually. Cha intercedes in a bureaucratic paper trail and uses bureaucratic reproduction processes, contributing to an ongoing material production event of gathering and redistributing information about herself and her family as the government does the same. In other words, Cha confronts the official record and rewrites it through the recontextualization offered by xerography.

Copying is a central action in our lives; as Hillel Schwartz notes, "Copying makes us what we are . . . our languages [take shape] from the mimicry of privileged sounds. . . . To copy cell for cell, word for word, image for image, is to make the known world our own" (1996, 211). Expressing a desire for alternative publication and archival outlets, and understanding the importance of scraps, ephemera, and, most of all, twentieth-century documentary culture (including familial photographs and letters, bureaucratic photocopies and other paperwork, and women's place within the bureaucracy), the work of Cha insists on its own materiality. By appropriating the low-status work of photocopying and elevating it to the status of bookmaking and art, she destabilizes assumptions regarding the inferiority and unimportance of this work, and redefines women's position in the workplace. Cha tells stories of transnationalism, citizenship, and postcoloniality through the bureaucratic tool of photocopying, subverting the standardizing reproduction medium to open up new possibilities for self-possession and identity formation in the diaspora.

Alison Fraser is assistant curator of the Poetry Collection of the University Libraries at the University at Buffalo, the State University of New York. She has edited *The Collages of Helen Adam* and other collections of Adam's work appearing in the *Chicago Review* and *Paideuma: Modern and Contemporary Poetry and Poetics*. Her current project is tentatively titled "Homemade Books: A Twentieth-Century Literary History." She can be reached at awfraser@buffalo.edu.

Notes

1. These artist's books are *absence* (1975), *presence/absence* (1975), *une action, une image* (1976), *Earth* (1976), *Father/Mother* (1977), *Population Ring* (1977), and *Untitled (the sand grain story)* (1980).
2. *Chronology* (1977) combines photographs found in *Father/Mother* and *presence/absence*, as well as photos not seen in her other work. Meant to hang on a wall, rather than be bound in a book, the pages of *Chronology* are photocopied, each with an image in indigo ink and a caption beneath in haphazard fonts.
3. In 1979 women represented over 80 percent of clericals, and in the two largest categories, secretaries and typists, women represented over 99 percent and 96 percent respectively (Wharton and Burris 1983, 113).
4. "In contrast to press copying or mimeographic reproduction," records archivist James O'Toole writes, "xerography did not require the intent to make a copy at the time one made an original. One no longer had to make that original in a particular way, using specific materials (special inks, for example) in order to be able to make a copy of it" (1994, 647–48).
5. In her artist's statement for the work, Cha explains that *Transcription* "is a documentation, a recording of events that has occurred in the past" (n.d.).
6. Cha's archivists suggest that "the photograph was possibly shot after their exile from Korea before their arrival in the U.S."—unlike the photographs in *Father/Mother*, which were likely taken in Korea (1975).
7. Other work by Cha also incorporates visual distortion; see for example the video *Mouth to Mouth* (1975), which shows Cha silently mouthing the eight Korean graphemes as video snow covers the image.
8. Perhaps not incidentally, Cha's films are most frequently composed of a series of stills.

Works Cited

Cha, Theresa Hak Kyung. 1975. *presence/absence.* The Theresa Cha Collection. Berkeley: University of California Berkeley Art Museum and Pacific Film Archive.

———. 1977a. *Father/Mother.* The Theresa Cha Collection. Berkeley: University of California Berkeley Art Museum and Pacific Film Archive.

———. 1977b. *Transcription from a Friend's Memory Word for Word.* The Theresa Cha Collection. Berkeley: University of California Berkeley Art Museum and Pacific Film Archive.

———. 1980. "Exilée." In *Hotel,* edited by William Reese, 133–90. New York: Tanam Press.

———. 1995. *Dictée*. Berkeley, CA: Third Woman Press.

———. n.d. "Untitled nd 1992.4.321." The Theresa Cha Collection. Berkeley: University of California Berkeley Art Museum and Pacific Film Archive.

Drucker, Johanna. 2004. *The Century of Artists' Books*. New York: Granary Books.

Gitelman, Lisa. 2014. *Paper Knowledge: Toward a Media History of Documents*. Durham, NC: Duke University Press.

Jeon, Joseph Jonghyun. 2012. *Radical Things, Radical Forms: Objecthood in Avant-Garde Asian American Poetry*. Iowa City: University of Iowa Press.

Jovanovich, William. 1971. "The Universal Xerox Life Compiler Machine." *The American Scholar* 40, no. 2: 249–55.

Lee, Christopher. 2012. *The Semblance of Identity: Aesthetic Mediation in Asian American Literature*. Stanford, CA: Stanford University Press.

Lowe, Lisa. 1996. *Immigrant Acts: On Asian American Cultural Politics*. Durham, NC: Duke University Press.

McKenzie, F. A. 1908. *The Tragedy of Korea*. New York: E. P. Dutton & Co.

McLuhan, Herbert Marshall. 1966. "Address at Vision 65." *The American Scholar* 35, no. 2: 196–205.

Meredith, Mamie J. 1955. "'Mimeo Minnie,' 'Sadie, the Office Secretary,' and Other Women Office Workers in America." *American Speech* 30, no. 4: 299–301.

Minh-ha, Trinh T. 2001. "White Spring." In *The Dream of the Audience*, edited by Constance Lewallen, 33–50. Berkeley: University of California Berkeley Art Museum.

Ngai, Mae M. 2004. *Impossible Subjects: Illegal Aliens and the Making of Modern America*. Princeton, NJ: Princeton University Press.

O'Toole, James M. 1994. "On the Idea of Uniqueness." *The American Archivist* 57, no. 4: 632–58.

Rinder, Lawrence R. 2001. "The Plurality of Entrances, the Opening of Networks, the Infinity of Languages." In *The Dream of the Audience*, edited by Constance Lewallen, 15–31. Berkeley: University of California Berkeley Art Museum.

Schwartz, Hillel. 1996. *The Culture of the Copy: Striking Likenesses, Unreasonable Facsimiles*. New York: Zone Books.

Spahr, Juliana. 2001. *Everybody's Autonomy: Connective Reading and Collective Identity*. Tuscaloosa: University of Alabama Press.

Stone-Richards, Michael. 2009. "A Commentary on Theresa Hak Kyung Cha's *Dictée*." *Glossator* 1: 145–210.

Tanselle, G. Thomas. 1998. *Literature and Artifacts*. Charlottesville, VA: Bibliographical Society of the University of Virginia.

Wharton, Amy, and Val Burris. 1983. "Office Automation and Its Impact on Women Workers." *Humboldt Journal of Social Relations* 10, no. 2: 112–26.
Yates, JoAnne. 1989. *Control through Communication: The Rise of System in American Management.* Baltimore: Johns Hopkins University Press.
Yu, Timothy. 2009. *Race and the Avant-Garde: Experimental and Asian American Poetry since 1965.* Stanford, CA: Stanford University Press.

"Something Like Kali and Durga Must've Rocked": Sri Lankan Femininity and the Poetics of Diaspora

Natassja B. Gunasena

Abstract: Reading feminist scholarship, ethnographic work, poetry, and personal narrative together, this essay charts a Sri Lankan "poetics of diaspora" to trouble the perceived gap between national and diasporic, Afro and Asian, feminine and transgressive. In so doing, this essay attempts to craft an interdisciplinary reading praxis that accounts for the complexities of Sri Lankan female subjectivity both nationally and diasporically.
Keywords: Sri Lanka, Sigiri frescoes, Sigiriya, Kali, Leah Lakshmi Piepzna-Samarasinha, South Asian nationalism, lesbianism, poetry, diaspora, femininity, anti-Blackness, Caribbean, Orisha

O my America! my new-found-land,
My kingdom, safeliest when with one man mann'd,
My Mine of precious stones, My Empirie,
How blest am I in this discovering thee!
—*John Donne, "To His Mistress Going to Bed"*

there is an unexploded landmine heart in us
under every breast chest
waiting for breath
tears a moan
to crack the land open
and let the stories come walking
out of the scar.
—*Leah Lakshmi Piepzna-Samarasinha,*
"Landmine Heart"

WSQ: Women's Studies Quarterly 47: 1 & 2 (Spring/Summer 2019)

A nation is enlivened by symbols. The symbolic gives meaning to the material and structural forces by which governing powers shape emerging nation-states and marshal their subjects into a collective consciousness which might constitute national identity. Female subjects of a nation often dwell in this complex and opaque terrain between the symbolic and the material, having to contend with the discursive limits of nationally sanctioned womanhood on the one hand and the danger in transgressing these limits on the other. Furthermore, these conditions gain new urgency during times of heightened upheaval: the withdrawal of an official colonial power, the establishing of a new country, ethnic violence and civil war. Anne McClintock describes how, during the advent of the colonial project, European male cartographers "ritualistically feminized borders and boundaries," installing female icons at "the ambiguous points of contact" and deploying feminine images as "mediating and threshold figures by means of which men oriented themselves in space" (2015, 24). This essay is concerned with such "mediating and threshold figures" of Sri Lankan national identity, specifically with the ways Sri Lankan women's subjectivity challenges and disrupts "the borders and boundaries" of nationalist hegemonies. Through examining three "texts" located at various "threshold" moments in the Lankan nationalist schema—the frescoes of Sri Lanka's famous Sigiriya fortress; my personal experience as a Sinhala-Buddhist, diasporic, lesbian subject; and the poetry of mixed-race, queer, diasporic poet Leah Lakshmi Piepzna-Samarasinha—this study articulates a Sri Lankan poetics of diaspora as an alternative to patriarchal, endogamous discourses of Sri Lankan nationhood and identity.

"Poetics of diaspora" is a term with cartographic purpose, mapping the migratory routes of those Asian subjects too often elided from traditional conceptualizations of Asian diasporas: the South Asian, the feminine, the queer, the Afro. It owes its conceptualization to Édouard Glissant's (1997) "poetics of relation," which he proposed as a framework for understanding the multiplicities of Caribbean subjectivity. The work of a poetics of diaspora is a "dialectics of rerouting": looking beyond traditional archives to those feminized symbols, iconographies, metaphors, images, and material cultures that circulate among both Atlantic and Indian Ocean diasporas (Glissant 1997, 16). It locates along this queerly plotted map what Black Caribbean feminist M. Jacqui Alexander calls "geographies of origin" that are historically and contemporarily overlapping (2005, 268) and argues for putting Sri Lanka in conversation with Black/Caribbean studies, both as an aesthetic and a political project that recognizes that not all Asian migration westward has been successful or even entirely voluntary, and that African slaves were also transported east to locations like Sri Lanka and the Maldives. It argues that placing these alternative routes and subjects of Asian diaspora in conversation with Black diasporic feminisms and queer studies might be generative and even transformative in that such conversations would necessitate a reformulation of Sri Lanka's currently insular and marginalized position within global Asian diasporas. This is not to suggest that diasporic voices evince a more expansive or "progressive" worldview than national ones, but rather to put diasporic women's expressive forms in conversation with national subjects' and to uncover the parallels and divergences, the weaving and departing, that constitute the fabric of Sri Lankan women's worldmaking. To map this fabric not only challenges hegemonic understandings of Sri Lankan femininity but also expands the scope of Sri Lankan womanness itself as a political and cultural project by gesturing toward its entanglement in global political economies.

When considering transnational, commodified icons of Sri Lankan femininity, the Sigiri frescoes spring prominently to mind. "Discovered" in 1875 by T. H. Blakesely, the frescoes perform the dual—if somewhat paradoxical—function of representing the Lankan nationalist feminine while also emanating the seductive appeal of exoticism that Sri Lanka, like many other Global South nations, offers Western tourists. This seeming paradox arguably resulted from the conditions under which the frescoes were contemporarily "discovered." I say "discovered" here not to elide a history of indigenous knowledge but to highlight Malathi de Alwis's argument that the Sigiri women in the Lankan popular imagination are best understood as a "colonial production, subsequently appropriated and contested by nationalists" (1996, 90). The discovery, restoration, and popularization of the frescoes occurred in the midst of rising nationalist sentiment and waning British authority, at the "threshold" of a new national identity. In many ways, the Sigiri frescoes offered the perfect symbolic field through which the new nation-state could articulate its existence, but not before they were marshalled into an appropriate nationalist framework of remembrance. Subsequently, the "struggles for interpretive power" ensued in a process of mutuality: the gendered, racial, and economic concerns of the emerging nation were retroactively mapped onto the frescoes, and the frescoes in turn gained life through nationalist desires (Franco 1989, ix).

The new state enlivened itself with feminine icons of a storied past, and the icons took shape in the contemporary Sri Lankan imaginary.

The discursive limits imposed on the frescoes by male nationalist scholars were threefold: they must be sexually circumspect, ethno-racially Aryan/Sinhalese, and answerable to patriarchal, heteronormative power. This proved a particular challenge as the women depicted in the frescoes were, in appearance, either bare breasted or very scantily clothed, drawn to emphasize the curving swell of breast, hip, and neck, inviting the gaze to linger on these voluptuary delights, while their varying hues of skin and hair evinced multiraciality. Finally, no images of men accompany them, such that the women in the frescoes seem sapphically content to share the flowers, food, and fruit they carry with each other. The very real possibility that they constituted the royal harem has been summarily dismissed from official studies, with some male scholars arguing that they were a party of courtly wives and maidens en route to a religious festival, while others insisted that these women were in fact not human women at all, but *apsaras* (celestial cloud and air spirits that take the shape of beautiful young maidens) gathered to bless and protect their king's reign (de Alwis 1996, 99–100). Meanwhile, English archaeologist H. C. P. Bell, and the self-styled "first" Sri Lankan anthropologist Nandadeva Wijesekera, both promulgated a system of racial stratification regarding the frescoes that not only girded colonial formulations of race but fortified upper-caste Sinhala-Buddhist hegemonies of Sri Lankan identity. Both based their conclusions on what they claimed was a depicted, colorist division of labor, with Bell stating that "the serving maids of 'unattractive mien' had been given a 'greenish complexion' as a 'badge of servitude' which clearly marked them off [from] . . . their 'mistresses' who were 'pale yellow blondes' or 'orange-hued brunettes'" (de Alwis 1996, 99). Wijesekera went even further according to de Alwis, who writes, "The Aryan typology he culled from these paintings included the 'more superior' features: long face, straight nose, delicate features and athletic body as opposed to the Dravidian typology: *largeness of frame, thick lips, dark eyes* and *matronly features*" (1996, 102; emphasis mine). This schema sought not only to cull "Aryan superiority" from the frescoes, but specifically to repudiate features colonially ascribed to Black women from the nationalist feminine imaginary (Hobson 2018).

This imaginary is cultivated and sustained through living female bodies. I come from a family of women who exactingly, lovingly, sometimes traumatically cultivate the perfection of a nationalist feminine. My grandmother, with her oval face and slender beauty, had never worked outside the home when she was widowed with five children and forced to sell her trousseau to support her family. Her daughters, all beautiful, all named after native flowers, leveraged their carefully curated femininity to secure wifely futures within a patriarchal schema. *Manage your hair, always wear perfume, never leave the house looking less than polished*: these were some of the tenets of the feminine ideal that was my family's only seeming currency. But there were other, more insidious laws too, ones governing weight, hair texture, and skin tone. *Fair and beautiful* versus *dark but attractive* were phrasings I grew up with alongside admonishments to stay out of the sun. Feminine curvaceousness was acceptable, but fatness was openly and harshly discouraged. Style and elegance in dress were revered, but overtly sexual displays were quickly stifled. Beauty and femininity were foregrounded as vital resources, but education and culturedness were also required. And of my female cousins, none exemplified these exacting requirements so perfectly as Sharani *akki,*[1] my elder by two years. Slender and golden skinned, gifted with a dancer's grace and long, rippling, silken hair, she seemed a Sigiri fresco come to life. Sharani akki was also an exemplary student, poised for academic success. Her death from dengue fever at the age of twelve devastated my maternal family. She died, and the dubious crown passed to me, now the oldest girl of a retinue of largely female cousins. Like the golden ankle bells she sometimes wore around the house whose delicate sound followed her everywhere, her absence trailed ahead of me, marking an enigmatic gap it seemed I could never fill.

I was a diligent student, but I had not inherited her slender form; my hair was too coarse and curly, my body too thick. Nevertheless, I was determined to fill the role of a successful and respectable Sri Lankan woman as envisioned by my family, and this determination saw me through four years of college in wintry Minnesota, and through a few more years of an emotionally and sexually abusive heterosexual marriage to a man. Our wedding took place, at my insistence, in Sri Lanka. I chose to wear the traditional *ossariya,* with white flowers in my hair and jewelry in the shape of golden lotuses. I was, on that day, as beautiful as I could ever hope to become in the shadow of nationalist, ethnic expectations. When less than a year later I was forced to confront the realities of my marriage and my own sexuality, I was first and most strongly apprehended by a fear of betraying familial expectations and, in doing so, betraying a part of my Sri Lankanness itself. "Anticolonial nationalism had taught us well about heterosexual loyalty, a need so great that it reneged on its promise of self-determination," writes Alexander, regarding her own terror about her lesbianism and "the fears of a dutiful daughter's jeopardizing middle-class respectability" (2005, 260–61). As a Sinhala-Buddhist woman from a middle-class family, the oldest girl in a family of complicatedly resilient women, confronting those fears meant reckoning with the ways I had been personally and politically defined within a model of Sri Lankan femininity that the Sigiri frescoes purportedly exemplify.

On a summer's night in 2014, as my mother looked on in confusion and disapproval, I cut off my long hair and threw it into the sea. Folded inside the offering, I also threw away my wedding ring. I remember a deep feeling of unmooredness, of a body stripped clean but also newly vulnerable. In *Pedagogies of Crossing,* Alexander (2005) charts a Black feminist politics of memory and rememory that foregrounds materiality and the body. Beginning with an analysis of erotic autonomy and patriarchal nationalisms in the Bahamas, Alexander carefully details her personal, political, and spiritual journey to and through Black Atlantic feminisms. Invoking the transformative work of Black, Xicana, and Indigenous women in the North Americas that first politicized her, she then remarks on her feelings of (dis)belonging to her native Bahamas and her eventual commitment to Afro-Atlantic spiritual systems as epistemological praxis. In the Lucumi religion of Orisha worship, originating in the Yoruba kingdoms of Nigeria and dispersed across the Atlantic world in the bodies and memories of enslaved peoples, Alexander locates a system of thought that models what Sri Lankan/Africana scholar Sureshi M. Jayawardene calls an Afrocentric epistemology constituted by the "coexisting nature of spirit, rhythm, and creativity" (2013, 700):

> The Divine knits together the quotidian in a way that compels attunement to its vagaries, making this the very process through which we come to know its existence. It is, therefore, the same process through which we come to know ourselves, as in the words of María, an espiritista: "Yo soy mis santos; mis santos soy yo" (I am my saints; my saints are me). How does one come to know oneself through and as Saints or Spirits? How does one not know oneself without them? What kind of labor makes this intelligibility possible? (Alexander 2005, 293)

Within this belief system, the body—and women's bodies—are not abstract symbols but key sites of knowledge production and esoteric realization. Unlike European imperial imaginaries that transposed feminine attributes onto ostensibly passive landscapes, Afro-Atlantic cosmological systems situate the body within an interconnected, dynamic system of nature, spirit, and flesh. When an "espiritista" channels spirits through her body, she taps into a web of transhistorical memory constituted by every form of life, from the leaves on the trees to the small creatures in the soil, to the unknown depths of the living ocean and the ancestors whose essence survived against all odds. According to this epistemic framework, the landscapes of our countries are more than mere earth and water, but repositories of memory. In the same vein, our bodies and our desires are not simply biological impulses, but pangs of consciousness that can lead us into deeper truths about who we are and how we choose to love. A Sri Lankan poetics of diaspora here is similarly about the "kind of labor [which] makes this intelligibility possible" (Alexander 2005, 293).

Ethereal and reified though they might appear, the Sigiri frescoes nevertheless labor to define and sustain the nation via discursive and economic means. De Alwis points out how the same state that routinely chastises women about modest dress, that publicly condemns their sexual displays, and more recently outlawed their right to purchase liquor (Agence France-Presse 2018), nevertheless "blithely touts the bare-breasted Sigiri women to the tourists" (1996, 105–6). And, when visitors walk the pathways leading to the frescoes, they are greeted by stall after stall peddling Sigiri-themed merchandise that traffics in the frescoes' imagery: "The most abundant items on display here are postcards of the Sigiri maidens and various souvenirs that are inscribed with their forms" (de Alwis 1996, 106). Living constantly at the "dangerous threshold" of war, Sri Lankan Tamil communities in the island's north also apprehended femininity and womanness in response to the chaos of destruction, but with a difference. With most Tamil men conscripted to the armed forces or imperiled by government campaigns of unlawful arrest and torture, Tamil women took up the task of maintaining communal bonds and collective identity in the face of impending annihilation. They performed this labor, Patricia Lawrence (2003) details, through worship and ritual engagement of the goddess Kali. Known alternatively as Pattirakaliyaman, Virakaliyamman, and Viramahakali, this goddess who is both protective mother and ferocious warrior is called upon by her *teyvam atumakkal* (deity dancers) and *vakku solluratu* (oracles) to ritually possess their bodies and speak through their mouths to her followers: Tamil men and women whose families have all been intimately touched by torture, violence, and death. In her ethnographic work, Lawrence witnessed the vakku solluratu, under possession by the goddess, answer her devotees' questions about the fate of sons, brothers, and husbands taken and imprisoned by government forces. In other instances, male devotees recounted Kali's intervention in procuring their release from imprisonment, and women whose family members returned safely propitiated the goddess through ritual mortification of their bodies in tribute to Kali's protection. Lawrence describes these acts as a kind of resignification of the terms of embodiment, a means by which people living under conditions of terrifying violence impose a sense of meaning to their lives and wrest back of the terms of subjectivity: "Torture is used to control 'punishable' people, to force them into submissiveness and obedience, but through ritual ceremonies that dignify the violated body-self . . . [the] body is resignified" (2003, 114). In a context where torture exposes the penetrability of all bodies, male and female, penetrability itself is resignified as transformative, even liberatory. Being comprised of women, the vakku sollaratu and teyvam attumakal reroute the openness of their bodies as vessels through which Kali bestows blessing, enunciates her demands, discloses the fate of disappeared family members, and bears witness to a community's collective trauma and grief. In the south, the Sigiri frescoes in both their divine and material capacity labor to uphold nationalist imaginaries and appeal to tourists, and in the north venerated feminine imaginaries perform the deeply vital labor of returning meaning to lives devastated by war.

During my childhood in Sri Lanka my family made the annual pilgrimage to Kataragama—a site of both Buddhist and Hindu veneration on the island—several times. The pilgrimage involved propitiating the gods and goddesses with various offerings ranging from fresh fruit to precious metals. Amid the haze of a child's recollection, I remember stepping into Kali's *devale* (shrine). I remember staring in awe at the floor-to-ceiling image of Daksinakali—Kali in her most iconic pose: standing in a cemetery of slain enemies, sword coated in blood, chest adorned with a garland of skulls, one foot balanced on the prostrate form of her husband Siva. It was Kali—not Lakshmi with her rain of golden coins, nor Durga in her royal-magenta sari, or even serene Saraswati with her lotus and sitar—I remember most vividly. She indexed, I now realize, more terrifying realities surrounding

Sri Lankan womanhood than my sheltered and naive Sinhalese childhood allowed. Shortly after, the civil war between Sinhalese government forces and Tamil separatists resulted in a spate of suicide bombings, including the assassination of prominent Sinhalese minister Gamini Dissanayake. In the weeks following his assassination, government officials photographed the severed head of an unidentified Tamil woman believed to have carried out the bombing and proliferated the image in posters across the capital, asking anyone who recognized her to come forward with information. No one in my family can recall this poster, nor have I been successful in tracing an official record of its existence. During those long years of terror and violence, with the fantasied image of a united Sri Lanka fracturing around us, the figures "mediating" boundaries of national identity grew equally uncertain. The conflict precipitated an exodus across the globe: Tamil families victimized by ethnic violence to Canada and Australia, and working-class Sri Lankan women as domestic workers to the newly rich Gulf countries (Ukwatta 2010). Though I had also seen the Sigiri frescoes as a young child, when I think of those last years in Sri Lanka, the quiet, quotidian encroachment of war and the eruptions of world-altering violence in the lives of Sri Lankan women, the figure that arises at the "dangerous threshold" is no ethereal apsara but Kali, garlanded in skulls, smiling with her foot upon the torso of the universe.

Some archaeologists speculate that during the height of its power, the Sigiri fortress featured over five hundred frescoes. The frescoes' chamber is accessed through a path flanked by a stretch of rock termed the "mirror wall" for its smooth, highly reflective surface that, in its glory days, multiplied and reflected the women's images to surround ascendants with visions of entrancing, divine beauty. In subsequent years, as the wall faded, visitors carved ardent poetry in honor of the frescoes across its surface, largely written in what scholars call Elu Sinhala, or Sinhala in its purest form (de Alwis 1996, 104). Richard Murphy, working off Senarath Paranavitana's translations of the Sigiri graffiti, based a poem on a verse attributed to a female visitor that reads, "as a woman I'll gladly / sing for these women / who are unable to speak" (Murphy 1989). Poetic expressions of Sri Lankan female subjectivity, addressed to other Sri Lankan women, written at the threshold of nation and identity, offer moments of "rerouting": instances where the governing logics of a patriarchal, militarized nation-state are troubled by the speech of those who regularly deemed "unable to speak." Neloufer de Mel writes of the "complex, poignant and contradictory constructions of female identities" in the poetry of three Sri Lankan women—Jean Arasanayagam, Kamala Wijeratne, and Sita Ranjini—where a context of war and ethnonationalism prompts each poet to meditate on the limitations of their variously located subjectivity (1996, 170). All three contemplate, with different implications, the conscription of the female body into reproducing fictions of nationhood and identity, and de Mel deftly identifies moments when each poet is forced to dwell in the contradictions of (dis)belonging to a nationalist patriarchal schema. This "rerouting" was also part of the labor of organizations like the Poorani Women's Center in Jaffna, founded in 1989 as a refuge for female victims of rape and sexual abuse in the warzone (Samuel 2006). Among the scant records of the Poorani women in their own voice that survived is a poem titled "Wartime" about the transgenerational impact of protracted violence: "our children come of age: / they lose / their childhood . . . / In fun / they tear the wings off / a captured dragonfly. / They play at war / with bits of stick / for guns. / As they play / they kill each other / laughing" (Samuel 2006, 34). The poet, Sivaramani, committed suicide in Jaffna, burning nearly all of her poetry.

> *This is why we stay with poetry. And despite our consenting to all the indisputable technologies; despite seeing the political leap that must be managed, the horror of hunger and ignorance, torture and massacre to be conquered. . . . We know ourselves as part and as crowd, in an unknown that does not terrify. We cry our cry of poetry. Our boats are open, and we sail them for everyone.*
>
> —*Édouard Glissant,* Poetics of Relation

Titled *Consensual Genocide,* the first published volume of poetry by femme, nonbinary, mixed-race diasporic Tamil Leah Lakshmi Piepzna-Samarasinha is dedicated to their family "lost and stolen, blood and chosen" (2006). In poignant, startling verse, Piepzna-Samarasinha weaves a poetics of identity, trauma, dispossession, and politics drawn from their lived experiences as the daughter of a working-class white woman and a disaffected, queer Sri Lankan man. Throughout the collection, Piepzna-Samarasinha contemplates their interpellation within global systems of race and gender through the lens of their and their father's fractured relationship to the homeland. These themes come most vividly together in a poem titled "Don't fuck anybody you wouldn't want to be," which opens with a defiant proclamation—"I gave up two things this New Year's / I gave up cigarettes and white boys"—that immediately likens imperial masculinity to a kind of fatal, long-term addiction. The reason the speaker cites for giving up "white boys" is their racial fetishism of them that emerges in their curiosity about "whether what they say 'bout colored pussy is really true." "Colored" invokes a constellation of anti-Black discourses on sexual excess, drawing our attention to the hatred and fear of Black femininity that animates discursive violence against varied groups of women of color. The speaker further clarifies that white men's fascination arises due to their proximity to the "exotic erotic mango sucking east" and because they're "just dark enuf to be sexy / not dark enuf to be scary." In rejecting the roving, Columbus-like masculinity of a white imperialism titillated by the racialized and gendered iconography of conquest, the poet also refutes the racialization of Sri Lankan femininity in the homeland that conscripted the iconic Sigiri frescoes into an anti-Back, colorist schema of Asian/Aryan superiority. This awareness shores up what S. M. Jayawardene names "the transmogrifying relationship" through which Euro-British colonialities transformed and renewed preexisting logics of biology and difference on the Indian subcontinent—namely those of caste and colorism—to produce contemporary iterations of racial power (2016). Within a Sri Lankan, diasporic context, anti-Black racial schemas function both globally and locally in tandem with—and sometimes incorporated into—anti-Tamil and casteist ideologies of nationhood and belonging.

However, rather than repudiate the symbolic registers of their Sri Lankanness in response to the fetishistic violence of a white male gaze, the poet reroutes them through a queer, diasporic trajectory. The phrase "mango sucking" might evoke the careless fetishization of brown women, but a closer look reveals that mangoes, so often used to stereotype South Asianness, are not only unabashedly cunnic but diasporic. In her political, anti-colonial choreopoetry, Kenyan-born poet Shailja Patel (2012) deploys the image of a mango held in the palm to invoke the precarity of the colonial condition. Mangoes, native to South Asia, also flourish abundantly in the Caribbean, ripening sweetly under the tropical sun, full of a silent history written in the flesh of indentured laborers transported to the archipelago for agricultural work (Alexander 2005, 262). In Jamaica Kincaid's (1996) *The Autobiography of My Mother,* a mysterious, female-bodied river spirit lures hapless schoolboys to their death with a ripe mango in her hand. "Mango sucking" thus indexes not only colonial disdain for the sexual proclivities of brown people but also colonial and nationalist fears of a transgressive, native femininity "sucking" and sustaining itself, as well as the global circulation of commodities, food, and laboring bodies that belie the myth of an endogamous national enclave.

The poetics deployed in Piepzna-Samarasinha's work perform what Gayatri Gopinath identifies as a queer disruption of nationalist hegemonies, one that rejects the repressive-home/progressive-diaspora binary by rerouting desire and queerness through—not despite—the symbolic field of "home," preventing "the reconstitution of patriarchal masculinity [by disturbing] the space of the heteronormative home *from within*" (Gopinath 2005, 84; emphasis mine). "I want someone whose armpits smell like my grandmother's kitchen," the poet declares, locating their desire in a homosocial space of rooted feminized materiality: a space where Sri Lankan women labor for the nourishment and pleasure of their and their families' bodies (Piepzna-Samarasinha 2006, 25). The speaker dreams of a lover "who isn't afraid of chili lips burning hers" (25); chili, of course, is widely and liberally used in Sri Lankan cooking to stall food spoilage in the relentless tropical heat, particularly in the northern, Tamil-majority regions that experience higher temperatures. But the culinary icons of home, here deployed to constitute pleasure between two brown feminine subjects, are also transformed under conditions of war, as detailed in Lawrence's ethnographic work. "They tied my hands and put chili powder on my face," a young Tamil man who escaped imprisonment reveals. Another was "stabbed in the thigh. . . . Then his torturers packed the large knife wound with salt and chili powder" (Lawrence 2003, 109–13). Afterward, he was suspended from the ceiling and "severely beaten with a large *akappai* (a wooden utensil for stirring large pots of rice)" (2003, 113). A Sri Lankan poetics of diaspora here necessitates attention to the imbricated symbology of belonging and exile, torture and joy, violence and sacralization marked on and by the bodies of those deemed "unable to speak," who nevertheless always already labor to renegotiate the terms of identity and embodiment.

In a similar fashion to those who resignify their bodies through ritual devotion to Kali, the poet continually resignifies the ecological body of Sri Lanka itself through an explicitly voiced, queer desire for a lover who shares their racial and political subjectivity. "The tamarind smells from her pussy match mine," Piepszna-Samarasinha writes, invoking the salty-sweet fruit which not only tastes cunnic but is used liberally in various foods throughout the island as well as to treat various digestive ailments and, in Ayurvedic medicine, to "cool" the body (2006, 26). And while tamarind grows so profusely across Asia one might think it indigenous, research suggests that the plant may in fact originate from tropical Africa, and was transplanted like mangoes to the Caribbean archipelago by white settlers (Diallo et al. 2007). Indeed, in a different poem, Piepzna-Samarasinha mails "a 99-cent package of tamarind candy" to her Sri Lankan father, whose own body is described as slack and empty from years of subsisting on cheap North American food. In mailing him the candy, a small piece of Sri Lanka, the poet instantiates a moment of queer reciprocality in their fraught relationship when their father subsequently calls them long-distance "weeping from tasting tamarind / for the first time in thirty years" (Piepzna-Samarasinha 2006, 1). Tamarind, also a natural laxative, here signifies the hollow ache of queer (dis)belonging, and reroutes itself through a diasporic poetics to create meaning between two disparately exiled subjects, their complicated relationship to Sri Lanka and to each other.

In detailing their desired lover and queer diasporic subjectivity, the poet writes, "and our hair naps into one forest of kinks / Our colors don't clash / as she lies on my earth / sucks coconut cream from my breast / nudges plantain all up in me / something like Kali and Durga must've rocked." Hair is the very pinnacle of Sri Lankan femininity, often a site of pain and shame as many Lankan women both nationally and diasporically pay money to chemically straighten their thick, wavy curls in an effort to look more East than South Asian, even while in the Americas this same thickness and waviness makes wigs and extensions of South Asian women's hair so desirable that "Indian Remy" is its own category. In Tamil Nadu and parts of Sri Lanka, women's unbound hair indexes wrathful anger (as exemplified in images of Kali where the goddess stands loose haired and grimly triumphant) but also death, as women (who died in greater numbers than men during the Boxing Day tsunami of 2004) drowned after catching their long hair on various debris, particularly in the north of Sri Lanka where both women's hair and long garments snagged on barbed wire fences left behind by military forces (de Mel and Ruwanpura 2006). In the poet's vision, the curly texture of some Lankan women's hair is not cause for shame but recognition, nor does hair shackle her to an ideal of heteronormative womanhood; instead, their beautiful naps curl into a "forest of kinks" with their lover's, into a rendering where queerness, Blackness, Tamilness, Sri Lankanness, and femininity weave complexly into both diasporic and national subjectivities. And as the poet's lover "nudges plantain all up in me," they invoke Kali, and in so doing invoke the hundreds of men and women in Sri Lanka's war-ravaged north opening themselves to penetration by the goddess by means of the *vayalaku* (mouth arrow), the *mullukavatti* (piercing of the back with fish hooks), and "walking the fire" (walking across hot coals) (Lawrence 2003, 111). Penetrability, femininity, and the liminality that haunts imperial imaginaries become a transformative terrain for subjectivities deemed unspeakable. "The people who are taken there normally get killed. Our Mother Kali released me. She appeared in a dream. . . . They beat me with a large stick. I could not bear it. I shouted 'Kaliyamma!' Then they stopped" (2003, 109). The symbolic and the material, conscripted on the body, create meaning out of chaos, reclaim belonging amid (dis) possession. "but i'm still going back home / This isn't home we can't go home" (Piepzna-Samarasinha, 2006, 26). The poetics of diaspora here refuses an easy notion of home, but turns instead to the queer feminine bodies that index rather than erase the complex facets of Sri Lankan female subjectivity. "but why don't you try making a home in these arms / where you can touch that place their cock never broke." At the "dangerous threshold" of war and upheaval, queerness and femininity, the poet says, "I want you to reach up through my cervix past my womb / wrap your hands round my heart / no longer / in exile" (26).

> *Who were my people? How does one know the stories and histories of one's people? Where does one learn them?*
>
> —*M. Jacqui Alexander,* Pedagogies of Crossing

Despite additions made to accommodate foot traffic, the ascent to view the frescoes remains precarious. A narrow spiral stairway shielded from the wind with metallic mesh offers little security this high on the rock face. Nevertheless, the promise of seeing them for a second time, after nearly two decades, compels me to keep climbing until we at least reach the secluded cave pocket where the frescoes adorn the walls. They appear to both float above you and look you in the eye, numinous and decayed, mysterious and serene. The tour guides hold their audiences in thrall with descriptions of the paint used (derived from local trees, designed to last centuries), praising the extraordinary dexterity of hands that mapped such beguiling forms onto the peculiarities of a rock face, and, of course, extolling the frescoes' beauty. Kassapa, the monarch to whom the fortress belonged and who oversaw its design, is styled a connoisseur of aesthetic pleasure, a king who surrounded himself with lavishness and indulgence in the form of beautiful women from all over the world. I wonder about the conditions under which these women—if they were indeed real—might have traveled to ancient Ceylon. Did they come alone? Did they leave sisters and mothers and fathers and brothers behind? What drove them into diaspora, and did they ever long to return to their own homelands? When Kassapa fell, did they scatter once again to the winds, or were they taken captive by his conquering brother, forced into another condition of servitude? Were they a comfort to each other during long nights and sweltering days? What record might there be of their friendships and trysts, their rivalries and alliances, of their daily, detailed lives? Would they have laughed at the absurdity of what their images had become? If they could tell their stories in their own tongues, make poetry out of everyday living, who would they be to us? "Look," our guide gestures, pointing at a shadowed corner of the cave, "that one is from Ethiopia." I peer at the half-faded figure, her disappearing smile, her outline eaten away by Time, her contours less polished, less looked after than the others. Her hair, a halo of curls.

Natassja B. Gunasena is currently a doctoral candidate in the Department of African and African Diaspora Studies at the University of Texas at Austin. Her research focuses on Afro/Asian humanities and queer diasporic formations. She can be reached at natassja.gunasena@gmail.com.

Notes

1. Akki/akka: a Sinhala suffix meaning "older sister," commonly used to address a woman a few years older than yourself, regardless of their biological relation to you.

Works Cited

Alexander, M. Jacqui. 2005. *Pedagogies of Crossing: Meditations on Feminism, Sexual Politics, Memory, and the Sacred.* Durham, NC: Duke University Press.

Agence France-Presse. 2018. "Sri Lanka reimposes ban on women buying alcohol—days after it was lifted." *The Guardian*, January 14, 2018. https://www.theguardian.com/world/2018/jan/15/sri-lanka-reimposes-ban-on-women-buying-alcohol-days-after-it-was-lifted/.

de Alwis, Malathi. 1996. "Sexuality in the Field of Vision: The Discursive Clothing of the Sigiriya Frescoes." In *Embodied Violence: Communalising Women's Sexuality in South Asia,* edited by Kumari Jayawardena and Malathi de Alwis, 89–112. London: Zed Books.

de Mel, Neloufer. 1996. "Static Signifiers? Metaphors of Women in Contemporary Sri Lankan War Poetry." In *Embodied Violence: Communalising Women's Sexuality in South Asia,* edited by Kumari Jayawardena and Malathi de Alwis, 168–89. London: Zed Books.

de Mel, Neloufer, and Kanchana N. Ruwanpura. 2006. *Gendering the Tsunami: Women's Experiences from Sri Lanka.* Colombo, LK: International Centre for Ethnic Studies.

Diallo, Boukary Ousmane, Hélène I. Joly, Doyle McKey, Martine Hossaert-McKey, and Marie Hélène Chevallier. 2007. "Genetic Diversity of *Tamarindus indica* Populations: Any Clues on the Origin from its Current Distribution?" *African Journal of Biotechnology* 6, no. 7: 853–60.

Franco, Jean. 1989. *Plotting Women: Gender and Representation in Mexico.* New York: Columbia University Press.

Glissant, Édouard. 1997. *Poetics of Relation.* Translated by Betsy Wing. Ann Arbor: University of Michigan Press.

Gopinath, Gayatri. 2005. *Impossible Desires: Queer Diasporas and South Asian Public Cultures.* Durham, NC: Duke University Press.

Hobson, Janell. 2018. "Remnants of Venus: Signifying Black Beauty and Sexuality." *WSQ* 46 (1/2): 105–20.

Jayawardene, Sureshi M. 2013. "Pushing the Paradigm: Locating Scholarship on the Siddis and Kaffirs." *Journal of Black Studies* 44, no. 7: 687–705.

———. 2016. "Racialized Casteism: Exposing the Relationship between Race, Caste, and Colorism through the Experiences of Africana People in India and Sri Lanka." *Journal of African American Studies* 20, no. 3: 323–45.

Kincaid, Jamaica. 1996. *The Autobiography of My Mother: A Novel.* New York: Farrar, Straus and Giroux.

Lawrence, Patricia. 2003. "Kali in a Context of Terror: The Tasks of a Goddess in Sri Lanka's Civil War." In *Encountering Kali: In the Margins, at the Center, in the West,* edited by Rachel Fell McDermott and Jeffrey J. Kripal, 100–23. Berkeley: University of California Press.

McClintock, Anne. 2015. *Imperial Leather: Race, Gender and Sexuality in the Colonial Contest.* New York: Routledge.

Murphy, Richard. 1989. *The Mirror Wall.* Winston-Salem, NC: Wake Forest University Press.

Patel, Shailja. 2012. *Migritude.* Translated by Meta Ottosson. Lund, Sweden: Celanders Förlag.

Piepzna-Samarasinha, Leah Lakshmi. 2006. *Consensual Genocide*. Toronto: TSAR Publications.

Samuel, Kumudini. 2006. *A Hidden History: Women's Activism for Peace in Sri Lanka, 1982–2002*. Colombo, LK: Social Scientists' Association.

Ukwatta, Swarna. 2010. "Sri Lankan Female Domestic Workers Overseas: Mothering Their Children from a Distance." *Journal of Population Research* 27, no. 2: 107–31.

A Question of Voice: Indo-Caribbean American Feminism through Music in New York City

Rupa Pillai

Abstract: Idolized as models of good Hindu women, Indo-Caribbean American women artists—dancers of *Kathak* and singers of classical Indian music and devotional songs—have the difficult task of performing and maintaining the authenticity of the Indianness of the Indo-Caribbean Americans living in New York. As they all vigilantly preserve and pass down the classical Indian arts, they also inhabit the interstices of their existence. Between immigrant and American, West Indian and East Indian, traditional and modern, religious and secular, these women crave to express their polycultural voice and to articulate an Indo-Caribbean American feminism. To appreciate the contradictions they live, this article examines these tensions to track the continued relevance of the *bhadramahila* or "respectable woman" concept devised during Indian independence to the experiences of the Indian diaspora. Also, by questioning the prevailing understanding of voice as empowering, this article considers how performance is not only transformative, but also disciplining.
Keywords: Indo-Caribbean, South Asian American, religion, performance, migration, ethnicity and race

As we sat in her cozy, sparsely decorated living room, Ranjitha,[1] a thirty-two-year-old Indo-Caribbean American singer and vocal teacher, reflected upon the issues we had discussed over the past hour:

> You know how heavy—*kafi*[2]—heavy these topics are. These are not little things. This is not like, let's feed the homeless and poor and maybe make a dent in that if we get corporate sponsorship. You're talking about ideals and tradition and . . . [*sighs*] I don't know what else to call it. Prejudices? Paradoxes? (Ranjitha, pers. comm.)

***WSQ: Women's Studies Quarterly* 47: 1 & 2 (Spring/Summer 2019)**

In sharing her history in New York City, Ranjitha had framed her experiences in terms of what it means to be an Indo-Caribbean American woman in the United States.[3] Her story echoes many I have heard from other Indo-Caribbean American women artists during my fieldwork. Idolized as models of good Hindu women,[4] these artists, dancers of *Kathak*[5] and singers of classical Indian music and devotional songs, have the difficult task of performing and maintaining the authenticity of the Indianness of the Indo-Caribbean Americans living in the city. As they all vigilantly preserve and pass down the classical Indian arts,[6] they also inhabit the interstices of their existence. Between immigrant and American, West Indian and East Indian, traditional and modern, religious and secular, these women crave to express their polycultural voice and to articulate an Indo-Caribbean American feminism which resolves the tensions between these binaries which impact their experience in New York.

To appreciate the contradictions they live, this article investigates these tensions by focusing on the experiences of Ranjitha. As will become apparent, Ranjitha's efforts to voice her polycultural self and realize an Indo-Caribbean American feminism through her art are thwarted by her community's history of twice migration, first from India to the Caribbean and then from the Caribbean to New York City. Because this history of twice migration renders their Indianness as less than, this double-diasporic community relies upon the authentic performances of classical Indian traditions to claim belonging to the Indian American diaspora and, by extension, access to the privileges associated with being acknowledged as a model minority in the United States.

Tasked with executing such performances of Indianness, Ranjitha and other Indo-Caribbean American women artists embody an ideal of a good Hindu, Indian woman akin to the *bhadramahila* or "respectable woman," an ideological construct that dates back to the Indian nationalist movement (Chatterjee 1993). Although the bhadramahila is unique to nineteenth-century Bengal, I will highlight in my discussion of recent scholarship how the larger ideology of respectable femininity embodied by the bhadramahila remains a productive lens for scholars of India and the Indian diaspora through time to examine the intersection of gender, nationalism, and race (Ramamurthy 2008; Radhakrishnan 2011; Reddy 2015). In particular, I will draw upon this scholarship to demonstrate the continued relevance of this figure to the Indo-Caribbean American community in New York City. By considering how this ideology and ideal are present in the experiences of Ranjitha, I will illustrate how Indo-Caribbean American women are central to the Indo-Caribbean American community's claims to Indianness and model minority status in the United States. Such an illustration is critical in appreciating the importance of gender in how Asian diasporas navigate notions of belonging and experiences of racialization in new locations. Also, my focus on the Indo-Caribbean American community highlights the "heterogeneity" and "multiplicity" of South Asian America (Lowe 1996). Further, I will show how this construct of the bhadramahila also presents questions about the prevailing formulation of voice as empowering, suggesting that at times performance is not transformative but disciplining.

Bhadramahila: Then and Now

In his book *The Nation and Its Fragments: Colonial and Postcolonial Histories,* Partha Chatterjee (1993) explores how gender is renegotiated during Indian independence by examining the response of the Bengali middle class in the 1920s. At that moment, anti-colonial nationalists and religious reformers collaborated to imagine a new woman ideal, known as the bhadramahila or "respectable woman," to counter the prevailing colonial discourse around Indian women. Rather than a victim of tradition requiring the civilizing intervention of British rule (Nandy 1983), this new woman ideal relied upon a new nationalist ideology in which India was superior to the West in the spiritual realm, a move that enabled Indian nationalists in the context of Bengal to selectively adopt aspects of Western modernity.[7] As Chatterjee argues, this ideology required the reforming of traditions in a manner that they could be "fortified against charges of barbarism and irrationality" (1993, 127). In other words, if tradition justified British colonial rule, tradition could justify Indian self-rule.

The subsequent reworking of traditions, which rendered certain forms of Indian art classical (Peterson and Soneji 2008), also required the re-imagining of Indian women as mediators between the material/spiritual, inner/outer, and modern/traditional.[8] To live in between such binaries, new forms of education and artistic training emerged that allowed middle-class women new access to public spaces (i.e., schools and performance stages). However, this new freedom was constructed in a manner that would not threaten their femininity nor jeopardize the inner, spiritual superiority that Indian nationalist ideology was predicated upon (Forbes 1996; Sangari and Vaid 1990). The bhadramahila, therefore, is restricted to a performance of respectable femininity often defined through binary opposition to other Indian women, a point I will return to later.

This model of gendered nationalism articulated by Chatterjee presents a compelling explanation for what transpired in nineteenth-century Bengal but, more importantly, offers insight into why and how culture is deployed in a manner to access self-determination and recognition from a hegemonic class. More recent scholarship extends this model in useful ways to demonstrate how this ideal and ideology lingers on in the contemporary moment, both in India and its diaspora, to structure and discipline gender. For instance, Smitha Radhakrishnan notes how Indian women IT workers in Silicon Valley and Bangalore negotiate the demands of work with maintaining a Hindu family at home to express a global Indianness, "a set of beliefs and practices that are at once tied to a global lifestyle and to a deep sense of belonging to the Indian nation" (2008, 9). This global Indianness echoes nationalist constructions of Indianness in its logic and ends by dividing the world in two, where success in the outside realm is predicated on moral superiority at home. These transnational, Indian, middle-class women feel respected for their ability to balance their work life and be good mothers and wives as it relates to a larger project of nation building, where India is a significant actor in the global economy.

Likewise, Anannya Bhattacharjee (1992) demonstrates how a version of this respectable femininity is constructed and performed by Indian middle-class immigrants in the United States in response to their racialization. Prior to immigrating, the middle- to upper-class Indians enjoyed the status and advantages of being unnamed or invisible. However, by immigrating these individuals were no longer anonymous and were defined by their difference, specifically race (Joshi 2006). In response, the Indian American middle class, through cultural and religious organizations, constructed a unified, homogenous Indian identity to redefine the meaning of their difference, not in terms of race, but ethnicity—a move that gives the community access to model minority status. Instead of challenging their racialization and the larger structural, racial inequalities of the United States, the community deploys their ethnicity and culture to demonstrate their worthiness as a minority community in order to access privileges (Omi and Winant 1994; Roshanravan 2009). Indian American women embody this Indianness by preserving, performing, and passing cultural knowledge to the next generation through art, fashion, and family in a manner similar to Chatterjee's bhadramahila. As a result, middle-class Indian American women of the United States perform "forms of femininity [that] cannot be disaggregated from but are also irreducible to the figure of the traditional-but-modern Indian woman that has been central to the shoring up of capitalist heteropatriarchies within a dominant national and diasporic imaginary" (Reddy 2015, 206).

However, in order for this diasporic Indian identity to succeed, traditions and festivals are standardized and performed for the American public, while certain histories and voices are silenced. While existing scholarship demonstrates the silencing of parts of the heterogeneous Indian American community whose experiences threaten this construction of Indianness through class and gender (Rudrappa 2004; Das Gupta 2006), this scholarship is limited to a conventional understanding of who is Indian American, ultimately failing to consider the experiences of double-diasporic communities such as the Indo-Caribbean American community of New York City (Puar and Rai 2004). By considering how the Indo-Caribbean American community deploys its own version of respectable femininity, I argue the community is simultaneously responding to a construction of Indianness described by Bhattacharjee and of bhadramahila described by Chatterjee. As I will explain, for this community to access the status of model minority achieved by Indian Americans in the United States, they first need to prove their Indianness.

A Minority within a Minority

Indo-Caribbeans are descendants of indentured laborers who left the Indian subcontinent from 1838 to 1917 for the British West Indies following the abolition of slavery. They started immigrating en masse to the United States in the 1960s to escape economic uncertainty and ethnic violence in their Caribbean homes of Guyana and Trinidad and Tobago (Vertovec 2000). Today, the majority of Indo-Caribbean Americans have settled in New York, with sizable communities in New Jersey, Georgia, Minnesota, and Texas (Ramey 2011; Schultz 2014).

Although Indo-Caribbean is an emerging political identity in the context of New York City, the community is largely invisible in the United States, especially in the Indian American community. This invisibility is due to an unawareness of Indo-Caribbean history, which leads to certain misconceptions about the community and their Indianness (Khandelwal 2002). As Ranjitha pointed out:

> I don't think a lot of East Indians knew who Guyanese, Trinidadians, or Indo-Caribbean people were. I mean, a lot of them, I'm sorry to say, some people were very ignorant to the fact that people were removed from India and were not considered slaves. Like they were indentured servants. . . . A lot of East Indian people never knew that happened. They were just completely unaware. "What do you mean you're Indian? What do you mean you're Guyanese? You're Caribbean? I don't get it."

In sharing her experience, Ranjitha indicated that the Indian American community has a lack of knowledge of Indo-Caribbean identity or history. This ignorance leads to misunderstandings about the nature of her ancestors' migration as indentured laborers in the late nineteenth century, which results in the questioning of their shared Indianness. In particular, this perception of indenture as synonymous to slavery resurrects the image of the "coolie." As indentured laborers, Indians who immigrated to the British West Indies in the late nineteenth and early twentieth centuries were reduced to and racialized as "coolie" or "an inferior person who simply labors for hire" (Prashad 2001, 72).[9] This construct of the "coolie" rendered indentured Indians as uncultured and devoid of respect (Kelly 1991). In fact, as part of their own decolonization, Indian nationalists recognized the importance of ending indenture and the debilitating image of the lowly "coolie" to their own right to self-determination in the Indian subcontinent (Seecharan 1992). In *Mobilizing India: Women, Music, and Migration between India and Trinidad*, Tejaswini Niranjana (2006) explores this connection by considering how the idea of the indentured Indian woman in Trinidad was constructed as a foil to the bhadramahila.

As mentioned earlier, the bhadramahila is restricted to a performance of respectable femininity often defined through binary opposition to other Indian women. In the context of the subcontinent, the bhadramahila functioned to offset the immorality of India's "common" woman, who was lower class, lower caste, vulgar, and uneducated. If the immorality of the "common" woman justified British colonialism, then the morality of the bhadramahila would justify self-rule (Chatterjee 1993). However, as Niranjana points out, indenture offered Indian women the opportunity to become modern through displacement rather than through Indian nationalism (2006, 78). In response, nationalists, such as Gandhi, viewed indentured women as "victim[s] of colonialism," with indenture as the root of their immorality, a move that disavowed their modernity and by extension their Indianness (Niranjana 2006, 78). For these women to be properly modern and part of the Indian nation, indenture needed to be abolished and India recentered in the imagination of Indians in the Caribbean through a focus on classical Indian arts and traditions (Seecharan 1992; Ruhomon 1998; Mohammed 1999).

As a result of this ideological intervention, Indianness in the Caribbean would only be recognized as authentic if direct connection to India could be established. Displays of Indianness influenced by the forces in the Caribbean context would be viewed as inauthentic (Niranjana 2006). For instance, Anusha Ragbir notes how Indo-Trinidadian women in Indo-Trinidadian beauty pageants opt to "present the fantasized Indian woman that is . . . pure, traditional, respectable and modern without displaying the facets of modernity that would have young women appear too Western and too creole" (2012, 14). The potential global audience of the pageant stage as well as the contested belonging of Indo-Trinidadians in the Trinidadian nation (Mohammed 2009) explain why Indianness is performed in this manner instead of displaying aspects of Indo-Caribbean culture that question such understandings of Indianness and illustrate the Caribbeanness of Indo-Caribbeans.[10]

This perception that the Caribbeanness of Indo-Caribbeans invalidates their Indianness is suggested in the questions Ranjitha often received when explaining her identity to Indian Americans in New York City, as mentioned earlier: "'What do you mean you're Indian? What do you mean you're Guyanese? You're Caribbean? I don't get it.'" These individuals seem perplexed by how one can be Indian and Caribbean simultaneously. Gina, an Indo-Caribbean American woman in her late forties, likewise shared how Indian Americans questioned her Indianness:

> I've been kind of looked down upon by people who left India, [who] could be considered Indians. . . . It wasn't much but they did look down upon those Indians who left India back then. . . . It was more like you're not really an Indian. (Gina, pers. comm.)

Although not an artist, Gina experienced prejudice from Indian Americans in her practice of Hinduism. Since her ancestors left India through indenture, her Indianness and Hinduism were deemed inauthentic. Likewise, Ajay, an Indo-Caribbean American musician in his early thirties, found that Indian Americans questioned the community's Indianness: "I know many *desi* people who are of the opinion that we have lost our culture and are therefore lost" (pers. comm.).[11]

The experiences of these Indo-Caribbean American individuals illustrate how the Indian American community questions their community's claims to Indianness. Like Indian nationalists in the nineteenth century, Indian Americans today invalidate Indo-Caribbean American Indianness on the basis of their migration. As Ranjitha complained:

> All they knew about Indo-Caribbeans [was] from channel 77 where the ones were dancing and doing chutney dances and they wanted to put you in that box.[12] "Oh, you must be like that. Really masala-ish kind of." (Ranjitha, pers. comm.)

The reduction of herself and by extension all Indo-Caribbean American women to a version of an Indian woman who suggestively dances to chutney music is offensive to Ranjitha. Also, the use of the word "masala-ish" suggests an impurity of her Indianness because of the presumed mixture with the Caribbean. In response, Ranjitha deployed respectable femininity to counter such questioning: "I'm like, no; I'm actually a classical musician and play the sitar" (pers. comm.) While her response defends her and her community's claims to Indianness, it is done so in a manner that fails to question such constructions of Indianness. By deploying her classical training as a defense, she misses an opportunity to correct these misconceptions in order to expand understandings of Indianness and render her community's history, experience, and culture visible.

Further, this failure to be recognized as Indian by Indian Americans renders real the critiques of her Indo-Caribbean American peers that Ranjitha shared with me:

> As a West Indian singing Indian composition, they're like, "Why you so serious? You're never really gonna, you're never really gonna push that bar. You're always going to be Caribbean," you know? (Ranjitha, pers. comm.)

Although uttered in attempts to persuade Ranjitha to stop practicing in order to socialize when she was a teen, such comments foreshadowed her experience as an Indo-Caribbean American artist and how the Indian American community might never accept her art or Indo-Caribbean Indianness in general as authentic in the United States. However, such performances and claims of Indianness are not about aligning with the Indian American community but rather about being perceived and recognized as Indian and by extension a model minority in the United States by the larger American community.

To help raise their visibility within New York City, the Indo-Caribbean American community ironically copied the efforts of the Indian community in the city. Inspired by the India Day parade held on India's Independence Day in Manhattan, the Indo-Caribbean American community decided to start their own parade. In 1989, in collaboration with two Indo-Caribbean American Hindu temples, the community held its first *Phagwah* parade. Phagwah, more commonly known as Holi, is a Hindu holiday of a carnivalesque nature. The first parade was a modest success, but each year it has grown to the extent that past parade marshals included Caribbean politicians and even former Mayor Bloomberg. In discussing how white Americans participate, Dhiraj, an Indo-Caribbean American man in his late fifties and a member of the organizing committee, also explained the parade's success:

> It has this visibility. This credibility. This respectability by the whole city of New York. The mayor came and now it is established. It is a big thing. . . . We want to bring a Bollywood star to give it more visibility. (Dhiraj, pers. comm.)

Such performances echo techniques utilized by the Indian American community discussed by Bhattacharjee (1992). Although an Indo-Caribbean American event, this distinct ethnic identity is illegible to an uninformed audience viewing the parade full of Indian clothing and Hindu deities, both icons of Indianness in the United States, which is the intent. Highlighting visual cues of Indianness recognized as such in the United States matters to gain the status as a model minority not being judged as authentic in relation to Indian American Indianness or global Indianness. But, as I will discuss in the final section, such concerns of authenticity plague the internal politics of the Indo-Caribbean American community, which restricts the possibilities of belonging and identity formation for Indo-Caribbean American women artists like Ranjitha.

Performing the Indian, Voicing the Future

Performing at local temples by the age of nine, Ranjitha represented not only for her parents, but also for the larger West Indian community, the future in which their Indian traditions would persist in the face of migration. Viewed as a "singing goddess" in the West Indian community of New York City, Ranjitha "could see that it was a sense of pride [for] the elder generation . . . [that] [their] tradition has been continued" (pers. comm.). A major part of our discussion focused upon Ranjitha's art: her training, her performing, her teaching, and her responsibility. She explained that, without music, she would not know herself nor truly connect with her Indian culture or her religion: "It was just a window into the Indian subcontinent that I had never had before." Through music, she found an avenue to express her emotion and to try to make sense of the hardships she had endured. From losing her mother to living with the stigma of being a divorcée, Ranjitha found solace in song, using music as a means to understand her polycultural[13] self, a self that is a product of different cultures. However, Ranjitha's attempted use of music to empower herself ultimately falters in the disciplining power of the audience:

> I can't even do what I do today because of all the politics involved. It is very sad. Yeah, I don't feel like the people are unified or united in any sense of the matter. . . . The promoters in this community . . . it's just crazy. (Ranjitha, pers. comm.)

As Ranjitha explained, the politics of her audience structure the dynamics of her stage. Internal divisions within the Indo-Caribbean American community around issues of class and ethnic status in the United States inform who promoters book, what music is appropriate to perform, and how a performer may express their identity and politics during a performance, a process which raises questions about "the relationship between voice, subjectivity, and agency" (Weidman 2003, 194).

In her ethnography of Carnatic music, Amanda Weidman (2006) examines how this South Indian music tradition became classical through the same process of modernity which created the bhadramahila. While she offers a fascinating history of how middle-class women access a new public (and new domesticity) by training in this tradition, what is most compelling about Weidman's analysis is her theorizing of voice. Instead of examining this process in terms of resistance, Weidman considers voice in relation to modernity, authenticity, and subjectivity, which enables us to reconsider the emancipatory potentials of voice and the assumed agency of speaking. By assuming one's agency and subjectivity through speaking, one fails to recognize the constructed nature of voice where "women learn to speak so that they will be heard in an arena already overdetermined by colonialism and nationalist politics" (Weidman 2006, 4). This intervention prompts an increased awareness of the context and type of voice being heard to assess agency and subjectivity. By exploring Ranjitha's music through Weidman's "politics of voice," one may consider how "practices of voice, while creative, are also a mode of discipline—embodied and performed—through which subjects are produced" (2006, 14).

As a singer, Ranjitha realizes the potentials of every stage she performs upon. With her microphone, she has the power to educate before entertaining and to share her political views to inspire her captive Indo-Caribbean American, middle-aged, middle-class audience to action:

> I get into trouble a lot. I get into trouble so much. There was a time I did a concert at city hall and I was just like, "We're not going to continue the arguments of old men." All the men wanted to funnel out. I got so much flak for that. Thank god the performance was killer so they couldn't say, "Well, if she could sing?" But what is up with all this drama? But the fact of the matter is it's not drama. How about we all stop turning the cheek? Let's stop turning the cheek and acting like there is nothing wrong. (Ranjitha, pers. comm.)

Frustrated by the petty feuds and toxic masculinity that plague the Indo-Caribbean American community, Ranjitha used the public forum a performance offers to call out these issues that not only impact her personally but other Indo-Caribbean American women.

Through voicing her politics, Ranjitha is asserting her agency and subjectivity. However, the audience's reaction to her statement captures the significance of Weidman's (2006) politics of voice. In violating the expectation of the performance context to deliver a political rant, Ranjitha is criticized for not voicing the appropriate voice, her Indian classical singing voice, and not performing and embodying Indian respectable femininity. It is only when she finally utilizes this appropriate voice and delivers a "killer" performance that showcases Indian respectable femininity that her indiscretion is forgiven or rather trivialized as "drama." The audience's response prevents, even disavows, the articulation of her Indo-Caribbean American feminist self that acknowledges the challenges the community faces internally and in the United States.

The dynamics of this episode problematize many of our normative assumptions of the transformative capabilities of performance. Yes, Ranjitha is visible and being heard, but the audience refuses to hear her as an Indo-Caribbean American calling for societal change. Their refusal denies Ranjitha the subjectivity implied by her statement. Like in her previous performances in the Indo-Caribbean American community, this audience had no interest in hearing about the issues she faces as a minority in New York City or how the community is complicit in domestic violence. They are concerned with the respectable Indian femininity embodied by the performer, not the performer herself.

By only hearing and recognizing her as an Indian classical singer, her Indo-Caribbean American audience restricts her agency, her voice, and her identity as an Indo-Caribbean American. For her audience, Indo-Caribbean American identity is limited to an ideal of Indianness to gain proximity to the model minority status of Indian American and to distance themselves from the negative markers given to Caribbean communities in the United States. They refuse to hear and acknowledge the issues Ranjitha refers to that highlight the heterogeneity of Indo-Caribbean American. As the embodiment of ideal Indianness, she is responsible for preserving, performing, and passing knowledge to the next generation. Any action that threatens their image of how a performer of Indian classical art should behave—the idealized epitome of respectable femininity—is a threat to the Indo-Caribbean American community's access to Indianness.

While her previous feminist challenge is forgiven through her performance, Ranjitha is aware of how the community is disciplining her voice by limiting the genre she sings:

> The people are not really supportive because they either want to hear their chutney soca, or they want to hear the SA RI GA MA. They don't want to hear you like Alicia Keys. But I'm from Brooklyn. I grew up with that. It was a Latino area at that time. I heard the congo drums, salsa, merengue every time I opened the window or went down the street to buy milk. There was a festivity, joy in the Latin people. And I was surrounded by so many different types of music. (Ranjitha, pers. comm.)

Describing herself as a "mosaic," her album recorded in 2012 attempts to voice that mosaic voice. Integrating salsa beats with Indian instruments and singing "like Alicia Keys," this album is a marked departure for her as an artist. Trying to expand her range as an artist and move beyond the devotional songs of her first album, Ranjitha is taking a big risk. By voicing her polycultural self instead of the authentic Indianness of the Indo-Caribbean American community, she is aware the community may not "embrace" her experiment. In departing from the approved genre and context as an Indo-Caribbean American woman singer, Ranjitha could lose her voice or her ability to perform this voice in public within her Indo-Caribbean American community. With her audience unwilling to hear this new voice, the promoters will not book her performance. Therefore, by denying her a stage and refusing to be her audience, the Indo-Caribbean American community's disengagement is an act of discipline. For her to be a performer within her Indo-Caribbean American community, she is pressured to be an Indian classical singer.

By exploring the history and mobilization of respectable femininity in different contexts to define Indianness, and using Weidman's (2006) politics of voice, I have argued that the community's larger desires to access an authentic sense of Indianness is disciplining and limiting Indo-Caribbean American singers, like Ranjitha, in the United States. Struggling to make sense of her hybrid identity where she exists in the interstices of many binaries, Ranjitha offered a simpler explanation for her experience as a singer:

> Someone told me you're just very Gandhi. I am in awe of him, this young lawyer. And I think he was able to accomplish this because he has the balls, literally, he was a man. People would listen. The minute a woman starts ranting or raving she is called a capital B. It doesn't matter what you're talking about. (Ranjitha, pers. comm.)

Despite many challenging factors in her life—the history of her ancestors' migration to the New World, the powerful (and sometimes limiting) influence of tradition in contemporary life, and the internal politics of Indianness in India and its diaspora—Ranjitha concluded that it is her gender that silences her in the communities she engages with. Ranjitha's performance and performer identity are disciplined within the Indo-Caribbean American community with the overwhelming responsibility to perform a respectable femininity so as to provide a platform for this community to gain wider recognition within the American community as a model minority and to establish Indian connection and authenticity within Indian American communities. As Ranjitha concludes, as an Indo-Caribbean American woman in her communities: "It's not easy to get *your* voice heard."

Acknowledgments

I want to thank the late Nadia Loan, Lamia Karim, Gabrielle Hosein, Lisa Outar, Carol Silverman, the anonymous reviewers, and the editors Lili Shi and Yadira Perez Hazel for their insightful comments. My deepest gratitude to the Indo-Caribbean American community who participated in this research.

Rupa Pillai is a lecturer in the Asian American studies program at the University of Pennsylvania. A cultural anthropologist, she investigates the intersections of religion, race, and migration in the Indo-Caribbean American community in New York City. She can be reached at rupillai@sas.upenn.edu.

Notes

1. Pseudonyms are used to protect the privacy of the individuals who graciously participated in this research. These individuals were interviewed in New York City between 2010 and 2016.
2. *Kafi* is the Hindi word for "heavy."
3. "Indo-Caribbean" refers to individuals of Indian descent who have a history of migration from the Caribbean, usually the nations of Guyana, Trinidad and Tobago, and Suriname.
4. Not all Indo-Caribbean American individuals are Hindus. Many are Muslims, Catholics, and Presbyterians. For the purpose of this article, I will limit my engagement to Indo-Caribbean Americans of the Hindu faith.
5. *Kathak* is a form of Indian classical dance from North India.
6. While Indian music and art never went through a classical period, the term "classical" "combined ideas about art and the artist with a notion of Indianness formed in opposition to the West" (Weidman 2006, 5). To be classical is to be Indian in a way that is modern, but still tied to a glorious past (Weidman 2012, 249–53).
7. Both colonial and national ideologies were based upon the division of the

world into inside and outside spaces. The material or outside domain, characterized by the economy and politics, was where the West is supreme. While this article will focus upon the new woman ideal in the Indian and Hindu context, there is a rich literature of a similar phenomenon in other postcolonial contexts. For a discussion of gender and nationalism in the Caribbean, see Mohammed 1997.

8. Indian nationalism countered colonial discourse by creating new versions of Indian masculinity and femininity. With the new Indian woman protecting the image of the nation, Indian nationalists remasculinized the Indian man to oppose colonialism in the outside realm. This new Indian man, in the image of the *kshatriya* (warrior caste), was at the forefront to counter the British colonizer, but also demonstrated how Indian nationals were trying "to defeat the West at its own game" (Nandy 1983, 80).
9. Emerging and acquiring its derogatory connotation during the imperial sugar schemes pursued worldwide, the construction of the category of "coolie" during the nineteenth century transformed both Indian and Chinese indentured laborers into a racialized, lower class that was pursued as a cheap, free labor force by European colonial powers (Jung 2006; Bahadur 2013).
10. Instead of finding a space within the national identity of Caribbean nations, middle-class Indo-Caribbeans tend to adopt the identity of the "other" (Mohammed 2009). By being the other, Indo-Caribbeans manipulate their culture and history to position themselves in a higher status than the rest of the nation. Or in other words, Indian culture is deployed as a shield against the creole nationalism which compels them toward blackness. See Niranjana 2006 for a further discussion of Indo-Caribbeans' position in creole nationalism and how some Indo-Caribbean women are subverting such ideals of Indianness through their performance of chutney and soca, musical traditions originating in the Caribbean.
11. To be *desi* is to be part of the South Asia diaspora or, in the context of this article, to be an immigrant or a child of an immigrant from India, Pakistan, or Bangladesh in the post-1965 wave of migration.
12. Channel 77 is a public access TV station in Queens that shows Hindu devotional programming as well as chutney/soca music videos. "Chutney dancing" refers to *wining*, which anthropologist Philip Scher defines as "the erotic gyration of hips, slightly bent knees, and rotations of the buttocks" (2003, 187).
13. "Polycultural" refers to "the process whereby cultural identities are multiple, multi-sited, and made through interactions with various communities of color" (Thangaraj 2010, 381).

Works Cited

Bahadur, Gaiutra. 2013. *Coolie Woman: The Odyssey of Indenture*. Chicago: University of Chicago Press.

Bhattacharjee, Anannya. 1992. "The Habit of Ex-Nomination: Nation, Woman, and the Indian Immigrant Bourgeoisie." *Public Culture* 5, no. 1: 19–44.

Chatterjee, Partha. 1993. *The Nation and Its Fragments: Colonial and Postcolonial Histories*. Princeton, NJ: Princeton University Press.

Das Gupta, Monisha. 2006. *Unruly Immigrants: Rights, Activism, and Transnational South Asian Politics in the United States*. Durham, NC: Duke University Press.

Forbes, Geraldine Hancock. 1996. *Women in Modern India*. Cambridge: Cambridge University Press.

Joshi, Khyati Y. 2006. "The Racialization of Hinduism, Islam, and Sikhism in the United States." *Equity & Excellence in Education* 39, no. 3: 211–26.

Jung, Moon-Ho. 2006. *Coolies and Cane: Race, Labor, and Sugar in the Age of Emancipation*. Baltimore: Johns Hopkins University Press.

Kelly, John Dunham. 1991. *A Politics of Virtue: Hinduism, Sexuality, and Countercolonial Discourse in Fiji*. Chicago: University of Chicago Press.

Khandelwal, Madhulika S. 2002. *Becoming American, Being Indian: An Immigrant Community in New York City*. Ithaca, NY: Cornell University Press.

Lowe, Lisa. 1996. *Immigrant Acts: On Asian American Cultural Politics*. Durham, NC: Duke University Press.

Mohammed, Patricia. 1997. "Midnight's Children and the Legacy of Nationalism." *Callaloo* 20, no. 4: 737–52.

———. 1999. "From Myth to Symbolism: The Construction of Indian Femininity and Masculinity in Post-Indentured Trinidad." In *Matikor: The Politics of Identity for Indo-Caribbean Women*, edited by Rosanne Kanhai, 62–99. St. Augustine, Trinidad and Tobago: University of the West Indies, School of Continuing Studies.

———. 2009. "The Asian 'Other' in the Caribbean." *Small Axe: A Caribbean Journal of Criticism* 13, no. 2: 57–71.

Nandy, Ashis. 1983. *The Intimate Enemy: Loss and Recovery of Self under Colonialism*. New Delhi: Oxford University Press.

Niranjana, Tejaswini. 2006. *Mobilizing India: Women, Music, and Migration between India and Trinidad*. Durham, NC: Duke University Press.

Omi, Michael, and Howard Winant. 1994. *Racial Formation in the United States: From the 1960s to the 1990s*. New York: Routledge.

Peterson, Indira Viswanathan, and Davesh Soneji. 2008. "Introduction." In *Performing Pasts: Reinventing the Arts in Modern South India*, edited by Indira Viswanathan Peterson and Davesh Soneji, 1–40. New Delhi: Oxford University Press.

Prashad, Vijay. 2001. *Everybody Was Kung Fu Fighting: Afro-Asian Connections and the Myth of Cultural Purity*. Boston: Beacon Press.

Puar, Jasbir K., and Amit S. Rai. 2004. "The Remaking of a Model Minority: Perverse Projectiles under the Specter of (Counter)Terrorism." *Social Text* 22, no. 3: 75–104.

Radhakrishnan, Smitha. 2008. "Examining the 'Global' Indian Middle Class: Gender and Culture in the Silicon Valley/Bangalore Circuit." *Journal of Intercultural Studies* 29, no. 1: 7–20.

———. 2011. *Appropriately Indian: Gender and Culture in a New Transnational Class*. Durham, NC: Duke University Press.

Ragbir, Anusha. 2012. "Fictions of the Past: Staging Indianness, Identity and Sexuality among Young Women in Indo-Trinidadian Beauty Pageants." *Caribbean Review of Gender Studies*, no. 6: 1–21.

Ramamurthy, Priti. 2008. "All-Consuming Nationalism: The Indian Modern Girl in the 1920s and 1930s." In *The Modern Girl Around the World: Consumption, Modernity, and Globalization*, edited by Alys Eve Weinbaum, Lynn M. Thomas, Priti Ramamurthy, Uta G. Poiger, Madeleine Yue Dong, and Tani E. Barlow, 147–73. Durham, NC: Duke University Press.

Ramey, Steven. 2011. "Hindu Minorities and the Limits of Hindu Inclusiveness: Sindhi and Indo-Caribbean Hindu Communities in Atlanta." *International Journal of Hindu Studies* 15, no. 2: 209–39.

Reddy, Vanita. 2015. *Fashioning Diaspora: Beauty, Femininity, and South Asian American Culture*. Philadelphia, PA: Temple University Press.

Roshanravan, Shireen M. 2009. "Passing-as-if: Model-Minority Subjectivity and Women of Color Identification." *Meridians: feminism, race, transnationalism* 10, no. 1: 1–31.

Rudrappa, Sharmila. 2004. *Ethnic Routes to Becoming American: Indian Immigrants and the Cultures of Citizenship*. New Brunswick, NJ: Rutgers University Press.

Ruhomon, Joseph. 1998. "India—The Progress of Her People at Home and Abroad, and How Those in British Guiana May Improve Themselves (1894)." In *They Came in Ships: An Anthology of Indo-Guyanese Prose and Poetry*, edited by Joel Benjamin, Lakshmi Kallicharan, Ian McDonald, and Lloyd Searwar, 44–50. Leeds, UK: Peepal Tree Press.

Sangari, Kumkum, and Sudesh Vaid, eds. 1990. *Recasting Women: Essays in Indian Colonial History*. New Brunswick, NJ: Rutgers University of Press.

Scher, Philip W. 2003. *Carnival and the Formation of a Caribbean Transnation*. Gainesville: University Press of Florida.

Schultz, Anna. 2014. "Bollywood *Bhajans*: Style as 'Air' in an Indian-Guyanese Twice-Migrant Community." *Ethnomusicology Forum* 23, no. 3: 383–404.

Seecharan, Clem. 1992. *India and the Shaping of the Indo-Guyanese Imagination, 1890s–1920s*. Leeds, UK: Peepal Tree Press.

Thangaraj, Stanley. 2010. "Ballin' Indo-Pak Style: Pleasures, Desires, and Expressive Practices of 'South Asian American' Masculinity." *International Review for the Sociology of Sport* 45, no. 3: 372–89.

Vertovec, Steven. 2000. *The Hindu Diaspora: Comparative Patterns*. London: Routledge.

Weidman, Amanda. 2003. "Gender and the Politics of Voice: Colonial Modernity and Classical Music in South India." *Cultural Anthropology* 18, no. 2: 194–232.

———. 2006. *Singing the Classical, Voicing the Modern: The Postcolonial Politics of Music in South India*. Durham, NC: Duke University Press.

———. 2012. "Musical Genres and National Identity." In *The Cambridge Companion to Modern Indian Culture*, edited by Vasudha Dalmia and Rashmi Sadana, 247–63. Cambridge Companions to Culture. Cambridge: Cambridge University Press.

American Movies

Grace M. Cho

I knew few things about my mother's past when I was young. Among them, I knew that American movies captivated her imagination when she was coming of age in 1960s South Korea. She credited the movies for teaching her English, as well as for giving her Western-style tips—a fashion sense she described as "high class." Her favorite films were *Doctor Zhivago* and anything starring Grace Kelly. If I had paid more attention I might have realized the depth of American cinema's impact on my mother's psyche, that through the movies she nurtured her most intimate desires—for glamour and intrigue and romance, and maybe above all, for recognition. When she sat in the dark, in front of that screen, the future was infinite, and her heart told her that she was destined for great things.

Life in America didn't live up to my mother's Technicolor dreams. There was no great love, no epic adventure in which she was the heroine, no resolution to her conflict. Whatever romance there might have once been between my father and her fizzled by the time I was five or six, and although she relished a few fleeting moments in which her movie-star good looks turned heads in our rural town, the mundane reality of her immigrant life was that it gave her more struggle than anything else. The Korean word I heard her say most often when she spoke to relatives was *gosaeng*. Hardship. Suffering.

Despite her nostalgia for the American movies of her girlhood, I hardly remember my mother going to the movies once we moved to the U.S. She was too busy working: piecing together income from cleaning houses and picking strawberries in Washington state, where we lived.

Although my father made a good income as a merchant marine, he didn't give her access to his money, and instead left her an allowance during

***WSQ: Women's Studies Quarterly* 47: 1 & 2 (Spring/Summer 2019)**

his months-long absences at sea. According to my mother, my father was a "stingy no-good son-of-a-bitch" and a "cheapskate" because it wasn't nearly enough to take care of a family. According to my father, she could make do if only she tried harder and gave up the things that he deemed unnecessary. Regardless, my mother felt compelled to earn her own money.

Eventually she landed a full-time job working the graveyard shift at the juvenile detention center, where her hours were 11:00 p.m. to 7:00 a.m. Then she would come home for her second shift—get us kids ready for school, clean the house, some days take a nap and other days work at another odd job, cook dinner, sleep for four hours before going to back to work. *Always I am working, working.*

Now I look back at her American theatergoing days and can count only four movies that she watched between 1981 and 1993, beginning and ending with films starring Harrison Ford.

The first one was *Raiders of the Lost Ark,* which we saw as part of the only birthday party I ever had as a kid. I had begged her all year for a real American birthday party, the kind where you invite other kids and go out for pizza, not the Korean kind, where you sit at home and eat a bowl of seaweed soup.

My mother sat in the middle of the row, with three girls on either side of her, and for some reason, seemed vaguely uncomfortable. When one of my guests leaned across me to ask her if she was enjoying the film, my mother mumbled, "It's all right." Her lukewarm response triggered a pang of guilt, as I knew that the birthday party was costing her "an arm and legs." I had wanted her to at least enjoy the movie. After that, I never asked for another birthday party, and we resumed our tradition of keeping birthday celebrations in the family.

Three years later, for my thirteenth birthday, I asked her to take me to see *Christine,* the film adaptation of Stephen King's novel about a demonic car. I was excited to see the movie, but about half an hour in, she began chastising me for my inappropriate choice of film.

"What kind of movie is this? All kind of filthy language!"

"Mom! Don't yell. Everybody's looking at us."

"I don't care! You are not watching this!" She grabbed my arm and dragged me out of the theater, and our second movie excursion was aborted.

I was baffled.

I knew it wasn't the violence that she objected to in *Christine* because we had a long tradition of enjoying scary movies together. She had introduced me to horror films when I was just six years old, when we started a Saturday night ritual of staying up late and watching *Sinister Cinema,* a weekly television broadcast of movies like *The House of Wax, Dracula's Daughter,* and *Trilogy of Terror.*

"All kind of filthy language," she had said, but the cursing wasn't any different from what I was used to hearing at home. Perhaps the most logical explanation would have been that the things she heard the characters say in *Christine* were not at all the same things I heard—maybe she heard them cursing directly at her, assaulting her with sexually violent words. *You fucking whore.*

But I couldn't have imagined that then. It would be another two years before I understood that she was hearing voices, another ten before I learned that she had been a sex worker for the U.S. military in Korea.

I was mortified after the *Christine* debacle, and there were many more incidents during my adolescence when my mother behaved in ways that embarrassed me. I made no further attempts to go see movies with her, or do anything else in public, for that matter. But one day, during my junior year of high school, she made a proposition.

"Grace-*ya,* will you go see a movie with me?"

"You want to see a movie?"

"There's a movie called *Can't Buy Me Love.* The title reminds me of your father," she said with indignation rising in her voice. She paused for a moment, recovering her calm and asked, "Do you want to go?"

"Not really," I said.

Her silence communicated her disappointment, but I didn't care. In those days, being with her was stressful, and all I wanted was to spend time with my boyfriend. Not until long after my mother had stopped going to the movie theater did I learn that she had seen *Can't Buy Me Love* by herself. Apparently, she had chosen the movie strictly based on the title and had no idea what it was about. My father had a history of exerting power over her with his money, starting with their first encounter in Korea, when he paid for her sexual labor. I think she had hoped the movie would tell her story, but it was just a silly teen rom-com.

The last time she saw a movie in the theater was in 1993, the year I graduated from college. She had recently separated from my father and moved to the East Coast to be close to my brother and me. My brother and his wife had just had a baby—my mother's first grandchild, though the circumstances in my family did not put my mother in the position of being an extra caregiver for the baby. Her mental health was steadily declining and she moved near us so that she herself could get extra care.

Nonetheless, her arrival was significant in that it brought my family together for a moment. One weekend, my brother and I decided to take her to see *The Fugitive*—*Domangja* in Korean—which had been one of her favorite TV series before she moved to the United States. It was the only time the three of us had ever gone to the movies together. Afterward, we asked her what she thought of the movie, and for the first time, she seemed utterly pleased by the experience.

"You remember?" she asked my brother. "We used to watch *Domangja* together in Korea! Yah, it's good. Lots of srill on 'em!"

My brother and I looked at each other trying to decipher that last sentence.

"What did she say?" my brother asked, under his breath.

"Lots of srill on 'em," she said. "Srill, srill."

"Ohhh. Thrills," I whispered. I was surprised to hear how much she liked the movie and wondered if there was more to her delight than the fond memories of Korea.

We emerged from the darkness of the theater into a brightly lit shopping mall, and my brother excused himself to go to the bathroom. The instant he had his back turned, my mother darted into a nearby J. C. Penney. I followed her into the baby section, where she was perusing quilts.

"Mom, what are you doing? Let's go."

"I'm getting present for baby."

"Don't get that. They don't need any more blankets. Let's go."

I'm not sure why I discouraged her from buying it. I think it was partly out of fear that, in her haste, she had chosen something that would get a chilly reception from my sister-in-law and that my mother would be disappointed, and partly out of my own impatience. I also worried that, because my brother didn't know where we had gone, our disappearance would cause unnecessary confusion. I tried to pull the package out of her hands, but she tightened her grip. We squabbled over it a moment longer, and then she raised her voice and said, "I want to get present for baby!" There were tears in her eyes.

A salesclerk looked up at us, and my mother's face flickered with shame. I was embarrassed that I had instigated an argument in public and even more so that I had made my mother's lack of authority so apparent. Who was I to deny her the pleasure of buying her only grandchild a gift, of doing what any other grandmother would do? She bought the blanket and we both slunk out of J. C. Penney not speaking a word. We got home and my mother presented the blanket to my sister-in-law, who opened the package, thumbed the fabric, and offered a half-hearted "thank you."

Though I had correctly foreseen my sister-in-law's less than effusive reaction, I later hated myself for my arrogance. At twenty-two, I knew almost nothing about the world and even less about my mother.

The remorse for having humiliated my mother lingered for days, but it took years to feel the full impact of my actions. I wish I had known then that we were running out of time. But the truth of the matter is that we had plenty of time left—years ahead of us in which I would contemplate the scope of my mother's life, years in which we would sit quietly together in her apartment longing for things to be different.

Hundreds of unwatched movies later, I realized what I had done that night—I put a damper on the best and last moviegoing experience I would ever have with my mother. About a week after we saw *The Fugitive,* she began having panic attacks every time she had to leave her house. She couldn't bear to go outside unless it was "absolutely necessary." Midway through 1994, she became so severely agoraphobic that she could no longer leave the house unaccompanied. She stopped shopping or running errands, and only emerged from her cocoon once every few months for someone to take her to her psychiatric appointments. It was around this time that she first tried to kill herself. "Because I feel worthless."

During the next fourteen years, the remainder of her life, I went to see lots of movies. If I saw one that she might like, I rented it for her when it came out on video. We watched thousands of movies—new movies and old movies, art house films and blockbusters, yet none of them made up for the sorrow I felt that we couldn't watch them together in the theater. The irony of my mother's American movie fantasies became even more bitter once I realized how her story was going to end.

For a time, I still had hope that one day she would be able to go out again. There was one moment in particular when it almost happened, about seven years into her life as a recluse. One day she decided that she wanted me to take her to the Korean grocery store in Manhattan's Koreatown. I was shocked and elated by the request. She got dressed, put on her makeup, and curled her hair, and the whole time we talked about everything she was going to buy. "*Misu karu.* Oh, I can't wait to taste *misu karu,*" she said, practically salivating at the memory of the sweet toasted grain drink of her childhood. The anticipation in the room was palpable. She was one beat away from opening the front door and taking a step outside before she changed her mind.

"Oh, never mind. It's a bad idea," she said.

"C'mon, Mom. Let's go. It'll be fun."

"I'd better not."

"Please, Mom. Let me take you out. I promise everything will be all right."

"No. It's okay." Her smile evaporated and she returned to her usual place on the couch, in the darkness of her living room.

As I grew into my twenties and thirties, I listened to my friends talk about all the things they did with their mothers. They spoke about mundane things like shopping and gardening and going out to eat, or extraordinary things like European vacations and wedding plans and being together for the birth of their children. Whatever it was, they completely took for granted that their mothers still lived in the world. I listened to them talk and tried to remember what it was like to be with my mother and not be confined to her one-room apartment. The memory that was always there, just below the surface of my consciousness, was of our last trip to the movies. I could still feel it in my skin—that sense of freedom and excitement we shared when we walked outside together in the open night air.

More than twenty years after we saw *The Fugitive*, after my mother died, I understood why it was so thrilling to her—she probably identified with Harrison Ford's character, Richard Kimble, a protagonist who was wrongly accused of a crime, persecuted by the authorities, and ultimately vindicated. This was a basic plotline in my mother's delusions. Maybe in *The Fugitive*, she was able to see herself, her life, as worthy.

I knew that I could never get my mother back—I had lost her long before her death—but I still wished that I could rewrite the memory of that night so that it ended with her still basking in the "srill," feeling like the star of an American movie.

Grace M. Cho is associate professor of sociology and anthropology at the College of Staten Island, CUNY. She is author of *Haunting the Korean Diaspora: Shame, Secrecy, and the Forgotten War*. Her creative nonfiction explores notions of hunger and survival in the context of immigration and U.S. imperialism. She can be reached at grace.cho@csi.cuny.edu.

Facebook Mama

Sokunthary Svay

As most refugee and immigrant children will tell you, it is not an unusual thing to have a parent call you in a panic about something their particular generation has yet to master.

"Chup, my phone not work. I not know why. I on the Facebook and it gone!"

And so begins a Friday afternoon saga wherein my mother, Yim Long, takes a train from the West Farms housing project in the Bronx, where she has lived since 1992 (when I was twelve), to have me, and only me, diagnose her device issues. We live in Forest Hills, Queens, which is in the middle of the borough of Queens and halfway toward Long Island. On a good day the commute can take just over an hour. During rush hour, it's closer to two. But my mother originally asked for Fridays and Saturdays off so that she could go to a myriad of doctor appointments without having to use up personal days. Fortunately, she was already off and able to spend the time and money to have her only daughter diagnose this phone issue.

As it happens, having her available on Fridays helps my partner and me have a date night that would otherwise add up to thousands of dollars a year. My daughter, Soriya, would be whisked off to her grandmother's in the Bronx on the subway as quickly as possible in order to avoid rush hour. The 4 and 5 subway lines on the Upper East Side have always been notorious for their crowding. As my mother ages into her midsixties, I worry for her bones and hope for a seat. She is more concerned about my near-eleven-year-old getting a seat. This is the Khmer way, the motherly-grandmotherly way, to care for others in place of oneself.

Which is why the desperation of her phone not working, and therefore her sudden isolation from Facebook, is out of character. I'm almost certain

WSQ: Women's Studies Quarterly 47: 1 & 2 (Spring/Summer 2019)

that if given the choice, my mother would prefer to never have anyone lift a finger for her. In any case, she shows up to my home with bao buns for Soriya, and chicken and rice from the halal cart for me (even though I specifically told her I wasn't hungry).

"Here. My friend he try to do say I need to add. I don't know . . ."

I wave off the explanation because it never really quite adds up to useful information. I would have to infer from the device itself. First, it's clear that the Facebook phone app is not there. It has somehow disappeared, so of course I go to the app store and try to download it. When I press the icon to download, the phone prompts me to enter the password for her Apple ID. There is where the meddlesome work begins. It's important to know that my mother has a low level of literacy (in the more traditional sense of reading and writing) as well as digital literacy. Still, she's pretty good for a woman who grew up in the rice fields with no electricity. Even so, all her social networking and device accounts have been set up by her husband, my father, Chy Svay. So in order for her to even use her iPhone and iPad (yes, she has an iPad, too), my father had to set up an Apple ID to log her in, as well as create accounts for Facebook. Apple updates are an especially confusing time for her since the phone stops functioning normally and instead is in limbo until the update is complete.

With a deep sigh, because I know there will be a lot of back-and-forth, I text my father to ask what her password is. He sends me one with my niece's name. "With a capital *S*," he clarifies. It doesn't work. So I try a different spelling, different capitalizations. It doesn't work. Meanwhile, my daughter has joined the saga and is watching from the counter, munching on the food her Yiey (Khmer for grandmother) has brought. My mother is watching carefully. She knows I'm capable of miracles.

I text my father again from her phone and tell him it doesn't work. He tells me to delete the account and make a new one. This seems to be a common response among Khmers of my parents' generation. If you know of any refugee/immigrant parents with more than one social networking account on the same platform, it's likely they did not save their password. So I sent a text to remind and chastise my father. Figure 1 is a screenshot of what I wrote to him, whom I lovingly dub "Old Man."

And it's completely true—my mother can't live without her Facebook. On so many levels now, it functions and completes her life in ways that would have taken so many other social circles and networks to overlap and culminate. Instead, this rice farmer from the province of Takeo has become

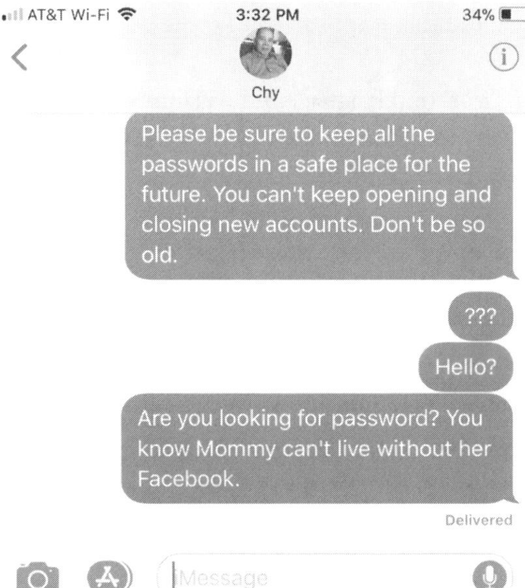

Fig. 1. iPhone screenshot of text conversation with the author and her father, 2018

reliant on her Apple devices and Facebook app for a large portion of her life. Let's take a look at the breakdown of the functions of Facebook in her life. And because I enjoy breaking conventions, I will use bullet points:

- Dissemination of information in the form of posts, typically with photos of herself and her family. Unlike the airmail letters she used to provide her family updates and money (the money she still sends that way or through people, but letters, not so much), she can get the word out quicker about how she's doing (i.e., prospering).
- Overall, a way to keep in touch with family, although she has also taken to FaceTime, a prospect so implausible in the eighties, it's incredible how normalized it has become.
- Sharing of posts functions as a way to reinforce her belief system (Buddhism) and her (limited) interest in the current politics of Cambodia, as well as opinions she wants to share.
- Interaction through her response to posts in the form of one-word replies such as "cute," "beautiful" (that was a difficult spelling to teach her), "how are u?" and "miss you."

(Bullet points aside, why is her dependency on the Facebook platform significant, so much so that I half-jokingly said that my "Mommy can't live without [it]"?)

Finally, my MA in language and literacy can be of some use:

- For a person who speaks a second language but has limited literacy in her native one and a much more limited literacy in her adopted country, Facebook has improved her digital literacy.

When we first had only desktops, they were these big clunky devices, yet another large piece of furniture for her to clean but otherwise inaccessible. These new compact devices have made it much more accessible for daily usage, without the need for more traditional forms of literacy. She knows how to turn on the device and open applications. Whatever she wants to learn, she actually seeks out instruction from someone she trusts (like me), and learns to upload photos and write specific words and phrases as needed for a given situation. Much like learning to read subway signs, a survival tactic for when she first came to this country, she learns to read signs, colors, and fonts. Digital literacy functions as a social survival tool.

- She establishes an online, social identity.

I've learned more new things about my mother and the way she interacts with the outside world through her Facebook activity. She is not a fan of Prime Minister Hun Sen; she shows concern about the ecological state of Cambodia and the persecution of those who protect the lands; she believes in sharing knowledge from her Buddhist background through images with texts, and even some animated videos of a Buddha.

- Most importantly, she is (re)connecting to a world that she was separated from early on.

My mother had an arranged marriage with my father at the age of fifteen. This was pretty common then, and you would be considered a spinster if you weren't married by eighteen. She dropped out of school after giving birth to my older brother, Sothy, after which she had another son, Sothear (who died from dysentery during the regime), and then was sent off to be a forced laborer under the Khmer Rouge regime. She and her family journeyed through the jungle to the refugee camp where I was born and then resettled in the United States, in the Bronx. The majority of Yim's adult life has been about survival and struggle. When did she get to be a youth? To flirt and dance? To get into trouble? Many of these socializing, educational (and hence economical) opportunities were lost the moment she got married and bore children. Her gender functioned as a way to keep her from economic advantages that her husband benefited from—he completed school (in French), joined the military and became a scribe, and picked up English more easily during resettlement because of his educational background. The doors that opened for my father were never open for her the moment she was married off, which was the only option for a woman at that time.

Facebook socialization has become a way for her to regain the things that she lost from growing up so quickly in what became such a tumultuous time in her country's history and in her personal life. She positions herself in the outside world through her limited words, her responses to specific family members and friends. When she sends a friend request, she is widening this circle, one closed to her because she couldn't log onto a website, or create an email account for an email she could never write, or because she didn't have time off from work to meet her children's friends.

She doesn't know how to type. But she has started texting my daughter. She uses emojis. Yim is an expressive woman, and the emojis seem especially appropriate for her. My mother has always been social, but her socialization has been limited to her coworkers and her next-door neighbor, sometimes a phone call or two with someone in the refugee community. Now, my mother has "friended" *my* friends. She has taken an interest in dog photos (she never mentioned dogs when I was growing up, but she recently admitted that there had been some strays hanging out beside her home that she liked).

I don't know if this is who my mother has always been or if it has been compounded by the presence of social media. I like to think it's a bit of both, part of her still growing as a person while she grows into these devices. Even as we speak about the dangers that lurk in these devices with children, I'm still so grateful to learn more of who my mother is. As I grew, at a certain point, I lost track of her and our relationship suffered, but I find myself tickled to learn some new aspect of her based on her Facebook posts.

Eventually my father gets me the correct password for the Apple ID login (note: it was the wrong granddaughter's name). Now I'm able to download the Facebook app. Unfortunately, once I open it up, I realize that I don't have the password for her account. I send a text to my father again and he tells me I should just get a new password. In this case, he was right. In a great security move, my mother's phone is recognized by the app and I'm able to get a new passcode to log in. My brow is relaxed and my mother is instantly relieved, though she hadn't been overly worried in the first place, because I am the daughter who performs miracles. The irony that my father and I are solving this problem through texts is not lost on me. This series of texts is more words than he will say to me in three months, but that's another story.

I show her the phone with her Facebook account logged in. She puts her hand in prayer position and thanks me like I'm the Buddha. She had been holding her breath this whole time thinking that her connection, her main link to her social life, might be forever gone. But it's not.

"Oh my god," she exclaims. "Outside the cloud so beautiful!"

It's a hilarious moment because the sky is dark and overcast, with a strong rain that just let up. But really her day had brightened and so she was being funny and poetic at the same time. LOL.

"Good Luck, Homey"

You know,
    my life
        good.
Now I know
It like I happy.
I use the skype,
    facebook
        and I not alone.

I take the picture
put on the facebook
and everybody like it.
I not know how to read before
but now
        I GOOD.

How you write "beautiful"?
I want to write when I see the

picture of my friend
say "how are you"

"look good, sister"

That how you spell?
Oh my god. I never know.
Now I know. You see,
I learn so much from you.

You see honey, you my good luck.

Sokunthary Svay is pursuing her PhD in English at the CUNY Graduate Center with a focus on Southeast Asian American sociopoetics. Her poetry collection, *Apsara in New York*, is available from Willow Books. She is a 2018 Poets House Fellow and can be reached at sokuntharysvay@gmail.com.

PART II. **DIASPORIC GEOGRAPHIES**

Diaspora Revisited: Toward a Transnational Feminist Critique

Cathy J. Schlund-Vials

Abstract: This essay explores how Operation Urgent Fury, the invasion of Grenada in 1983, shapes diasporic subjectivity. Examining Audre Lorde's "Grenada Revisited" (1984) and Monica Sok's "Yearning" (2016), the author argues that these two texts dialogically form a diasporic feminist synthesis that refuses—in the face of overpowering American military might, bellicose melancholy, diasporic loss, and pervasive indifference—to disremember. Ultimately, it is through this subtle manipulation of interpretive poetics, memory work, and recollective labor that Sok and Lorde engender a new way of seeing the legacies of war and the ongoingness of conflict. **Keywords:** Operation Fury, Grenada, Audre Lorde, Monica Sok, diaspora, memory

The first time I came to Grenada I came seeking "home" for this was my mother's birthplace and she had always defined it so for me. Vivid images remained of what I saw there and of what I knew it could become . . .

The second time I came to Grenada I came in mourning and fear that this land which I was learning had been savaged, invaded, its people maneuvered into saying thank you to their invaders.

—*Audre Lorde, "Grenada Revisited: An Interim Report"*

I want to know the names of things
only the names in Khmer.
I want to know the names of trees
whose roots grow on temple roofs.

WSQ: Women's Studies Quarterly **47: 1 & 2 (Spring/Summer 2019)**

I don't want to know my uncle was never found.
When my aunts looked for his face, his was not there.
I don't want to learn my aunt's twin sister died.
Or why Bong Soto's father got killed.
—*Monica Sok, "Yearning"*

On October 25, 1983, at approximately 5:00 a.m., American troops and coalitional Caribbean forces—under the militarized auspices of the U.S.-led Operation Urgent Fury—were deployed en masse from Grantley Adams International Airport (Barbados) to Grenada, a small island nation located roughly one hundred miles north of Venezuela. Colloquially referred to by locals as "just south of paradise, just north of frustration," and euphemistically known as "the Spice Isle" (due to its international status as a key exporting hub for nutmeg and mace), Grenada—and its population of 91,000 (the demographic equivalent of contemporaneous Fargo, North Dakota)—was a decidedly *unexpected* setting and domestic audience for the first major operation conducted by the U.S. military since the Vietnam War (1959–1975).[1] Ineludibly, as the United States grappled with the all-too-recent memory of the failed Southeast Asian endeavor, struggled to maintain its economic prominence on a world stage (increasingly dominated by deindustrialization and Japanese trade war), strived to adjust to unpredictable Soviet regime shifts (via a dizzying succession of communist party leaders), and strained to respond to heightened Middle East conflict (which included bombings of U.S. embassies and on-site American military installations), Grenada was to most Americans—prior to Operation Urgent Fury—an infrequently accessed tourist location and largely unknown Atlantic Ocean atoll.

On the one hand, this geographic dismissiveness with regard to island and nation explicitly underscores a now-recognizable and oft-deployed U.S.-centrism vis-à-vis other countries; such American exceptionalism, more often than not, is rendered evident in the court of public opinion and made tragically apparent on the battlefield. When Operation Urgent Fury commenced, 63 percent of Americans supported the campaign. Such assuredness with regard to international military maneuver, however, was not matched on the ground; illustratively, U.S. Marines reportedly relied on old tourist maps of the island, dramatically underscoring a lack of military preparedness (History.com 2009). On the other hand, and in a more implicit vein, such indifference by means of strategic amnesia transects with what Lisa Lowe (2015) has recently termed the incontrovertible "intimacies"—via palimpsestic colonialisms and interconnected politics—of seemingly disparate locales and ostensibly disjointed archives. As this transnational, transatlantic, and transpacific reflection subsequently makes clear, these recollected intimacies—comprised of undermined histories and personal reflections—evocatively encapsulate the work featured in this special issue about Asian diasporas and feminist critique. Congruently, as guest editors Lili Shi and Yadira Perez Hazel of this special issue of *WSQ* constructively contend, integral to imagining and narrating Asian diasporas is ultimately an intersectional, feminist examination that—to draw directly from the issue's original "call for papers"—refracts, reflects, and recalibrates "gendering spaces and times that intertwine stories of race, transnationalism, citizenship, and postcoloniality" (Shi and Hazel 2017). Accordingly, Shi and Hazel—via their capacious refusals to monolithically read "Asia" as merely a "geographic term"—compellingly reason (along with the contributors included herein) that the notion of "Asia" is necessarily a "comparative one . . . the collective sum of heterogeneous racial, regional and transhistorical politics that transcends bodies and identities of 'Asia' across Global South and North" (2017).

In so doing, Shi and Hazel build on Kuan-Hsing Chen's (2010) influential conceptualization of "Asia" not as a cartographically defined place but rather a dynamically variegated space wherein politics and cultural production extend in global fashion beyond the limiting parameters of the traditional nation-state. As the essays in this *WSQ* special issue make clear, at stake in reseeing transnational affect and recasting diasporic subjects is what Chen characterizes as a deimperializing, decolonizing "Asia as method." As Chen clarifies, "Decolonization is the attempt of the previously colonized to reflectively work out a historical relation with the former colonizer, culturally, politically, and economically" (2010, 3). Set against a backdrop of past/present colonialism and unchecked neocolonialism, such reflexive "memory work" lays bare the ongoing relevance of transnational feminist critique.[2] As this essay ultimately maintains (by way of conclusion), to comprehend Monica Sok's invocation of "yearning" (as Cambodian/American hermeneutic) in the introductory epigraph, one must engage a syncretic evaluation of the historical, diasporic, and political interconnectedness embedded in Audre Lorde's above-excerpted

"Grenada Revisited." Consistent with the transnational vision and diasporic conceptualization that animate this special issue, such comparative analyses and evaluative pairings take solemnly and centrally the role art plays in the making of agentic feminist subjects (Espiritu 2014).

Recollecting Grenada: Operation Urgent Fury and Audre Lorde's "Grenada Revisited"

"Discovered" by Christopher Columbus on his third voyage to the New World in 1498, Grenada was originally named "La Concepción" (to honor the Virgin Mary); one year later, Amerigo Vespucci purportedly rechristened the island "Mayo." During the 1520s, the Spanish renamed the territory's northerly islands "Los Granadillos"; soon after, the name "Mayo" was replaced by "Grenada" on Spanish maps. Following French settlement and colonization in the mid-sixteenth century, the seven-island archipelago was known as "La Grenade." Ceded in 1763 to the British as a territorial "spoil" of the Seven Years' War (1757–1763), Grenada would remain a Commonwealth territory until February 7, 1974, when—roughly two decades after its colonial counterparts in Asia and Africa—it was granted political independence.[3]

To be sure, Grenada's sovereignty was by no means secure nor was its newly institutionalized governance without conflict. Soon after Eric Gairy assumed the role of prime minister, a political back-and-forth commenced between the left-of-center Grenada United Labour Party and the New Joint Endeavor for Welfare, Education, and Liberation (a.k.a., New JEWEL Movement, or NJM), a Marxist-Leninist vanguard led by Maurice Bishop. While Gairy and his party claimed victory via a 1976 general election, the opposition maintained otherwise, presaging a tense period of widespread street violence and pervasive political unrest. On March 13, 1979, Bishop and the NJM engaged a successful coup d'état and established the People's Revolutionary Government, which suspended Grenada's constitution and ruled by decree until October 14, 1983, when a party faction led by Deputy Prime Minister Bernard Coard assumed control. Bishop was summarily placed under house arrest, prompting in-country protests. Amid ensuing chaos, the former head of state escaped, though Bishop was eventually captured and executed (along with other loyal government officials). The country, now under General Hudson Austin, dismantled the People's Revolutionary Government and instituted a four-day curfew total wherein anyone found in the nation's streets would face the possibility of summary execution (BBC News 2012).

Notwithstanding the violent politics and vexed dynamics which brought the martial government "into being," General Austin's regime only lasted six days due to the aforementioned Operation Urgent Fury, a multilateral, pan-regional late–Cold War military campaign. Even with President Ronald Reagan's assurances that the U.S.-driven siege was a response to "an urgent request from five member nations of the Organization of Eastern Caribbean States," the U.S invasion of Grenada was at the time critically characterized as "extreme" and intercontinentally unpopular (Reagan 1983). Predicated on the false assumption that Grenada's recently completed Point Salines International Airport was a cover for a Soviet-Cuban airstrip, and hegemonically consistent with the imperial tenets of the 1823 Monroe Doctrine, the U.S. invasion married Cold War realpolitik to long-standing notions of American hemispheric influence.[4] Cynics, critics, and skeptics alike noted that the U.S. invasion of Grenada occurred two days after discernible diplomatic disaster in Beirut: expressly, on October 23, 1983, two trucks—loaded with munitions—crashed into barracks housing Multinational Force in Lebanon peacekeepers, claiming 307 lives (241 Americans, 58 French, 6 civilians, and the 2 suicide bombers).

Regardless of extant foreign policy concerns, the invasion initially struck a problematic chord insofar as the United Kingdom and Canada had provided funds to construct the aforementioned Grenadian airport. Correspondingly, British prime minister Margaret Thatcher (a stalwart U.S. ally) privately voiced concern over the invasion though publicly stressed support; Canadian authorities were confessedly less ambiguous in their denunciation of the U.S. invasion. Perhaps most telling was the response issued by the United Nations General Assembly, which condemned the invasion as a "flagrant violation of international law" by a 108–9 vote (Bernstein 1983). Consistent with the course of U.S. war-making over the course of the twentieth century, the so-termed "invasion of Grenada" was euphemistically cast by Reagan as "a joint effort to restore order and democracy on the island" (Reagan 1983). Accordingly couched by Reagan as a campaign meant to "protect innocent lives, including 1,000 Americans," "forestall further chaos," and "assist the restoration of conditions of law and order and the governmental institutions to the island of Grenada," Operation Urgent Fury vis-à-vis presidential rhetoric and foreign policy justification tactically eschewed military objective in favor of humanitarian intervention (Reagan 1983). Nevertheless, Operation Urgent Fury was an incontrovertible military endeavor, an effort comprised of 7,600 troops (inclusive of U.S. soldiers and Jamaican combatants, along with members of the recently created Regional Security System) assisted by profound mechanized might (e.g., government-owned helicopters and federally deployed gunships). Dramatically, Operation Urgent Fury as militarized conflict and swift Cold War campaign lived up to its exigent name: the U.S.-supported endeavor lasted a mere four days (October 25–29, 1983) and was marked by relatively few reported civilian casualties (twenty-four), a paucity of American deaths (nineteen), and the quick deposal of General Hudson's government. Notwithstanding the campaign's short duration, and despite international criticism, President Reagan declared the U.S. invasion of Grenada a foreign policy success, characterizing it as the first "rollback" of communist influence in the Cold War era (1945–1989).[5]

Despite such triumphant declarations, and notwithstanding the commemorative fact that the invasion is memorialized as a national holiday ("Thanksgiving Day"), Operation Urgent Fury is—as Audre Lorde's "Grenada Revisited" accentuates—by no means a "settled" narrative nor was it a campaign without collateral cost. As diasporic subject and feminist theorist, Lorde potently accesses a melancholic reading of her "mother's birthplace," wherein the vividness of life is supplanted by a palpable "mourning" and "fear" emblematic of a postintervention "savaged" imaginary (1984, 22). Militating against politicized "otherwise" claims of American-led democraticization and U.S.-sanctioned liberation, Lorde's return "home" intersects with what M. Jacqui Alexander maintains is foundational to "different geographies of feminism," which enable a reinvigorated reevaluation of and pertinent negotiation with "multiple operations of power, of gendered and sexualized power that is simultaneously raced and classed yet not practiced within [the] hermetically sealed or epistemically partial borders of the nation-state" (Alexander 2006, 4). Accordingly, Lorde's negotiations with "multiple operations of power"—which commence with a pre-invasion remembrance of her mother's homeland and conclude with post-invasion dystopic reportage—converge on a transnational feminist sensibility that dialogically brings to light the forgotten dimensions and misremembered aspects of U.S. intervention.

Conclusion: Diasporic Yearning and Transnational Feminist Critique

Lorde's tactical remembrance of the collateral costs of U.S. intervention via state-authorized invasion inadvertently yet potently presages the recollective stakes of Monica Sok's "making visible"—through the purposeful juxtaposition of past and present—the extent to which war is, to revise Chris Hedge's suggestive articulation, a process that brings both Lorde and Sok "into being" as transnational, diasporic subjects (Hedges 2003). With regard to Lorde, such subjectivity is born out of U.S. invasion and euphemistically named humanitarianism; in terms of Sok, this positionality is attributable to the expansive reaches of the Vietnam War, which despite "contained" nomenclature was waged in neighboring Cambodia (via illegal bombings of the nation's countryside) and Laos (which, during the conflict, was a significant CIA hub and remains the most bombed country in the world).[6] Both Grenada and Cambodia were established militarized zones insofar as they were featured keenly in Cold War operations (namely the aforementioned Operation Urgent Fury and President Richard M. Nixon's "Operation Menu," an illicit campaign intended to target National Liberation Front strongholds in Cambodia). Last, but certainly not least, Grenada and Cambodia—despite great distance and the considerable passage of time—function as necessary settings for Lorde's memory-oriented thesis (about U.S. war-making) and Sok's resistive antithesis. Taken together, "Grenada Revisited" and "Yearning" dialogically form a diasporic feminist synthesis that refuses—in the face of overpowering American military might, bellicose melancholy, diasporic loss, and pervasive indifference—to disremember.

Whereas the first stanza of Sok's "Yearning" is characterized by two affirmative statements concerning language (Khmer) and nomenclature (for flora), the next is marked by a series of negative assertions which pivot on "not knowing" and not wanting to know the truth behind the deaths of family members and close friends (inclusive of aunts, siblings, and fathers). As further complication, Sok deliberately employs, then strategically subverts, a litotic construction in the first line of the second stanza: Sok writes, "I don't want to know my uncle was never found" (2016, 10). Connotative of a sardonic understatement wherein an oppositional affirmative is conveyed via a contradictory negative statement (for instance, "not bad," which in conversation means "good" or "serviceable"), litotes are frequently fixed to specific cultural contexts. In writing that she does not "want to know [that] my uncle was never found," Sok makes clear that despite grammatical elision, she does in fact "know" this familial fact. Similarly, when Sok avers that she does not "want to learn" about her aunt's death nor does she desire to know "why Bong Soto's father got killed," the poet's original declaration about not "wanting to learn" is contrastingly undermined by the inclusion of specific loss (e.g., the aunt's twin sister) and adverbial usage (via the use of "why").

In drawing to a close, as antithetical composition, Sok's "Yearning" is simultaneously decontextualized and historicized; while the causes behind such losses are chiefly allusive, the collection's title (*Year Zero*) and its mention of Khmer, temple roofs, and *Bong* (a Cambodian word for "older brother," "older sister," or "older friend") draw tacit attention to what those in Cambodia refer to as "Pol Pot time" and those outside Cambodia recognize as the "Killing Fields era." Between 1975 and 1979, under the catastrophic Khmer Rouge regime, an estimated 1.7 million Cambodians (roughly 21–25 percent of the extant population) perished as a result of disease, starvation, forced labor, execution, and torture. In addition, out of 550 doctors, only forty-eight survived; 90 percent of Khmer court musicians/dancers were killed; and 75 percent of teachers were executed. Despite the passage of four decades since the deposal of the Khmer Rouge regime by Vietnamese forces on January 7, 1979, only three former officials (Kaing Guek Eav, Khieu Samphan, and Nuon Chea) have been found guilty of crimes against humanity and war crimes.[7]

Despite its focus in numerous memoirs, documentaries, and film, "life under the Khmer Rouge" remains at best a predictable narrative (wherein the emphasis concerns life before regime shift, experiences in Cambodia's Killing Fields, and postconflict asylum) and at worst a forgotten story. Acknowledging historical differences and political divergences, it nevertheless becomes apparent that without articulation and in the absence of widespread remembrance, Grenada and Cambodia—as interlinked Cold War combat zones—would tragically fade from cultural view. Hence, it is through this subtle manipulation of interpretive poetics, memory work, and recollective labor that Sok and Lorde engender a new way of seeing the legacies of war and the ongoingness of conflict. In turn, these inheritances—a direct outcome of U.S. militarization, an indirect consequence of "Asia-oriented" Cold War policy, and (in the case of Sok) the result of forced displacement—foreground a connective "yearning" and diasporic (non)belonging that is foundational to a distinctly feminist transnational subjectivity.

Cathy J. Schlund-Vials is professor of English and Asian/Asian American studies at the University of Connecticut; she is also associate dean for Humanities and Diversity, Equity, and Inclusion in UConn's College of Liberal Arts and Sciences. In addition to published book chapters, articles, reviews, and edited collections, she is the author of two monographs: *Modeling Citizenship: Jewish and Asian American Writing* and *War, Genocide, and Justice: Cambodian American Memory Work*. She is a coeditor for Temple University Press's Asian American History and Culture series and was the president of the Association for Asian American Studies (AAAS, 2016–2018). She can be reached at cathy.schlund-vials@uconn.edu.

Notes

1. Nutmeg was introduced to Grenada in 1843 by a merchant ship headed to England. The nutmeg tree (*Myristica fragrans*) is indigenous to the Banda Islands in Indonesia.
2. The use of "memory work" in this instance accesses James Young's *Texture of Memory* (1993), focused on Holocaust memorials. To quickly summarize, the efficacy and effectiveness of a memorial is measured according to the debates raised about historical events and present-day access. This particular notion figures keenly in *War, Genocide, and Justice: Cambodian American Memory Work* (Schlund-Vials 2012).
3. What follows is a brief listing of other countries that had gained independence in the immediate decade or so after World War II: Ethiopia (1951), Sudan (1956), Ghana (1957), Iraq (1958), Guinea (1958), Democratic Republic of Congo, Benin, Upper Volta, Chad, Niger, Central African Republic, Mauritania, Madagascar, Cameroon, and Ivory Coast (1960), Algeria (1962), Kenya, (1963), Malaysia and Singapore (1963), Tanzania (1964), and Zambia (1964).
4. The Monroe Doctrine refers to a U.S. policy involving European colonial engagements in the Americas. Expressly, the doctrine—enacted on December 2, 1823—attempted to delimit European influences on territories in Latin America. To quote the *Oxford English Dictionary*, such colonial acts would be considered "the manifestation of an unfriendly disposition toward the United States." The doctrine was promulgated at a time when most of Spain and Portugal's colonies in the "New World" had gained independence.
5. "Rollback" refers to the forced political shift of a state, usually via the removal of one regime and the installation of another; this Cold War tactic operates

in contrast to "containment," which is a policy wherein the primary objective is to prevent the expansion of a state and its regional influence (Gwertzman 1983).

6. While there was considerable CIA (Central Intelligence Agency) engagement in Cambodia, such personnel were not directly responsible for Laos's infamous designation as the most bombed country in the world. Instead, this characterization is in large part the consequence of a policy wherein pilots were not allowed to bring unexploded ordnance back to the base; pilots were encouraged to drop remaining payloads over Laos.
7. Kaing Guek Eav (a.k.a., Comrade Duch) was the former head warden for S-21 Prison (Tuol Sleng Prison). Of the roughly twelve thousand individuals detained, a little over two hundred survived. Duch's verdict was delivered on July 26, 2010, as per "Case 001" of the Extraordinary Chambers in the Courts of Cambodia. Of the almost twelve thousand inmates interned at S-21, approximately two hundred survived. On August 7, 2014, under the auspices of "Case 002/01," Chea and Samphan (former Khmer Rouge Prime Minister) were convicted and received life sentences for crimes against humanity during the Khmer Rouge era. Chea and Samphan are currently facing crimes of genocide under the rubric of Case 002/02; Case 002 was divided to delineate between crimes against humanity and crimes of genocide.

Works Cited

Alexander, M. Jacqui. 2006. *Pedagogies of Crossing: Meditations on Feminism, Sexual Politics, Memory, and the Sacred*. Durham, NC: Duke University Press.

BBC News. 2012. "Timeline: Grenada." August 7, 2012. http://news.bbc.co.uk/2/hi/americas/1209649.stm.

Bernstein, Richard. 1983. "U.S. Vetoes U.N. Resolution 'Deploring' Grenada Invasion." *New York Times*, October 29, 1983. https://www.nytimes.com/1983/10/29/world/us-vetoes-un-resolution-deploring-grenada-invasion.html.

Chen, Kuan-Hsing. 2010. *Asia as Method: Toward Deimperialization*. Durham, NC: Duke University Press.

Espiritu, Yên Lé. 2014. *Body Counts: The Vietnam War and Militarized Refuge(es)*. Berkeley: University of California Press.

Gwertzman, Bernard. 1983. "Reagan Gains by Grenada, But Mostly on His Own Turf." *New York Times*, November 6, 1983. https://www.nytimes.com/1983/11/06/weekinreview/reagan-gains-by-grenada-but-mostly-on-his-own-turf.html.

Hedges, Chris. 2003. *War Is a Force That Gives Us Meaning*. New York: Anchor Press.

History.com Editors. 2009. "United States Invades Grenada." History.com. Last modified December 13, 2018. https://www.history.com/this-day-in-history/united-states-invades-grenada.

Lorde, Audre. 1984. "Grenada Revisited: An Interim Report." *The Black Scholar* 15, no. 1: 21–29.

Lowe, Lisa. 2015. *The Intimacies of Four Continents*. Durham, NC: Duke University Press.

Schlund-Vials, Cathy J. 2012. *War, Genocide, and Justice: Cambodian American Memory Work*. Minneapolis: University of Minnesota Press.

Shi, Lili, and Yadira Perez Hazel. 2017. "Call for Papers, Poetry, and Prose: *WSQ Asian Diasporas* Issue." https://call-for papers.sas.upenn.edu/cfp/2017/12/16/call-for-papers-poetry-prose-wsq-asian-diasporas-issue.

Sok, Monica. 2016. "Yearning." In *Year Zero*, 10. New York: Poetry Society of America.

Reagan, Ronald. 1983. "Text of Reagan's Statement on Marines Landing in Grenada (October 23, 1983)." *UPI Archives*. https://www.upi.com/Archives/1983/10/25/Text-of-Reagans-statement-on-Marines-landing-in-Grenada/6947178182102/.

Young, James. 1993. *Texture of Memory: Holocaust Memorials and Meaning*. New Haven, CT: Yale University Press.

Cowboys and Indians: Indian Priests in Rural Montana

Sonja Thomas

Abstract: In this article, I examine Catholic missionary priests from India in rural Montana. I begin with an overview of Asian settler colonialism and gender, sexuality, and racialization in the rural. I then discuss the dimensions of religious worker migration, racism, and settler colonialism. Using a *comparative racialization* framework, I locate how privileged groups use notions of victimization to deploy ideas of place-based belonging against racial "others"—the dispossessed and foreign "import." I conclude by examining global connections between white cowboys and Indian priests. The Asian diaspora in rural Montana provides context for the ways in which the Asian diaspora, settler colonialism, and comparative racializations function in the U.S. **Keywords**: transnational feminisms, Asian settler colonialism, queer ruralism, comparative racialization, Native feminisms

On a windy day in June 2016, I am in the passenger's seat of an old car driving across the beautiful landscape of central Montana speaking with Fr. Willie D'Souza. We are driving on a two-lane highway from the small town of Fort Benton to the even smaller town of Geraldine so he can celebrate Mass. Fr. Willie is a priest from India, but has become incardinated into the diocese of Great Falls–Billings in Montana.

As the wind pushes on the car a bit, I say, "Whoa, this must be terrible to drive in the winter."

"Oh yes," he replies. "When I first came to Montana, I was unaware of how difficult it would be to drive in the winter. One time my car went off the road. I had no mobile signal. Luckily, a motorist passed by soon after and stopped to help" (Fr. Willie 2016, pers. comm.).

***WSQ: Women's Studies Quarterly* 47: 1 & 2 (Spring/Summer 2019)**

"Luckily!" I respond. I look down and check my own cell phone. No signal.

St. Margaret's in Geraldine is a small church. While Fr. Willie prepares for Mass, I read a history of the parish priests who served at St. Margaret's, from Reverend Edward C. Morgan in 1916 to Fr. Willie, who arrived at St. Margaret's in 2012. Two congregants arrive, and the Mass begins. At the close of the Mass, Fr. Willie announces my name and tells the two congregants that I am a professor studying Indian priests in Montana. "If you'd like to stay, I'm sure she'll have some questions for you" (Fr. Willie 2016, pers. comm.). As Fr. Willie retreats to the sacristy to remove his vestments, the two congregants, Susan and Caroline, readily make their way to me to shower praise on Fr. Willie. One remarks, "Fr. Willie may do things a bit different than other priests. At first, his accent was hard to understand. But you get used to it. We're so blessed to have him. Without Fr. Willie, they might close our church. That would devastate the Catholics here." "That would devastate the town!" the other congregant exclaims. "The town depends on the church. Whether you are Catholic or not!" (2016, pers. comm.).

I marvel at the complexity of all this. Rural "flyover" communities impacted by out-migration and now facing a declining and aging population, farmers and ranchers both struggling with and welcoming a priest from India, the centrality of a church for rural communities, Indian priests learning how to drive in snow, and the difficult adjustment of an Indian priest to rural American life. Of white cowboys, many who support border walls and anti-immigration policies; and Indians, South Asian priests who serve as missionaries in rural areas of the U.S.

In this article, I examine missionary priests from India in rural Montana through a feminist lens. Using an anti-racist self-reflexive praxis, I contribute to emerging feminist research on the South Asian diaspora, transnational feminisms, queer ruralism, and settler colonialism. Borrowing from Hong and Ferguson's (2011) work on women of color feminisms and queer of color critique, I use a *comparative racialization* framework, examining how privileged groups can use notions of place and victimization to deploy ideas of belonging against racial "others"—the dispossessed and foreign "import"—while simultaneously connecting with racial "others" in and through faith-based communities and practices.[1]

When examining the relationship between cowboys and Indians, I argue that it is critical to understand the ways in which settler colonialism and "legitimate immigration" shape the Asian diaspora. In rural Montana, racialization is produced alongside a history of the genocide of Native Americans and the lauding of a particular white immigrant story as a move to settler colonial innocence that I will discuss in depth in this article. Asian missionary priests may enter into a racialized placemaking that offers little space to understand how spiritual labor and comparative racializations function. Therefore, I center my analysis on Asian presence within an area of the country that Winona LaDuke has called the "Deep North" (2017) and the connections between Indian priests and their largely white congregants.

If ever there was an "insider" to a research project, it is my relationship to Indian priests and Catholicism in Montana. I myself am an upper-caste South Asian American, born and raised in the small town of Glendive, Montana near the North Dakota border. My parents were immigrants and came from the Syro-Malabar Catholic rite based in the state of Kerala, India. Syro-Malabar Catholics are part of an upper-caste Christian community known as the "St. Thomas Christians" or "Syrian Christians" (Thomas 2018). Many, but not all, of the Indian Catholic priests in the United States are from Kerala, India and come from the upper-caste Syrian Christian community. Based on my upbringing in a devout upper-caste South Asian American Catholic family in eastern Montana, I have good deal of personal experience with the Indian Catholic community and its traditions, with Catholicism in eastern Montana, and with the challenges that Indian priests face in rural America.

For this study, I conducted a total of forty interviews all over central and eastern Montana from 2016 to 2018. Eleven of those interviews were with priests—six Indian priests currently serving, two Indian priests who served in the diocese and returned to India, and three American-born white priests including the bishop of the Great Falls–Billings diocese, Michael Warfel. Participants' names have been changed and the names of towns omitted unless participants agreed to be quoted directly.

Asian Settler Colonialism and the Queer Rural

There is new and emerging feminist work on the relationship between Asian diasporas, people of color, and settler colonialism in the U.S. and Canada. Lawrence and Dua (2005) have argued that immigrants and people of color play into settler colonial logics especially by subscribing to a formal-equality politic that has historically worked to dispossess Native peoples of their lands/sovereignty, a process which continues into the present. They suggest that people of color and immigrants, by conforming to nation-state colonialism, are complicit in settler colonialism themselves (Lawrence and Dua 2005). Others have critiqued the paradigm that "all immigrants are settlers." Such a paradigm may deny the history of migration of Native peoples and the current migration of indigenous peoples forced from lands because of postcolonial nationalisms (Sharma and Wright 2008–9). People of color may have a different settler colonial logic than white settlers and/or racial solidarity with Natives which forms as a response to white supremacy, but it would be all too easy to assume racial solidarity based solely on racial oppression. Jonathan Okamura has discussed ethnic identity construction and privileged Asian groups in Hawai'i in relation to other ethnic groups and Native Hawai'ians (Okamura 2008a, 2008b). Similarly, Dean Itsuji Saranillio points out that power doesn't just target oppressed communities, but operates *through* practices of communities and

> offers a way of examining other dynamics of power such as labor, exploitation, anti-immigrant laws and sentiment, and imperialist wars that have historically shaped diverse Asian American groups without misrecognizing the context for framing Asian settlers on Native lands seized by the US settler state. (2016, 108)

I follow Saranillio's assessment that what is needed is not a flattening of differences, assumptions of solidarity, or arguing over who is and is not a settler, but an understanding of power, intersectional oppressions, and the situating of different histories within context (101).

I differ slightly in my analysis from studies on Asian settler colonialism because I am specifically interested in the unique spiritual labor of priests and their migration patterns to rural areas devoid of large Asian communities. Most of the studies on migration do not encapsulate the realities of spiritual leaders who come to rural areas on religious worker visas, some staying for only a limited time, who are not migrating for family reunification, and who do not choose their migration location (Gautier et al. 2014, 29). While scholars of Asian settler colonialism argue for settlers to stand behind Natives and challenge settler practices in their own Asian communities (Fujikane 2018, 30), the same sorts of communities do not exist for priests in rural Montana. On the mainland, the Asian diaspora is often understood through a bicoastal and/or California-centric paradigm which makes it difficult to understand the racialized historical and contemporary presence of Asian Americans outside these geographical spaces (Joshi and Desai 2013, 2). Joshi and Desai argue that Asian American presence in the American South should make us reconsider discourses of race—not through a mere recovery of Asian American histories in the South, but as a productive disruption that should impact how scholars understand race relations, empire, cosmopolitanism, and transnationalism (2013, 3). I would argue that the rural and settler colonialism should also make us reconsider discourses on race especially because so many Native reservations are in rural areas. The Great Falls–Billings diocese, for instance, covers an area of central and eastern Montana where five different reservations and eight different (U.S. recognized) tribes are located.[2] Works on the South Asian diaspora and religion in the U.S. tend to focus on urban areas and assume the racial homogeneity of worshippers (Bhatia 2007; Joshi 2006). Studies specifically on the South Asian Christian diaspora in the U.S. center on upper-caste South Asian Christian churches and upper-caste South Asian American congregants in urban enclaves rather than on the unique spiritual labor of Indian priests and settler colonialism in rural areas of the country (Kurien 2012, 2013; George 2005; Galbraith 2016).

All this complexity is layered onto gendered and sexual norms that frame how South Asian priests may be perceived in rural America. For Catholics especially, the priesthood itself is imbibed with masculinity. The Catholic Church is invested in the idea of complementarity, which stresses that men and women have different, but complementary, roles in Catholicism (Case 2016, 156).[3] The Vatican has argued against ordaining women because women do not possess a "natural resemblance" to Jesus Christ—a natural resemblance that "men" supposedly have in their innate difference from "women" (Raab 2000, 35–38). Congregants might additionally assume that South Asian priests come from a more "traditional" society with clear patriarchal gender roles (Bracke and Paternotte 2016).

But as brown men in rural areas, Indian priests may not be fully able to access the specific white and hypermasculinized narrative of the settler cowboy (Jafri 2013; Glenn 2015, 58). As Beenash Jafri points out,

> What makes the relationship between racialized subjects and settler colonialism so challenging to tease out is that even as racialized subjects access

> colonial power in settler states—for example, through political representation—they remain socially and politically unrecognized as settlers (and thus, unrecognized as wholly human). This failed recognition has implications for how mis- or unrecognized subjects negotiate their place within settler colonialities. (2013, 76)

Further, Stanley Thangaraj has argued that the category of South Asian American may exist outside both the dominant black/white paradigm and the Asian American "model minority" racial logics of American racism (2015, 17–18). Different from (East/Southeast) Asian Americans, South Asian American men in post-9/11 America may experience what Thangaraj has called "Muslim looking" racial formations, whereby South Asian American men are perceived to have a dangerous, excessive masculinity "with the potential to unravel the cultural-political fabric of the US" (2013, 245). This is buttressed by a history of television and movies drawing from orientalist images depicting Arabs and Muslims—often portrayed by South Asian/American actors—as patriarchal, misogynistic, and as terrorists (Alsultany 2012, 7–10). I am attentive, therefore, to the *intersectional* aspects of comparative racialization that impacts the ways in which gender norms, labor, and Indian missionary priests are understood in rural America.

The rural has become an object of inquiry in feminist studies under the rubric of the "queer rural." Much of the work on queer ruralism has centered on queer communities and queer activism in rural areas—areas assumed to be hyperreligious (Evangelical Christian) and homophobic. Studies on queer ruralism have explored rural stylistics that are set against queer urbanism (Herring 2010). As work on the queer rural has shown, "the spatial politics of gender and sexuality are enormously complicated" and a critique of queer "metronormativity" is needed (Johnson, Gilley, and Gray 2016, 6). Uncomforted in the queer rural, however, is the perceived perversity of Catholic priests. Catholic priests may be perceived as particularly "queer"—linked to repressed sexuality, homosexuality, or to pedophilia in the wake of lawsuits and increased media attention on sexual abuse and the cover-ups/protection of abusers by the Catholic hierarchy. In Montana, it is now being reported that many Native children faced sexual abuse in boarding schools with Montana reservations serving as a "dumping ground" for abuser priests (Larson 2017). The Great Falls–Billings diocese has declared bankruptcy due to sexual abuse lawsuits, many brought by Native survivors. How does Asian presence, settler colonialism, and (non-Evangelical) Christianity fit/not fit within the queer rural scholarship? How would queer ruralism understand the "queer" body of a South Asian priest in Montana?

Jasbir K. Puar's (2007) work on American sexual exceptionalism has discussed how South Asian queer diasporic subjects need to produce themselves as exceptional homonormative American subjects especially post-9/11. However, the turbaned bodies of South Asian American Sikh men, often mistaken as Muslim, and attached to hypermasculinity, perverse heterosexuality, and warrior militancy faces a limit. The turbaned body is rendered "neither within the bounds of respectable queer subjecthood nor worthy of a queer intervention that would stage a reclamation of sexual-racial perversity, suggesting that it is a body almost *too perverse to be read as queer*" (Puar 2007, 169). Like the Sikh turbaned body, the body of a South Asian diasporic Catholic priest enters a similar realm of the "almost too perverse to be read as queer" because this body is not considered a "legitimate immigrant" exemplified in settler cowboy masculinity *and* may be seen as a sexually perverse body. Indian priests in rural America should not merely be a strange addition to studies on Asian settler colonialism and/or the queer rural. Rather, Asian presence in the rural exposes the limits of and expands the scope of theoretical inquiry on both the queer rural and Asian settler colonialism. I therefore turn now to that Asian presence and the spiritual labor of Indian priests in rural Montana.

Indian Priests in Montana

Currently, there are over 6,500 international priests serving in the U.S. (Center for Applied Research 2014, 1, 11). The largest number of those priests, 972 of them, come from India (11). Indian priests in the U.S. are either diocesan priests or religious-order priests. Religious-order priests belong to a religious order such as the Capuchins or the Heralds of the Good News. These priests go where their religious order sends them. Indian diocesan priests, on the other hand, belong to a diocese in India and serve for a limited time on missions to the U.S. The majority of international priests in the U.S. today are diocesan priests (Hoge and Okure 2006a, 11). In order for an Indian priest to become a diocesan priest in rural Montana, a connection must somehow be made between the originating diocese and Great Falls–Billings. Once a connection is established, there could be multiple priests who come to a U.S. diocese from that particular Indian diocese. The Great Falls–Billings diocese has had a close connection to the Sagar diocese in India.

International priests enter on a religious order visa (R-1) which grants stay in the U.S. for two and a half years. However, priests usually stay in the Great Falls–Billings diocese for about five to six years. As Bishop Warfel explained to me, the diocese tries to get a permanent visa for Indian diocesan priests immediately because once an investment in a priest is made, it does not make sense economically or resource-wise to start the whole process again after only two years (2016, pers. comm.). Some priests from India become incardinated into the diocese. This means that they change bishops, moving from working under a bishop in India to working under a bishop in the U.S. There are four priests from India who became incardinated into the diocese so far. Incardination can also lead to naturalization. There are currently ten priests from India in the Great Falls–Billings diocese and a number of others who have served in the diocese and returned to India after their mission.

The diocese of Great Falls–Billings covers central and eastern Montana and is the fourth-largest diocese in the United States area-wise (Larsen 2003, 9). Despite the vast territory, the diocese only has a total of 57,000 Catholics (9). Churches in extremely small towns (with a population of roughly 100–2,000) are considered mission churches—served by priests who usually reside in a larger town (with a population of roughly 2,000–8,000).[4] In rural Montana, the work of a priest can be especially daunting because priests travel to one or sometimes two mission churches throughout the week. They celebrate Mass, perform ceremonies like baptisms, funerals, and weddings, council parishioners and hear confessions, and participate in various community and church events in both parish churches and mission churches. The Great Falls–Billings diocese tries to make sure that Indian priests are stationed with an American-born white priest in larger towns when they arrive to help facilitate their transition. Ideally, the two priests share the workload and travel demands.

The Great Falls–Billings diocese does not force closures on churches that are economically viable even if they aren't pastorally viable. That is, if a church can keep the lights on, it will have a priest. The closing of a Catholic church in a sparsely populated area is not the same as the closing of ethnic churches in urban areas where there is another Catholic church just down the road. The closing of a Catholic church would mean that parishioners would have to travel sometimes over forty miles to another church. Parish halls are often rented out for a variety of community functions because they store chairs and tables, and have large kitchens. For both Catholics and non-Catholics, the closing of a Catholic church can be the closing of a town's very identity especially as Protestant churches and schools in small towns have already shut their doors.[5] For many mission towns in the Great Falls–Billings diocese, the acceptance of Indian priests may be tied to the realization that without them, the church could close. According to a white American-born priest, Fr. A., "Parishes are learning to understand them. And they appreciate their spirituality. . . . They also know that this might be the last priest they see. So they better hang on to him. Because there isn't a lot of depth behind. So if they abuse a priest, that doesn't mean they're gonna get Jesus Christ next, it might mean they might get closed next" (2016, pers. comm.).

The limited research on international priests in the U.S. speaks at length about accents or cultural misunderstandings (Hoge and Okure 2006a, 2006b; Gautier et al. 2014). But they stop short of discussing any of this through the lens of America's racist history or current anti-immigrant political rhetoric. Nothing is said about settler colonialism and the racial differences between Indian priests and their largely white congregants in the "Deep North." I don't want to argue that everyone is racist in rural areas of the country. However, it is important to note the ways in which anti-immigrant sentiments play out especially because the research on Indian priests seems to bury the discussion of racism within the more benign rubric of "cultural mismatches" (Gautier et al. 2014, 59).

Racism and Asian American Presence in Rural Montana

Indian priests are entering a Montana that has recently been in the news for the increasing rise in white supremacy and anti-immigrant sentiments during the 2016 election and its aftermath. These include white supremacist literature cropping up in Bozeman, Missoula, and Great Falls, a white student wearing a "white power/Trump 2016 white pride" T-shirt at Polson High School on the Blackfeet Indian Reservation, and racist comments against Native students at Montana State University–Northern in Havre, Montana (see Szpaller 2016; Bermes 2017; Manning 2018; Devlin 2016; Hudson 2017). The Montana Human Rights Network reported an uptick in the number of racist incidents in Montana post–Trump election—from usually a dozen reports in an entire year, to a dozen reports in less than three weeks after the election (O'Brien 2017). Perhaps most widely reported is the fact that Whitefish, Montana, is the home of the white supremacist Richard Spencer. Spencer gained national attention when a video of him shouting "Hail Trump" and audience members responding with a Nazi salute went viral just days after the 2016 election.

The racism of the "Deep North" is not merely something that came along with the election of Donald Trump. Despite knowing many wonderful and loving people in eastern Montana, my own experiences of racism in the region prompted me to leave Montana and (for many years) never look back. I cannot even count how many times my family and I were told to "go back to our own country." As a child, I was forced to be "the slave" when girls in my class played house with Cabbage Patch dolls. When I was in high school teaching tap dance to small children, a mother angrily grabbed her young daughter and led her away from me saying that my family and I were "dirty." My siblings and I have repeatedly had the N-word thrown at us. Patients refused to be seen by my late father, a doctor, because of his skin color. Sharon, an Asian American Catholic who grew up in the region, had this to say about being a minority in eastern Montana:

> One time at a party, one person kept hitting me with a broom saying "no chinks or gooks allowed" until I finally left. . . . It's kinda like you don't want to mention you are a minority. It's just like you are hoping they will forget [*laughter*], which is an insane thing to say, but it was the mentality. . . . I felt like it was really obvious that I was Asian and I went through that whole phase where I wanted to ignore it. And if I ignored it, maybe it wouldn't actually exist. (2016, pers. comm.)

Sharon was very supportive of Indian priests in Montana especially because they could act as a role model for any youth of color and especially for Native youth. Someone who could help children of color "deal with the big things, not just another white guy telling you how things are" (2016, pers. comm.).

There is a particular immigrant story that is celebrated in this area of the country: one that privileges the experiences of homesteading European migrants of the late nineteenth and early twentieth centuries. Many Catholic, Lutheran, and Mennonite families in central and eastern Montana have a specific double immigrant story. In the 1760s, tens of thousands of

Germans migrated to Russia and cultivated wildlands near the Volga River. Known as the "Volga Germans," or "Germans from Russia," these German farmers faced discrimination in Russia and after a few generations, began emigrating to Montana and North Dakota, as well as Alberta, Canada. Their migration coincided with the 1909 Enlarged Homestead Act which increased the 1862 Homestead Act land grants from 160 acres to 320 acres in central and eastern Montana. In 1900, Montana had a population of 243,329; by 1920, that number had grown to 548,889 (Myers 1990, 219). Homesteaders "claimed" over fifty-four million acres of what was said to be public and Northern Pacific railway land (Myers 1990, 219).

Because of farm mechanization and the boom of World War I wheat exports, many of these homesteaders prospered. However, after World War I, crop prices fell, and the area experienced a drought. The following Great Depression years wiped many of the homesteaders out. The farmers and ranchers who managed to remain subscribe to a narrative in which immense hardship was overcome by perseverance and hard work two times over. First in Russia, cultivating wild areas and discriminated against by Russians because they were German, and then in Montana, cultivating a semi-arid desert and facing drought and foreclosures. These immigrants became hardworking victims par excellence, and this narrative helps shape a dominant idea of what "legitimate immigration" looks like.

Of course, these lands were not empty, nor were they wholly inhabited by Germans from Russia. Montana was/is home to the Chippewa, Cree, Gros Ventre, Assiniboine, Crow, Northern Cheyenne, Sioux, Blackfeet, Salish, Pend d'Oreille, and Kootenai. There was also a Chinese population in Montana. By 1870, 10 percent of the population of the Montana territory was Chinese, many who came to the area as miners or employed as service workers (Merritt 2017, 3). Although the Chinese miners faced racial discrimination, their experiences were framed in different terms in comparison to Native populations. Examining diaries of white women settlers in the late nineteenth century, Sheila McManus has shown that in northern Montana, Native Americans were linked to the physical landscape by white settlers (2001, 74). But since Chinese migrants were not so linked to the land, white settler racialization placed the Chinese as nonthreatening "others" while Native Americans were depicted as hostile and a threat to settlement (2001, 80). Thus, the perceived Native spatialized threat created a Native/white settler racial logic a bit different from the dominant black/white racial binary we may be accustomed to when approaching the presence of the Asian diaspora in the U.S.

What emerges from this narrative of "legitimate immigration" is a rewriting of history which makes the settler the victim and courageous conqueror of the American frontier, while injustices and violence against Native peoples are thoroughly erased. Further, over time, Native peoples' claims to land become seen as less valid as settlers take over as the "true" inhabitants (Arvin, Tuck, and Morrill 2013, 12–13). As settlers become the native owners of the place, any discussion of the injustices that Native Americans face today may be treated with extreme hostility from descendants of "victim" settlers. For example, in the 1980s when the Great Falls–Billings Bishop Anthony Malone attempted to support the Crow tribe's water rights of the Bighorn River, he received hate mail from non-Native Montana Catholics (Larsen 2003, 43).

Indian priests are asked to step into a landscape where placemaking racialization and settler victimization legitimizes presence. For American Catholics, the idea of a "missionary priest" may invoke colonial fantasies of white clergymen preaching to savage heathens. In turn, this positions Indian missionary priests as subpar temporary proxies against the white American-born priests who are the hegemonic standard. In this frame, Asian priests are mere replaceable commodities or "imports." In 1997 Fr. Richard P. McBrien argued against the "importing" of priests (McBrien 1997). In response to Fr. McBrien, Fr. Cosmas K. Okechukwu-Nwosuh wrote, "I find it ironic that when American and European priests and religious set out to preach the gospel in Africa, Asia and Latin America they are called 'missionaries.' But when the reverse is the case, they become 'imported goods'" (Okechukwu-Nwoshuh 1998; see also Hoge and Okure 2006a, 36–37). Even a decade after this exchange, we seem to still be using the language of "import/export": in 2008 the *New York Times* described the entire country of India as an "exporter of priests" (Goodstein 2008).

Unrecognized as settlers and with little contextualization of their presence, pushback against Indian priests can be strong by white parishioners. A white American-born priest told me that when an Indian priest was introduced into a neighboring parish, the American-born priest suddenly had five to ten white "refugees" start attending his Mass every week (Fr. A 2016, pers. comm.). Similarly, Michael, a congregant, recounted, "In particular I do remember one of the gentlemen I worked with on the railroad. I remember him telling me one day, 'I'm not goin' back to the

Catholic Church as long as they have that priest from India here'" (2016, pers. comm.). Another white American-born priest revealed to me that the arrival of Indian priests in the diocese has actually created more work for him. Parishioners, he told me, started specially requesting the white priest for funerals, confessions, and other services because of the strong prejudices they held against Indian priests (Fr. B 2016, pers. comm.).

But a priest is not your typical migrant. People make a connection with the priest who baptized their child, the priest who married them, the priest who came to their house for anointing of the sick, or to oversee a family member's funeral. As Michelle, a Catholic woman in a parish town, remarked, "Like any other changes in our society, getting Indian priests was one that was very necessary in order for the Catholic church to keep going, particularly in Montana. But number two, it has lent people who had lived here in Montana all their lives an opportunity to get a picture out in the world of who else lives on our planet with us" (2016, pers. comm.). Despite the racism that is a feature of the "Deep North," global connections are being made almost because of the unique labor of a Catholic priest.

Global Connections

In this section, I highlight the ways in which Indian priests have engendered travel, charity, and prayers between Montana and India in a comparative global sense. I intentionally use "global" instead of the term "transnational" because of the ways in which the transnational should be understood as a more complex phenomenon of "scattered hegemonies" examining "the histories of how people in different locations and circumstances are linked by the spread of and resistance to modern capitalist social formation even as their experiences of these phenomena are not all the same or equal" (Grewal and Kaplan 1994, 5). Unfortunately, the complexity of "transnational" in feminist studies is all too often diluted into a surface understanding of the non-West with little area studies engagement or depth. In turn, such a limited view of the "transnational" may prevent feminist scholars from understanding how Native nations are transnational. Renya Ramirez (2007) has noted that urban Native Americans have a sense of tribal collectivity even if they live outside the reservations. Thus, she uses the term "transnational" to disrupt normative binaries between majority and minority populations (Ramirez 2007, 13–14). Luana Ross has further argued that "Native nations have a nation-to-nation relationship with each other, the United States, and other countries. We are transnational by definition because we are nations" (2009, 47–48). Since Indian priests also serve in towns on or near five different reservations in Montana, I think it is important to not confuse "global" connections between cowboys and Indians with "transnational" cultural and capital flows, asymmetrical links, transnational organizing, and border crossings.

Indian priests have created opportunities for Montanans to participate in global travel. (Of course, U.S. citizenship and money make the opportunities for such travel easier for some Montanans than others.) Fr. Ben Lobo, the first Indian priest to serve in the Great Falls–Billings diocese, took a group of Montana parishioners to the Holy Land in 1996. Fr. Ben Lobo served in many different parishes in Montana, became incardinated in the diocese, and then retired in India where he passed away in January 2016. Over the years, Fr. Ben kept in close contact with Montana parishioners. Many of my research participants shared stories of Fr. Ben's hospitality. For instance, Susan was a child when Fr. Ben served in Montana, but her family stayed in contact with Fr. Ben for years. When Susan went to college, she decided to spend a winter break with Fr. Ben in India, focusing her three-week trip on education in India. Fr. Ben took her to Catholic schools in the city of Mangalore and rural schools as well so she could see the inequalities between schools (Susan 2017, pers. comm.). Elsa, a Montanan who loves to travel, stayed with Fr. Ben in India three times. On one of these visits, Elsa was joined by two Montanans who had been traveling from Thailand and stopped to say hi to Fr. Ben in India. "It was clear they knew Fr. Ben, and made sure to stop in India and stay with him" (Elsa 2017, pers. comm.). In 2009 Fr. Ben celebrated his jubilee year and some Montanans made the trip to India. One rancher I interviewed, Kelly, was especially close to Fr. Ben and had this to say:

> When Fr. Lobo went back to India, he probably asked for our address before he left. And then we'd write back and forth, I don't know, usually at least once a month. He would write to us. He must have told us that he did some different work over there or something to help out with the poor. So we started sending him, I tried to send him fifty to one hundred dollars a month to kinda help him with the stuff he was doing over there. And he'd send us pictures. . . . [For his jubilee celebration in India], he sent us videos. DVDs of it, hours long! And of course, I couldn't understand a word of it! He invited us to go to his jubilee in India. And I don't know, "Where

> would we stay, Father?" "Well, you would stay here!" [*laughter*] Yeah, he'd be that welcoming to let us stay at his house. That was how Fr. Lobo was. Of course, I had never flown anywhere. I mean, I never gone anywhere! And the thought of going clear over to India was a little bit intimidating. We even got our passports and everything. And at the last minute, and kinda the expense . . . [*trails off, crying*]. (2016, pers. comm.)

For Kelly, who has never flown anywhere, to consider her very first plane trip to be a transatlantic flight to India is a bit more than just a connection. It is truly a cross-racial friendship that impacted her deeply. And it disrupts our notion of "flyover" zones being devoid of cosmopolitanism and marked only by racism.

Fr. Alex and Fr. Jolly—both priests from the state of Kerala, India, who served in Montana and then returned to India after their mission—led Montanans on a three-week trip to India. This trip was not your average Taj Mahal trip. Rather, the Montana tourists visited a number of Christian sites in India including churches, missions, schools, hospitals, and orphanages. As Rebecca, who went on the tour of India, shared:

> It was just so magnificent. And he really tried to squeeze in a lot of information. We saw a lot of things in Kerala. And then we went up to [the] Sagar [diocese in North India], where the divine mercy chapel and statue were built. Some parishioners had donated money for that chapel, so we were happy to see it in person. We went to the missions, the schools, and we met a lot of the nuns and priests doing good work. (2016, pers. comm.)

The chapel and statue Rebecca discusses were of particular note for many of my research participants, both for those who traveled to India and others who did not. Many eastern and central Montana parishioners sent donations to the Sagar diocese for its construction. Still other Montana Catholics are sending donations to help Indian Catholics in need. Some Indian priests have brought handicrafts made by Indian women and sold them to parishioners in the Great Falls–Billings diocese or asked Montana parishioners to consider donating money to particular causes in India; like Kelly, the Montanan rancher who considered traveling to India for Fr. Ben's jubilee, who donated fifty to one hundred dollars a month to Fr. Ben's causes after he retired in India. Seminarians in India are being sponsored by Montana Catholics. As Bishop Warfel explained,

> We have parishioners, mostly I think in Glendive area and Circle, all those small places, they were sending out money to support seminarians, too. I like to see the fact that there are more people open to accepting outside nationalities and cultures, as far as what they're used to. You know. And that was a real broadening of a life experience, and I think real important connections, too. (2016, pers. comm.)

My hometown of Glendive, Montana, was recently given the honor of being the second-most "in the middle of nowhere" towns by *Nature* (Weiss et al. 2018) while nearby Circle, Montana (forty-nine miles northwest of Glendive), has a population of only 615. These farming/ranching small towns are not exactly teeming with diversity or with money. Thus, it is quite a thing to see parishioners in towns like Glendive and Circle sending money to India to support seminarians. In some parishes in Montana, Mass intentions—or Mass said in remembrance of a loved one who's passed away—are being "outsourced" to India when the calendar days are filled in Montana parishes.

Examining the presence of Indian priests in rural Montana can help in understanding the complexity of Asian diaspora and faith-based communities in the U.S. The unique labor and migration patterns of priests beg an analysis of rural areas, place-based comparative racialization, and settler colonialism. There are a number of issues that come up with these global connections, to be sure. For instance, it is much cheaper for a priest to go through seminary training in India than in the U.S. And there may be prejudices against priests who are trained in India because they may be seen as less qualified than American seminarians. On the other hand, seminarians trained in India stand to make more money as missionaries in the U.S. than as parish priests in India. Are the cost-cutting measures of having priests trained in India, the prejudices associated with that training, or the salaries of Indian priests in Montana discussed when Montanans sponsor an Indian seminarian? The global connections engendered therefore requires careful analysis of *transnational* cultural and capital flows.

That said, the realities of Indian priests in rural areas of the U.S. should help us think through race, settler colonialism, and how feminists theorize Asian diasporas among other diasporas and subordinated communities. In this article, I have argued that the Asian diaspora in rural areas helps to contextualize how Asian settler colonialism functions through complex histories and intersectional oppressions. As I only touched on the perceived perversity and the "queer" bodies of South Asian priests in the rural, much more needs to be discussed and theorized in this regard. This article offers a starting point for further research on the relationship between settler colonialism, religious workers/immigration, and the queer rural. The story of Indian priest migration is not merely about adding a quirky anecdote of migration to the larger story of Asian diaspora. Rather, the Asian diaspora in rural Montana troubles conventional notions of black/white and Asian as foreign racial paradigms and provides context for the actual ways in which Asian settler colonialism and comparative racializations function in the U.S.

Sonja Thomas is an associate professor of women's studies at Colby College. She teaches courses on South Asian feminisms, feminist theory, critical race feminisms, and postcolonial and native feminisms. She is the author of *Privileged Minorities: Syrian Christianity, Gender, and Minority Rights in Postcolonial India*. She can be reached at smthomas@colby.edu.

Notes

1. I draw from Grace Kyungwon Hong and Roderick Ferguson's discussion of comparative methodology in the introduction to *Strange Affinities*. Hong and Ferguson use women of color feminisms and queer of color critique to discuss a comparative analytic rather than a description of different identities. As Hong and Ferguson explain: "This comparative methodology allows us to see moments when certain racial groups could articulate a demand for incorporation, albeit unevenly, over and against other racial groups as complexly interrelated to the processes by which subjects, within racial collectivities, are differentially incorporated or excluded from the class, gender, and sexual norms of respectability, morality, and propriety and thus placed on different sides of the dividing line between valued and devalued" (2011, 2–3).
2. In the mid-nineteenth century, the area now known as Montana was home to the Pend d'Oreille and Salish, Blackfeet and Gros Ventre, Crow, Assiniboine, Hidatsa, Mandan and Arikara, and Sioux. The five reservations in central and eastern Montana are Rocky Boy (Chippewa and Cree), Fort Belknap (Gros Ventre and Assiniboine), Crow (Crow), Northern Cheyenne (Northern Cheyenne), and Fort Peck (Assiniboine and Sioux). The two reservations in Western Montana (Helena diocese) are the Blackfeet Reservation (Blackfeet) and Flathead Reservation (Confederated Salish, Pend d'Oreille, and Kootenai).
3. As Mary Anne Case has shown, complementarity is a mid-twentieth-century

innovation and came especially in response to Catholic opposition to contraception, homosexuality, and women's ordination (2016, 156).

4. Depending on the number of priests in the diocese and the needs of the mission churches, the place where a priest is stationed by the bishop may change, as may the mission churches assigned to a parish.
5. Schools in rural Montana are closing and consolidating. Enticing teachers to the region has also been difficult. Some, taking a cue from the diocese, have tried to recruit teachers from overseas (Hoffman 2016). Likewise, Protestant churches have faced difficulties in recruiting/retaining pastors, and have also been closing their doors (Olp 2017).

Works Cited

Alsultany, Evelyn. 2012. *Arabs and Muslims in the Media: Race and Representation after 9/11.* New York: NYU Press.

Arvin, Maile, Eve Tuck, and Angie Morrill. 2013. "Decolonizing Feminism: Challenging Connections between Settler Colonialism and Heteropatriarchy." *Feminist Formations* 25, no. 1: 8–34.

Bermes, Whitney. 2017. "Anti-Semitic 'White Genocide' Fliers Distributed in Bozeman." *Bozeman Daily Chronicle,* May 8, 2017. https://www.bozemandailychronicle.com/news/anti-semitic-white-genocide-fliers-distributed-in-bozeman/article_30c2a754-f062-5543-b5eb-89fa6656435d.html.

Bhatia, Sunil. 2007. *American Karma: Race, Culture, and Identity in the Indian Diaspora.* New York: NYU Press.

Bracke, Sarah, and David Paternotte. 2016. "Unpacking the Sin of Gender." *Religion & Gender* 6, no. 2: 143–54.

Case, Mary Anne. 2016. "The Role of the Popes in the Invention of Complementarity and the Vatican's Anathematization of Gender." *Religion & Gender* 6, no. 2: 156–71.

Center for Applied Research in the Apostolate. 2014. "International Priests Are Now 'Bridging the Gap.'" *The CARA Report* 20, no. 2: 1–11.

Devlin, Vince. 2016. "Social Media Erupts after Polson Student Wears 'White Power' Shirt to School." *Missoulian,* September 27, 2016. https://missoulian.com/news/state-and-regional/social-media-erupts-after-polson-student-wears-white-power-shirt/article_57649a10-3298-5394-a50a-2d01b6d1fae2.html.

Fujikane, Candace. 2008. "Introduction: Asian Settler Colonialism in the U.S. Colony of Hawai'i." In *Asian Settler Colonialism: From Local Governance to the Habits of Everyday Life in Hawai'i,* edited by Candace Fujikane and Jonathan Y. Okamura, 1–42. Honolulu: University of Hawai'i Press.

Galbraith, Elizabeth Cameron. 2016. "The Culture of Asian Indian Catholicism in North America." In *South Asian Christian Diaspora: Invisible Diaspora in Europe and North America*, edited by Knut A. Jacobsen and Selva J. Raj, 171–82. New York: Routledge.

Gautier, Mary L., Melissa A. Cidade, Paul M. Perl, and Mark M. Gray. 2014. *Bridging the Gap: The Opportunities and Challenges of International Priests Ministering in the United States*. Huntington, IN: Our Sunday Visitor Publishing Division.

George, Sheeba Mariam. 2005. *When Women Come First: Gender and Class in Transnational Migration*. Berkeley: University of California Press.

Goodstein, Laurie. 2008. "India, An Exporter of Priests, May Keep Them." *New York Times*, December 29, 2008. https://www.nytimes.com/2008/12/30/us/30priest.html.

Glenn, Evelyn Nakano. 2015. "Settler Colonialism as Structure: A Framework for Comparative Studies of U.S. Race and Gender Formation." *Sociology of Race and Ethnicity* 1, no. 1: 52–72.

Grewal, Inderpal, and Caren Kaplan. 1994. "Introduction: Transnational Feminist Practices and Questions of Postmodernity." In *Scattered Hegemonies: Postmodernity and Transnational Feminist Practices*, edited by Inderpal Grewal and Caren Kaplan, 1–33. Minneapolis: University of Minnesota Press.

Herring, Scott. 2010. *Another Country: Queer Anti-Urbanism*. New York: NYU Press.

Hoffman, Matt. 2016. "Help Wanted: Montana Schools Are Struggling to Find and Keep Teachers." *Billings Gazette*, September 25, 2016. https://billingsgazette.com/help-wanted-montana-schools-are-struggling-to-find-and-keep/link_4dc0de2f-ba45-5288-9d0a-45ff09b9def0.html.

Hoge, Dean R., and Aniedi Okure. 2006a. *International Priests in America: Challenges and Opportunities*. Collegeville, MN: Liturgical Press.

———. 2006b. "International Priests in America: Two Coming Issues." *New Theology Review* 19, no. 2: 14–22.

Hong, Grace Kyungwon, and Roderick A. Ferguson. 2011. "Introduction." In *Strange Affinities: The Gender and Sexual Politics of Comparative Racialization*, 1–22. Durham, NC: Duke University Press.

Hudson, Matt. 2017. "Racial Comments Expose Rift between Native Students, Northern Administration." *Billings Gazette*, April 26. https://billingsgazette.com/news/state-and-regional/montana/racial-comments-expose-rift-between-native-students-northern-administration/article_dd27bb85-72ca-5f83-b5c5-e5d3baf8ea82.html.

Jafri, Beenash. 2013. "Desire, Settler Colonialism, and the Racialized Cowboy." *American Indian Culture and Research Journal* 37, no. 2: 73–86.

Johnson, Colin R., Brian J. Gilley, and Mary L. Gray. 2016. "Introduction." In

Queering the Countryside: New Frontiers in Rural Queer Studies, 1–21. New York: NYU Press.

Joshi, Khyati Y. 2006. *New Roots in America's Sacred Ground: Religion, Race, and Ethnicity in Indian America.* New Brunswick, NJ: Rutgers University Press.

Joshi, Khyati Y., and Jigna Desai. 2013. "Asian Americans in Dixie: Asian Americans and the South." In *Asian Americans in Dixie: Race and Migration in the South*, edited by Khyati Y. Joshi and Jigna Desai, 1–30. Urbana: University of Illinois Press.

Kurien, Prema. 2012. "Decoupling Religion and Ethnicity: Second-Generation Indian American Christians." *Qualitative Sociology* 35, no. 4: 447–68.

———. 2013. "Religion, Social Incorporation, and Civic Engagement: Second-Generation Indian American Christians." *Review of Religious Research* 55, no. 1: 81–104.

LaDuke, Winona. 2017. Public lecture at Colby College, Waterville, Maine, April 10.

Larsen, Kim. 2003. *From Age to Age: A History of the Catholic Church in Eastern Montana*. Strasbourg, FR: Editions du Signe.

Larson, Seaborn. 2017. "Montana Reservations Reportedly 'Dumping Grounds' for Predatory Priests." *Great Falls Tribune*, August 16, 2017. https://www.greatfallstribune.com/story/news/2017/08/16/montanas-reservations-were-dumping-grounds-predatory-priests-suit-alleges/504576001/.

Lawrence, Bonita, and Enakshi Dua. 2005. "Decolonizing Antiracism." *Social Justice* 32, no. 4: 120–43.

Manning, Tyler. 2018. "White Nationalist Group's Helena Recruiting Attempts Quickly Shut Down." *Billings Gazette*, October 31, 2018. https://billingsgazette.com/news/state-and-regional/white-nationalist-group-s-helena-recruiting-attempts-quickly-shut-down/article_f4061bcc-3c30-57ba-8417-7d78296f34f3.html?utm_content=buffer9dc99&utm_medium=social&utm_source=twitter.com&utm_campaign=LEEDCC#tracking-source=home-the-latest.

McBrien, Richard P. 1997. "Importing Priests to U.S. a Poor Solution." *National Catholic Reporter*, November 14, 1997, 21.

McManus, Sheila. 2001. "Mapping the Alberta-Montana Borderlands: Race, Ethnicity and Gender in the Late Nineteenth Century." *Journal of American Ethnic History* 20, no. 3: 71–87.

Merritt, Christopher W. 2017. *The Coming Man from Canton: Chinese Experience in Montana, 1862–1943*. Lincoln: University of Nebraska Press.

Myers, Rex C. 1990. "Homestead on the Range: The Emergence of Community in Eastern Montana, 1900–1925." *Great Plains Quarterly* 10, no. 4: 218–27.

O'Brien, Edward. 2017. "Hate Groups on the Rise in Montana, MHRN Says."

Montana Public Radio, February 16, 2017. http://www.mtpr.org/post/hate-groups-rise-montana-mhrn-says.

Okamura, Jonathan Y. 2008a. *Ethnicity and Inequality in Hawai'i*. Philadelphia: Temple University Press.

———. 2008b. "Ethnic Boundary Construction in the Japanese American Community in Hawai'i." In *Asian Settler Colonialism: From Local Governance to the Habits of Everyday Life in Hawai'i*, edited by Candace Fujikane and Jonathan Y. Okamura, 233–55. Honolulu: University of Hawai'i Press.

Okechukwu-Nwosuh, Cosmas K. 1998. "Is He a Missionary or 'Imported Goods'?" *National Catholic Reporter*, January 9, 1998, 18.

Olp, Susan. 2017. "As Church Leaders Grow Older, Fewer Young People Are Stepping Up." *Billings Gazette*, June 14, 2017. https://billingsgazette.com/news/local/as-church-leaders-grow-older-fewer-young-people-are-stepping/article_7abdd054-a74c-599b-934f-9d6afd5d412b.html.

Puar, Jasbir K. 2007. *Terrorist Assemblages: Homonationalism in Queer Times.* Durham, NC: Duke University Press.

Raab, Kelley A. 2000. *When Women Become Priests: The Catholic Women's Ordination Debate.* New York: Columbia University Press.

Ramirez, Renya K. 2007. *Native Hubs: Culture, Community, and Belonging in Silicon Valley and Beyond.* Durham, NC: Duke University Press.

Ross, Luana. 2009. "From the 'F' Word to Indigenous/Feminisms." *Wicazo Sa Review* 24, no. 2: 39–52.

Saranillio, Dean Itsuji. 2016. "Why Asian Settler Colonialism Matters: A Thought Piece on Critiques, Debates, and Indigenous Difference." In *The Settler Complex: Recuperating Binarism in Colonial Studies*, edited by Patrick Wolfe, 99–116. Los Angeles: UCLA American Indian Studies Center.

Sharma, Nandita, and Cynthia Wright. 2008–9. "Decolonizing Resistance, Challenging Colonial States." *Social Justice* 35, no. 3 (113): 120–138.

Szpaller, Keila. 2016. "Racist Activity Crops Up in Montana over the Weekend; Acts of Kindness Reported as Well." *Billings Gazette*, November 15, 2016. https://billingsgazette.com/news/state-and-regional/montana/racist-activity-crops-up-in-montana-over-the-weekend-acts/article_0acb6a08-6675-5109-8dba-03ca84362c00.html.

Thangaraj, Stanley. 2013. "Competing Masculinities: South Asian American Identity Formation in Asian American Basketball Leagues." *South Asian Popular Culture* 11, no. 3: 243–55.

———. 2015. *Desi Hoop Dreams: Pickup Basketball and the Making of Asian American Masculinity.* New York: NYU Press.

Thomas, Sonja. 2018. *Privileged Minorities: Gender, Syrian Christianity, and Mi-*

nority Rights in Postcolonial India. Seattle: University of Washington Press.

Weiss, D. J., A. Nelson, H. S. Gibson, W. Temperley, S. Peedell, A. Lieber, M. Hancher, E. Poyart, S. Belchior, N. Fullman, B. Mappin, U. Dalrymple, J. Rozier, T. C. D. Lucas, R. E. Howes, L. S. Tusting, S. Y. Kang, E. Cameron, D. Bisanzio, K. E. Battle, S. Bhatt, and P. W. Gething. 2018. "A Global Map of Travel Time to Cities to Assess Inequalities in Accessibility in 2015." *Nature* 553: 333–343.

Shop Talk and Everyday Sites of Resistance to Gentrification in Manhattan's Chinatown

Diane Wong

Abstract: Chinatowns have been important destination points for new and old Asian diasporic communities, however many of these neighborhoods have experienced demographic changes and major shifts in land use due to gentrification. This study examines the political implications of gentrification by focusing on how Chinese American women are responding to the process on a daily basis. Drawing from two years of ethnographic research, archival research, and oral history interviews, I reveal how ordinary neighborhood spaces like Wing on Wo & Co. (永安和), the oldest store in Manhattan's Chinatown, can serve as the foundation for intergenerational grassroots action and particularly for the mobilization of women in the neighborhood. I suggest that actively listening to what women in the neighborhood talk about on a regular basis provides tremendous insight and critical perspective on how political consciousness, values, ideologies, and practices are formed or negotiated over time. This paper reveals how a younger generation of Chinese American women in Manhattan's Chinatown are using informal conversations or what I call "shop talk" to engage elders in discourses of collective memory, resistance, dissent, movement, and hope for the future of the neighborhood.
Keywords: Chinese diaspora, women, gentrification, urban politics, democratic citizenship

Introduction

Located at 26 Mott Street, Wing on Wo & Co. (永安和) is the oldest continually run store in Manhattan's Chinatown. The humble red-painted porcelain shop is filled with rows of ceramics and porcelain that artfully decorate its wooden shelves. The first time I stepped foot into the store was in December 2015, when I started research in New York City and was in the process of interviewing small business owners about their thoughts on the gentrification in the neighborhood. It wasn't until I returned to the store a few weeks later that I met Mei Lum, who is the fifth-generation shopkeeper of 永安和. During our first conversation, Mei had not yet taken over the position and she told me that her family was actually about to sell the six-story red brick tenement building along with the porcelain business that had been in the neighborhood since the late 1800s. The burden of increasing property taxes, maintenance costs, and operating fees made it exceedingly difficult for her family to keep the property afloat while trying to earn a livelihood. My conversations with Mei complicated the way that I understood gentrification because they compelled me to think more centrally about the role of small multigenerational family-owned businesses in the midst of these neighborhood changes. As Manhattan's Chinatown continues to experience gentrification and mass displacement, family-owned businesses are among the first to bear its effects and are often forced to close due to rent increases and demographic shifts. A ten-minute walk down on the once vibrant Canal, Broadway, and Bowery Streets now reveals vacant storefronts shuttered with For Lease signs and corridors overshadowed by new eighty-story luxury skyscrapers. Longtime residents and small businesses like 永安和 that have been in Manhattan's Chinatown for generations are now under pressure to close or relocate to make way for even more changes that are transforming the heart and soul of the city.

If you ask anyone who grew up in Manhattan's Chinatown what the neighborhood was like in the 1960s, they would tell you that it was no larger than six square blocks, with Mott Street at its geographic heart. Due to discrimination and federal restrictions on Chinese immigration, housing, and employment, for much of the twentieth century Manhattan's Chinatown was a bachelor society consisting of transient low-wage working Chinese men and merchants. Walter Eng was a paper son who sailed to Manhattan's Chinatown from Taishan in Guangdong province of China in 1867.[1] With assistance from the Eng Family Association, Walter opened the doors of 永安和 in 1880 on 13 Mott Street as a general store, selling everything to new immigrants such as canned goods, cookware, medicinal herbs, vegetables, seeds, and roasted pork. The general store had wire racks that functioned as a makeshift post office to receive mail from China and temporary sleeping quarters for those passing through in search for work. The move across the street from 13 to 26 Mott Street occurred in

1925 when Walter purchased the six-story red brick tenement building from Irish owners for $68,000. The new location allowed him to expand the scope of the general store, even hiring a traditional herbalist to fill medicine prescriptions for customers. There was also a trapdoor in the backroom kitchen, which had stairs that led to a basement oven room used for roasting whole pigs on occasions like Lunar New Year. Throughout the decades, 永安和 extended a lifeline to some of the earliest Chinese immigrants in the city who otherwise were isolated from the rest of society.

When Walter Eng passed away in 1964, he left 26 Mott Street to his daughter Nancy Eng. Despite having a full-time job elsewhere and no formal training, Nancy decided to keep the store open and taught herself the basics of running a small business. She eliminated the sale of groceries to focus her energies on shaping 永安和 into an exclusive porcelain shop, sourcing inventory from Japanese companies who sent their supplies through Hong Kong, since at the time China had yet to trade with the United States. Nancy balanced running the porcelain store with her full-time job as secretary to the assistant commissioner at the Health Department. She worked out a schedule with her brother Tungnan Eng where he ran the store for several hours in the afternoon until she was off work at six, keeping the business open until eleven at night. In early 1972, President Nixon's widely publicized trip to China led to foreign policies that promoted trade between the two countries. A year later Nancy and her husband Shuck Seid began their biannual business trips to Hong Kong to self-curate and source porcelain for the shop. Nancy sent giant wooden crates of decorative plates, ceramic teapots, vases, and other selections from Yue Hua, a Hong Kong department store, directly to the Port of New York. In the 1980s, cities across the country began to host museum exhibits and trade shows that focused on Chinese cultural arts and ceramics, which sparked national curiosity and brought more tourists into Manhattan's Chinatown. As business picked up, Nancy left her full-time job at the Health Department in 1986 and with the help of her sister Betty Eng, she decided to focus attention entirely on the store. Over the years, the shop has continued to serve as a space for Chinatown residents to congregate, share information, and participate in public life.

Nancy managed 永安和 for five decades as she watched her children raise another generation inside the shop. However, things began to change when the business, along with the rest of the neighborhood, became impacted by 9/11 and post-9/11 policies. Manhattan's Chinatown is one of the closest residential areas in proximity to Ground Zero; spatially the neighborhood is less than ten blocks away. The social, economic, and health consequences were catastrophic for residents in the months and years that followed. In the weeks after 9/11, all transportation was suspended and the police placed checkpoints throughout Chinatown, making the area a frozen zone where residents had to carry identification in order to leave or enter the neighborhood. Within the first two weeks, 75 percent of the workforce in Chinatown was temporarily dislocated or unemployed (AAFNY 2002). By the end of the first year, sixty-five garment factories shut down completely and 20 percent of businesses including restaurants, barbershops, and small retail shops did not survive the economic downturn (AAFNY 2002). Although millions of federal dollars in recovery assistance were poured into Lower Manhattan, the Lower Manhattan Development Corporation, a public-private corporation tasked to distribute these assistance funds, provided disproportionate support to corporations on Wall Street over small businesses in adjacent neighborhoods like the Lower East Side or Chinatown. In the decade after 9/11, Mayor Bloomberg targeted Lower Manhattan including the Lower East Side and Chinatown for redevelopment not just to rebuild but to encourage upscale reconstruction and market rate development. Dozens of former garment factories were converted into multimillion-dollar lofts by developers, effectively increasing real estate speculation and the costs of living for existing tenants who are predominately low-income Chinese immigrant families and seniors who live below the poverty threshold. Despite these gentrification-led changes, Nancy kept 永安和 open until November of 2015 when she stood at a crossroads on whether or not to keep or to sell it along with the building that her father had bought in 1925. After conversations with family members and close friends in Chinatown whom she confided in, Nancy decided that she was exhausted and it was time to close the doors of 26 Mott Street.

This decision would have ended five generations of family ownership of the store. Mei Lum, who is the second youngest of the Eng family's five grandchildren, learned about her grandmother's decision when she received a call from her father while she was abroad working in China. Fearful of the rapid changes happening in Chinatown, Mei immediately considered the risks of a developer or large chain store purchasing 26 Mott Street, which would change the landscape of the entire block. Mei also thought of the many buildings that she had seen in Manhattan's Chinatown that have been sold to developers who have either demolished them to construct hotel towers or left them vacant for speculation. By the time their 26 Mott Street building was on the market for an asking price of ten million dollars, Mei had already applied to graduate school and had been accepted into a program to study international development. However, not ready to part with such an integral part of her childhood and family legacy, Mei turned down graduate school to take over the shop from her grandmother as the fifth-generation shopkeeper. As I sat down with Mei for a one-year reflection interview in the backroom kitchen of the store in March 2017, she told me why she decided to take over the store:

> The situation my family was going through was larger than us. If we sold the business, it would affect our block, our neighborhood, our community. I started thinking about how I could, as a single person, reinvent the store and put new energy into it. I wanted to turn it into a space where residents could share their stories and creatively strategize around issues like gentrification. The work I did abroad set me up for the work I have to do in Chinatown. I can't make changes in other parts of the world if there is so much to be done at home. (Mei Lum, pers. comm., February 4, 2016)

Inspired by her grandmother's commitment to preserve and grow community through the store, Mei has since transformed 永安和 into a women-run space for intergenerational dialogue and grassroots resistance to gentrification through the W.O.W. Project, a community-based initiative located inside the store to address neighborhood issues outside.

The story of 永安和 importantly tells the often overlooked narrative of women in American Chinatowns and their extensive role in preserving community structures, cultivating social networks, and mobilizing collective action. Drawing from oral history interviews over the span of two years and a series of informal conversations organized by the W.O.W. Project, this article explores how ordinary shop spaces can serve as a catalyst for intergenerational organizing and particularly for the political mobilization of women in Manhattan's Chinatown. In an attempt to bridge feminist theory to lessons on the ground, I advocate for the viability of everyday neighborhood spaces as sites for transformative change and political possibilities for women. Rather than focus on traditional sites and modes of participation in politics, I shift attention to focus on how women in the neighborhood are using informal community dialogue or what I call "shop talk" to strategize around gentrification. In the following sections I contextualize the gentrification happening in Manhattan's Chinatown and draw from critical feminist scholarship to set the theoretical foundation for this study. I suggest that actively listening to what women talk about on an everyday basis offers tremendous insight into the ways in which political values, ideologies, and practices are formed or negotiated over time in urban immigrant communities. I proceed to illustrate how Mei and other Chinese American women cultural workers, residents, and activists involved with the W.O.W. Project are using shop talk to generate new arenas for democratic participation and engagement around issues of displacement and dispossession in the city. Fundamentally, the research and methods used in this study broaden the scope of how we conceptualize feminist politics and where it unfolds on the ground, importantly shaping how both scholars and practitioners understand the relationship between women in immigrant communities, democratic citizenship, and political possibilities.

Contextualizing the Gentrification in Manhattan's Chinatown

Manhattan's Chinatown continues to be an important destination for newly arrived Asian immigrants, although it now faces major transformations due to gentrification. Being in such close proximity to Tribeca, SoHo, the Financial District, and the newly renovated East River waterfront promenade, Chinatown has been advertised as the "final frontier" for development by city officials, developers, financial institutions, and media outlets. In the years directly after 9/11, housing and land use policies accelerated the gentrification of Manhattan's Chinatown by allowing for upzoning and developers to build without any accountability to existing residents (Kwong and Stein 2015). In 2008 the New York City Council approved Mayor Bloomberg's rezoning of the East Village, the third-largest rezoning plan since the city's adoption of the 1961 Zoning Resolution. The rezoning aimed to preserve the neighborhood scale and established character of the East Village area by mandating height limits on new building development projects and affordable housing incentives for developers within a 111-block area, excluding all of Chinatown, the Lower East Side, the Bowery, and NYCHA public housing. Hundreds of residents and housing advocates came together to protest the rezoning plan, arguing that it would push gentrification further into Chinatown and negatively impact the lives and livelihoods of low-income residents who rely on rent-regulated housing.[2] Since then, there have been dozens of luxury hotels and as-of-right developments that have been built in Chinatown without public hearings, environmental impact studies, or input from the local community.

Between 2000 and 2010, the number of Asian residents in Manhattan's Chinatown dropped 18 percent largely due to unaffordable rent increases and evictions (Urban Justice Center 2008). Many predatory landlords have deliberately purchased buildings with Chinese tenants who live in rent-regulated units and have taken advantage of the fact that most are low-income, speak limited English, and/or undocumented to push them out of their homes. Chinatown has seen its affordable housing stock decline drastically: it has lost nearly 20 percent or 11,000 rent-regulated units within the last ten years (Gafvert and Weber 2011). The number of residents earning between $25,000 and $50,000 has decreased by 24 percent, indicating that there are now fewer low-income residents and families who can afford to live in the neighborhood (AAFNY 2008). In addition, nearly 12 percent of businesses in Manhattan's Chinatown are classified as "high-end" including over 150 new clothing boutiques and upscale restaurants (AALDEF 2013). As of 2015, 40 percent of all new galleries in the city have opened up in Chinatown, outpacing Chelsea, Bushwick, the Upper East Side, and other areas with art scenes. There are over 140 galleries in Manhattan's Chinatown which include artist-run spaces, WhiteBox galleries, galleries run out of apartments, and arts nonprofits (Moy 2016). A lion's share of these galleries have opened up in clusters along Delancey, Orchard, Eldridge, Rivington, and Chrystie Streets, contributing to real estate speculation, increasing rents, and massive displacement of existing residents and small businesses. Even though some have argued that these changes happening in Chinatown are inevitable, there is nothing natural about policies and practices that have uprooted thousands of families from the places they called home for generations. While the dominant narrative is that people are being pushed out of their homes without a fight, this is simply untrue as many Chinatown residents, younger generations, shop owners, local artists, and organizers are fighting to stop gentrification. In the next section I draw theoretical inspiration from feminist scholarship to show how Mei and other women in the neighborhood are using ordinary shop spaces like 永安和 to resist gentrification and all forms of dispossession.

"Shop Talk" and Everyday Sites of Politics in Manhattan's Chinatown

The question of how an individual becomes active in politics cannot be separated from the question of where politics happens on the ground, especially since the two are mutually reinforcing. To date, however, much of the dialogue on where politics unfolds centers the elite and the electoral realms, which tend to privilege traditional sites of political involvement such as civic organizations, churches, educational institutions, and electoral campaigns. Importantly complicating this body of literature are feminist scholars, who have suggested that politics extends beyond formal political institutions and happens in the places that are closest to our daily lives (hooks 1990; Mansbridge 1999; Collins 2008). There have been numerous pieces written by feminist scholars that have expanded the scope of conventional political studies to conceptualize what happens in ordinary spaces as politics. In *Barbershops, Bibles, and BET: Everyday Talk and Black Political Thought,* Black feminist political scientist Melissa Harris-Lacewell draws on the everyday talk that happens in barbershops to learn about Black political ideologies and public opinion. Through experimental and ethnographic research, Harris-Lacewell reveals that the daily face-to-face conversations that people have with each other are essential to understanding Black political thought development (2006, 17). In order to uncover the nuances of political life that are often overlooked in conventional studies of voting patterns, partisan affiliation, or organizational membership, a closer look at everyday talk in quotidian spaces like the barbershop reveals a wealth of information about salient neighborhood issues and how political ideologies are developed or expressed over time.

Feminist scholars have also written about how intimate spaces like the home can function as a critical site of politics for women. In *Yearning: Race, Gender, and Cultural Politics,* feminist theorist and activist bell hooks (1990) writes about how the home or homeplace constitutes a site of resistance and contains a radical political dimension of subversion, renewal, self-recovery, and healing. She writes, "I want to speak about the importance of homeplace in the midst of oppression and domination, of homeplace as a site of resistance and liberatory struggle. . . . Whatever the shape and direction of black liberation struggle, domestic space has been a crucial site for organizing, for forming political solidarity" (1990, 388). Following bell hooks, political theorist Iris Marion Young has also written about the intimacies of the home as a liberatory site of politics for women to subvert dominant social structures and to transform daily life into an arena of political contest. Although the home has in many ways been oppressive to women as sites of violence, distrust, and confinement, Young suggests that "the material values of home can nevertheless provide leverage for radical social critique. . . . Home can have a political meaning as a site of dignity and resistance and should be democratised rather than rejected" (2005, 157). These feminist frameworks allow for a more fluid conception of politics and represent what political scientist Cathy Cohen (2004) calls a paradigmatic shift in how we think, write, and talk about the politics of those most vulnerable in our communities. Drawing inspiration from these frameworks, I illustrate how 永安和 as a porcelain store and as home to three generations of Chinese American women embodies a critical yet intimate site of political engagement where family, friends, and neighbors can gather under one roof to openly participate in discussions, in negotiations, in vulnerability, and in a commitment to solidarity with each other to address fundamental issues like gentrification.

Historically in Manhattan's Chinatown, family-owned markets, hand laundries, bakeries, and curio stores have served as important spaces for residents and especially women in the community to converge and talk about their lives, family, work, and politics. In fact many of the socially engaged activist and women-run collectives that emerged in the 1970s and 1980s—like the Basement Workshop, Godzilla, and Asian American Arts Centre—resulted from informal conversations held in basements, restaurants, and other everyday spaces in Chinatown. The kind of work that the W.O.W. Project does continues in this lineage because it generates space for women organizers, cultural workers, and small shop owners to cultivate new relationships rooted in a memory of collective resistance. Mei currently runs the W.O.W. Project, and it operates as a loose collective that includes interns, volunteers, and artists who come together to host workshops and public programs including the Homeward Bound series, which highlights everyday resilience in Chinatowns around the world. For Mei, a focus on daily conversations or "shop talk" does not mean ignoring the existing challenges and material conditions that residents in Manhattan's Chinatown continue to face but it means firmly believing that residents have the power to change their immediate surroundings. It means creating neighborhood spaces that never existed before, bringing those who never interacted together, sharing knowledge in ways that are accessible to everyone, and dreaming out loud to get things done. In the span of three years, the W.O.W. Project has curated a series of intergenerational dialogues, launched a youth-led arts activism program called Resist Recycle Regenerate, established an Asian American storefront artist-in-residency program, and sustained relationships with residents in other Chinatowns facing similar changes from gentrification including Vancouver, San Francisco, Los Angeles, Seattle, Philadelphia, and Boston. In the following section I draw from one specific conversation held at 永安和 to show how Mei and other women are using shop talk to creatively and collectively resist gentrification through shared stories, reflections, laughter, memories, solidarities, and hopes for the future.

Chinatown Women and Building across Generations through Shop Talk

The significance of the W.O.W. Project lies within the fact that it disrupts the erasure of women in narratives of activism in Manhattan's Chinatown and that it creates an intentional space for women across three generations to cultivate relationships with one another. The contributions of women in Manhattan's Chinatown are often overlooked due to the patriarchal structures that has been firmly entrenched in the social and political institutions of the neighborhood. As Jack Tchen and Mary Ting Li Lui delineate in their respective writings, Manhattan's Chinatown is not only a racialized space but is gendered in terms of how women experience and move through it on a daily basis (Tchen 2001; Lui 2007). Recognizing that gentrification disproportionately impacts women in the community, Mei decided to transform 永安和 into a space to encourage dialogue between women from across generations to share experiences of working at various historical junctures in the neighborhood and lessons learned from the past that might be useful in addressing contemporary issues.

On Saturday, December 10, 2016, a talk was held at 永安和 that involved women all with deep activist roots in Chinatown. The talk included Ching Yeh Chen, cofounder of Pearl River Mart; May Ying Chen, organizer for the International Ladies' Garment Workers' Union Local 23–25 Workers United; Cynthia Lee, vice president of Exhibitions, Programs, and Collections at the Museum of Chinese in America; and Sophia Ng, vice president and second-generation owner of Po Wing Hong Food Market. The talk was guided by Lena Sze, a cultural worker from the neighborhood involved with the Asian American Writers' Workshop. On the night of the conversation, 永安和 was packed to capacity and forty people crowded into the store space, including longtime neighborhood activist women like Alice Yip, organizer at Garment Workers' Union Local 23–25; Betty Yu, cofounder of the Chinatown Art Brigade; and Liz OuYang, director of the Organization of Chinese Americans–New York. For three hours 永安和 was turned into a women-run space of storytelling, listening, healing, activating, and building. I draw from parts of the dialogue to illustrate the extraordinary work that these women are doing to preserve one of New York City's last affordable neighborhoods. These conversations importantly broaden the scope of how we conceptualize feminist politics and where it unfolds on the ground in Asian immigrant communities.

Mei began the talk by introducing the W.O.W. Project and reasons for bringing everyone together:

> This discussion was inspired by my grandmother and watching how she worked through the challenges of taking on a leadership role in a male-run neighborhood. We can learn a lot from across generations and from the struggles we have overcome in the past to look towards the future, especially in this political moment. Today we are going to create space to reflect on particular historical moments in our past to celebrate the strategies and the approaches we as women have used to overcome. (Mei Lum, pers. comm., December 10, 2016)

Ching Yeh Chen was the first to speak about her early roots in Chinatown as an activist through her family's second-generation-owned store Pearl River Mart. For Ms. Chen, the most practiced form of resistance to gentrification for small shop owners like her is to embrace the new ideas, abilities, and values of the next generation. As one of the first Maoist-inspired "friendship stores" in the United States, Pearl River Mart opened its doors on Catherine Street on September 1, 1971. For the first two decades of its existence, the store was an anchor for restaurant and garment workers. It sold specialty products from China and was a gathering place for activists involved in groups like the Chinese Hand Laundry Association. Ms. Chen and her husband, Ming Yi Chen, were active in supporting low-wage immigrant workers, joining the fight for garment workers' rights, affordable housing, and health care. She reflected:

> You can take Pearl River out of Chinatown but you can't take Chinatown out of Pearl River. Many people have asked us why we haven't moved out of Chinatown. There used to be garment factories in Chinatown. Garment workers were the main revenue source for us. I grew close to the women

> but many of them stopped coming after a while and I assumed they left. But sometimes some of them come back and it makes me think they haven't moved too far. If we leave how can they find us? (Ching Yeh Chen, pers. comm., December 10, 2016)

Prior to the 1990s, Pearl River Mart primarily served garment workers who would visit after factory hours to buy steamers, washcloths, and soap, but the clientele has changed due to gentrification. Ms. Chen shared her experiences with gentrification from moving the business to Catherine Street to Elizabeth Street to Canal Street and then finally to Broadway, where the store recently experienced a fivefold rent increase from $100,000 to $500,000 a month. In order to survive the increasing rents, Ms. Chen has been more intentional about engaging the next generation in their family business. Too often the narrative of success in immigrant communities like Manhattan's Chinatown is for the next generation to uproot and move onto different career paths, but Ms. Chen is challenging the idea that leaving a place equates success. Over the last several years she has actively encouraged the next generation to carry out their store legacy by sharing her knowledge and expertise in operating a small business. Pearl River Mart is now run by Joanne Kwong who is the second-generation shop owner. Joanne has introduced social media, community outreach, and inventory that showcases local Asian American artists. By embracing new ideas and practices from the next generation, stores like Pearl River Mart and 永安和 are doing critical work to reimagine what it means to be a mom-and-pop shop in New York City while at the same time holding together the social and economic fabric of the community. In Chinatown, small multigenerational businesses are more than transactional spaces because they continue to persist as lifelines where new immigrants can find jobs and residents can build human connections and deepen their relationships within a community.

A significant part of the discussion focused on the role of cultural production as resistance to gentrification. Betty Yu, cofounder of the Chinatown Art Brigade (CAB), discussed her relationship to creative resistance work in the neighborhood. CAB is a women-run collective of Asian American artists, media makers, residents, and activists driven by the fundamental belief that cultural modes of production have the power to advance positive social change. Since the group was established in December 2015 by artists ManSee Kong, Tomie Arai, and Betty Yu, CAB has facilitated a series of responses to gentrification created in collaboration with CAAAV: Organizing Asian Communities and their Chinatown Tenants Union membership.[3] One of CAB's immediate goals is to address the hyperdevelopment and new galleries that are placing the livelihoods of low-income Chinese residents at risk. Betty expressed:

> A family of four only makes $32,000 a year in Chinatown so rent has to be $900 to be affordable, yet rent goes up to as much as six or seven thousand dollars. The average rent is $5,000 now for a one-bedroom apartment. When we talk about neighborhood preservation, we have to talk about people who make up this place. What can we do to protect Chinatown for future generations, not just the facade, but the people who live and work here. (Betty Yu, pers. comm., December 10, 2016)

CAB's cultural production work is rooted in a long history of women-led resistance and art activism in the neighborhood. Betty reflected:

> It is funny when people buy into this stereotype of the passive immigrant woman because in Chinatown, Chinese immigrant women have always been at the leadership of everything, of all these movements, of all this work. As a women-led cultural collective we continue in this tradition. CAB challenges the notion that this neighborhood needs cultural revitalization because there is a culture that already exists. We are not just fighting day-to-day conditions, we are fighting for a community rezoning plan that would bring protections to families who have been here for generations. We are sending messages to new art galleries by asking critical questions like, Who did you displace to be here? This fight determines the future of Chinatown. (Betty Yu, pres. comm., December 10, 2016)

CAB's "Here to Stay" Placekeeping Project involves a series of tenant-led storytelling workshops, mapping exercises, placekeeping walks, and large-scale outdoor mobile projections that highlight stories of tenant resistance to gentrification. Given that cultural change oftentimes proceeds political change, the work that the women in CAB engage in is critical because it allows for those most impacted to creatively reconfigure what the neighborhood can look like even in the face of displacement.

May Ying Chen, an organizer for the International Ladies' Garment Workers' Union Local 23–25 Workers United, joined the discussion and shared her organizing experiences of working for unions representing garment workers. Drawing from her experiences as a labor organizer for three decades in Chinatown, May indicated that another important approach to combat gentrification is to hold coethnic landlords accountable for their complicity. Influenced by the Third World liberation movement, May began working as a union organizer with the International Ladies' Garment Workers' Union (ILGWU) and Local 23–25 Union of Needletrades, Industrial, and Textile Employees (UNITE) in the early 1980s and rose through the ranks to become the international vice president of UNITE HERE. In the early 1960s there were fifty garment factories in Chinatown that employed two thousand workers; however, by 1982 there were five hundred garment factories that employed twenty thousand workers who were mostly new immigrant women from Fujian and Guangdong (Chin 2015). In the 1980s as rents doubled and offshore production increased local competition, many coethnic garment factory owners in Manhattan's Chinatown reduced worker wages and hired nonunion labor to keep costs low. In response to deteriorating labor conditions and stalled worker contracts, Local 23–25 of ILGWU organized the largest strike in Manhattan's Chinatown in which twenty thousand Chinese immigrant women who worked in garment factories flooded the streets to demand better work conditions from their coethnic employers (Chin 2015). May spoke about how she became a full-time labor organizer after participating in the 1982 labor strikes:

> Chinese bosses thought they could play the coethnic card but many of the women in the union already knew about the benefits they have. I was blown away because the Chinatown women really came out and fought for things like daycare and other community services. Many of them served in the PTA and continue to be active in the neighborhood as retirees. These immigrant women taught me a lot in my experience as a younger woman and as a young mother. (May Ying Chen, pers. comm., December 10, 2016)

What May shared from her experiences of working as a labor organizer reveals the cycles of coethnic exploitation that happens in Chinatown from owners, bosses, and landlords. Many Chinese landlords in Manhattan's Chinatown have used a variety of predatory tactics to force coethnic tenants out of their homes from refusing to provide heat, hot water, and basic repairs to using hazardous construction as a form of systematic harassment. It is not enough to keep people in their homes or in the neighborhood by fighting external forces; there must also be a coordinated effort to hold those within the community accountable for their role as agents of mass displacement.

Conclusion

This article importantly bridges feminist theory to lessons learned from on the ground and advances the viability of ordinary neighborhood spaces as sites for transformative social change and political possibilities for women. The talks held inside 永安和 have resulted in new insights and new strategies to approach gentrification, and have also helped to deepen interpersonal relationships among women across three generations. As the oldest continually run store in Manhattan's Chinatown, 永安和 creates space for residents, organizers, cultural workers, and elders to cultivate relationships, generate new political knowledge, and share strategies of resistance through dialogue. Rather than focus on traditional sites and modes of participation in politics, I shift attention to focus on how women in the neighborhood are using informal community dialogue or what I call "shop talk" to develop mutual understandings around the issue of gentrification. I reveal how listening to what women in the neighborhood talk about on a regular basis provides critical insight and tremendous perspective on how political consciousness, values, and practices are formed or negotiated over time. The kinds of conversations happening in 永安和 indicate that political possibilities are most deeply rooted in the circumstances of people's daily lives, their pasts, and the environments in which they are born, grow, work, live, and age. Since this talk was held at 永安和, Mei and the rest of the W.O.W. Project team have organized other public programming events including an Asian American women filmmakers series in collaboration with the Third World Newsreel and another on Chinatown's newest galleries in collaboration with the Chinatown Art Brigade. The intergenerational work that Mei and the W.O.W. Project have done for Manhattan's Chinatown has caught wind in other Chinatowns, inspiring similar conversations across cities.

Diane Wong is an assistant professor and faculty fellow in the Gallatin School of Individualized Study at New York University. She holds a PhD in American Politics and an MA in Comparative Race, Ethnicity, and Immigration from Cornell University. She can be reached at dw465@cornell.edu.

Notes

1. From the 1900s to the mid-1950s, thousands of Chinese men gained entry into the United States by purchasing false papers identifying them as relatives to Chinese Americans who had citizenship, making them sons on paper.
2. In the fall of 2008, sixty organizations came together to draft the Chinatown Working Group, a community-led rezoning plan that would preserve affordable housing and small businesses.
3. CAAAV: Organizing Asian Communities works on a range of systemic issues including police violence, poverty, and worker exploitation. Their Chinatown Tenants Union (CTU) was founded in 2005 to organize residents around displacement.

Works Cited

Asian American Federation of New York (AAFNY). 2002. *Chinatown One Year after September 11th: An Economic Impact Study*. November 2002. https://www.aafny.org/doc/ChinatownOneYearAfter911.pdf.

———. 2008. *Working but Poor: Asian American Poverty in New York City*. October 2008. https://www.aafny.org/doc/WorkingButPoor.pdf.

Asian American Legal Defense and Education Fund (AALDEF). 2013. *Chinatown Then and Now: Gentrification in Boston, New York, and Philadelphia*.

Chin, Margaret May. 2015. *Sewing Women: Immigrants and the New York City Garment Industry*. New York: Columbia University Press.

Cohen, Cathy J. 2004. "Deviance as Resistance: A New Research Agenda for the Study of Black Politics." *Du Bois Review: Social Science Research on Race* 1, no.1: 27–45.

Collins, Patricia Hill. 2008. *Black Feminist Thought: Knowledge, Consciousness, and the Politics of Empowerment*. New York: Routledge Classics.

Gafvert, Rebecca, and R Weber Consulting. 2011. "Framework to Preserve Chinatown/Lower East Side." A Study for Two Bridges Neighborhood Council.

Harris-Lacewell, Melissa. 2006. *Barbershops, Bibles, and BET: Everyday Talk and Black Political Thought*. Princeton, NJ: Princeton University Press.

hooks, bell. 1990. *Yearning: Race, Gender, and Cultural Politics*. Boston: South End Press.

Kwong, Peter, and Samuel Stein. 2015. "Preserve and Protect Chinatown." Published for Roosevelt House Policy Institute at Hunter College.

Mansbridge, Jane. 1999. "Everyday Talk in the Deliberative System." In *Deliberative Politics: Essays on Democracy and Disagreement*, edited by Stephen Macedo. Oxford, UK: Oxford University Press.

Moy, Liz. 2016. "Site of Mass Displacement: A Chinatown Gentrified by Galleries." *Bowery Boogie*, October 21, 2016. https://www.boweryboogie.com/2016/10/site-mass-displacement-chinatown-gentrified-galleries-op-ed/.

Ting Yi Lui, Mary. 2007. *The Chinatown Trunk Mystery: Murder, Miscegenation, and Other Dangerous Encounters in Turn-of-the-Century New York City.* Princeton, NJ: Princeton University Press.

Tchen, John Kuo Wei. 2001. *New York before Chinatown: Orientalism and the Shaping of American Culture, 1776–1882.* Baltimore: John Hopkins University Press.

Urban Justice Center. 2008. "Converting Chinatown: Snapshot of a Neighborhood Becoming Unaffordable and Unlivable." Report published in collaboration with CAAAV: Organizing Asian Communities.

Young, Iris Marion. 2005. *On Female Body Experience: "Throwing Like a Girl" and Other Essays.* Oxford, UK: Oxford University Press.

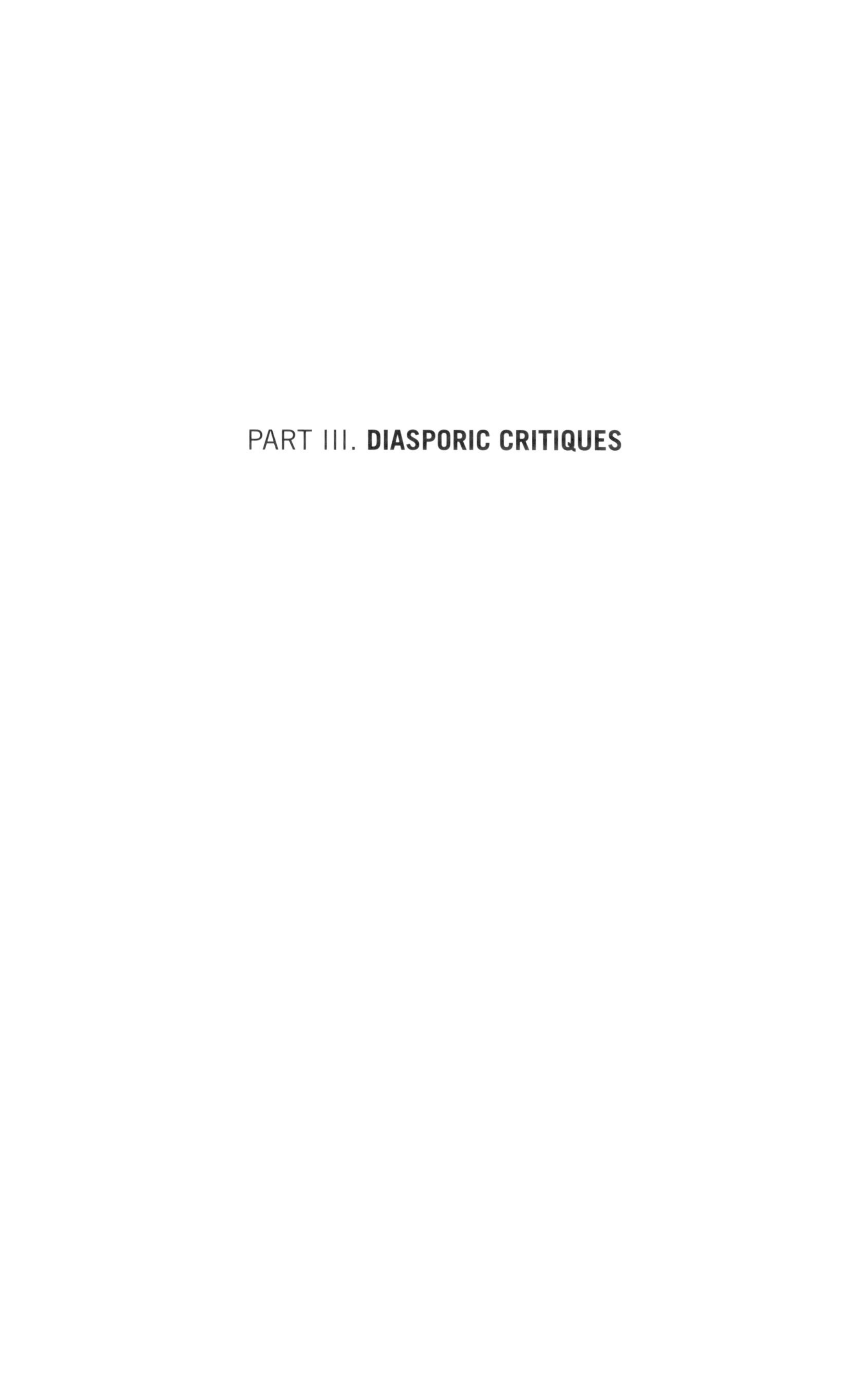

PART III. **DIASPORIC CRITIQUES**

Turning Diaspora to Dirt: Addiction and Illness in Asian American Critique

Peggy Lee

Abstract: This article locates the Asian addict in global capitalism and argues that drug addiction and illness point to the limitations of diaspora in Asian American criticism. Through a reading of Nami Mun's 2009 novel, *Miles from Nowhere,* where "dirt" configures as a central trope, this article theorizes "diasporic dirt" as a framework to challenge the rehabilitative impulse within identitarian politics and narratives of diasporic "uplift" often valorized in Asian Americanist critique. **Keywords:** diaspora, dirt, home, addiction, illness, debt, memoir, Asian American women's literature, neoliberalism, literary criticism

Introduction: Diasporic Dirt

In Nami Mun's novel, *Miles from Nowhere,* the teenage protagonist, Joon, recalls her mother's psychotic episodes, or her struggles with dirt. She remembers her mother lying still in the backyard garden after one of her father's habitual disappearances. Attempting to wake her mother from this catatonic state, Joon begins to playfully bury her mother's legs and feet with the dirt, digging up tiny pebbles to line around her neck, with no response. Joon's last memory of her mother's encounter with dirt coincides with her father's final disappearance, which, she narrates, turns her mother crazy. Obsessively digging a large hole in the backyard, as if she was trying to dig her way back to Korea, her mother throws all her father's belongings into it and lights them on fire. She attempts to fall into the flames before Joon quickly pulls her away. When she returns from hospitalization, her mother does not talk despite Joon's desperate attempts to get her to engage. After six months of impenetrable silence, Joon runs away from home

WSQ: Women's Studies Quarterly 47: 1 & 2 (Spring/Summer 2019)

in the Bronx at the age of thirteen. Years later, while in jail for stealing from a Korean-owned fruit and vegetable grocery store, Joon learns of her mother's death in a car accident from her public defender. She thinks to herself, "She was dead now. Her nose filled with dirt" (2009, 212).

The novel begins with Joon's memory of her mother, digging, talking, and listening to dirt. Dirt reappears in the novel as the very substance of Joon's connection to her mother. Dirt, an anonymous yet ubiquitous organic material, captures the mystery Joon grapples with of her mother's mental illness, a narrative and diagnosis that remains opaque for the reader to its conclusion. Dirt, as Mary Douglas once famously put it, is "matter out of place" (1966, 35). For Douglas, dirt instigates a constant project of reordering and monitoring that ensures cultural conceptions of cleanliness and purity are ritualized and felt. She describes dirt "as a kind of compendium category for all events which blur, smudge, contradict, or otherwise confuse accepted classifications. The underlying feeling is that a system of values which is habitually expressed in a given arrangement of things has been violated" (1966, 51). Dirt is indistinct, runaway material.

Marketed as a coming-of-age and runaway novel, Joon's experiences of homelessness, engagement in survival work, and heroin usage attend to another social dimension of "dirt" that she is witness to in the setting of 1980s New York City. Her mother's introductory question directed at the dirt—"What do you think God does to people like you?"—reverberates in another way, one charged with a religious condemnation seemingly reserved for people engaged in survival crime and addiction. Social conceptions of dirt, as Douglas (1966) illuminates, reveal theories on order and control. Joon's mother's question also acts as foreshadowing for Joon's own difficulties to come. The repeated trope of dirt, citing this "nowhere" in *Miles from Nowhere,* contoured by its own anonymity, provides a peculiar approach to the question of homeland and diaspora in second-generation Asian American women's literature in the following ways. First, for Joon, home, in its domestic and Korean diasporic sense, like dirt, is nebulous, discharged of any longing, nostalgia, and sentimentality. In other words, if Korean American women's literature, as Laura Kang observes, has a "sustained, if terribly strained, investment in the Korean homeland" that troubles the notion of the return, Mun's novel turns this home, in all its iterations, into dirt (2002, 40). Second, this unfeeling of diaspora, so to speak, makes apparent the conventions of racial and ethnic uplift that can prevail in diasporic narratives, one that is repeatedly challenged by Joon's character. Lastly, this novel, often reviewed closely with the harrowing genre of the addiction memoir, brings to the fore the figure of the Asian addict, a character who seldom appears in contemporary Asian American literary discourse. Alongside a mentally ill mother and neglectful father, Joon's story could be read as a confessional, of life's "dirt" and family "dirt." In these various crossings of meaning, this article brings together dirt with diaspora to theorize how the framework of "diasporic dirt" can situate Nami Mun's novel and the Asian addict beyond an individualized, atypical narrative of an Asian American girl, but whose experience illuminates the violent contradictions of global capitalism.

Published by Riverhead Press in 2009, *Miles from Nowhere* is a story of runaway and addict Joon-Mee, a Korean American teenage girl who immigrated to the Bronx, New York City, from Korea at eight years of age. The novel follows her from age thirteen as a runaway, until age eighteen, when she becomes sober and finds stable employment through a job officer willing to overlook her past. Similar to the conventions of the addiction memoir, Joon's experience on the streets are made up of a series of "chances" she either takes or leaves; the novel stages how her reception as an Asian girl, often coded by others as a particularity—whether as a runaway or prisoner—reifies how state apparatuses especially confine and project criminality onto black, brown, and queer bodies. Set in an era of New York City when historic displacement and deteriorating public infrastructure heightened the criminalization of poor communities of color, Joon negotiates model minority discipline by betraying its impotence as a narrative that can hold her mother's illness and her addiction struggles.

Following Mun's novel and the trope of dirt, this article suggests that Asian American criticism may implicitly valorize narratives of diasporic "uplift." Insofar as diaspora is characterized by movement, disruption, and displacement resulting from political and historical events that in retrospect produce its own narrative forms, I understand Mun's novel and its strategy of turning "uplift" to "dirt," as an example of a "difficult diaspora" (Pinto 2013, 4–5). Coined by literary scholar Samantha Pinto in her work on black feminist writers, "difficult diaspora" refers to the interpretive strategies enabled by the proliferation of forms; in other words, diaspora is defined by its disorder more so than its geographic movements (4–5). By beginning with dirt, which signifies the unstable and unpredictable locations and embodiments of illness and addiction, "diasporic dirt" considers the difficulty of gathering these narratives under the cohesive guise of

Korean/Asian American literature writ large. Mun's novel provides an opportunity for Asian American cultural criticism to take into account the location of the Asian addict during the rise of Reagan neoliberalism and the development of predatory transnationalism, as well as on a global scale.

From the recent "opioid crisis" in the United States to the "drug war" in the Philippines, the "addict" has reemerged as a focus in the reordering of U.S.-Pacific geopolitical interests. And yet, there has been little critical attention paid to cultural conceptions of the Asian addict beyond the binary conceptualization of rebel/model minority. I argue that addiction and illness point to a limitation in the Asian American critical framework, as they challenge the valorization of diasporic uplift narratives. My article interprets "diasporic dirt" with the legacies of the U.S. "drug war" and its circulation within the U.S. Pacific to better understand the role of the Asian addict in the intertwining of addiction and debt during the expansion of Pacific capital. Mun's novel provides an opportunity to contextualize the Asian addict in literary and historical discourses, which is underexamined in Asian American critique.

Racial Capitalism of the Addict and Debtor

Representations of the "addict" have reemerged as a global lynchpin, indexing human rights, economic development, and militarization during the unsettling reordering of U.S.-Pacific geopolitical interests—with the United States and Philippines in the global spotlight. In December 2017, U.S.-based international debt watcher Fitch Ratings upgraded the national credit rating of the Philippines, putting its solvency on par with Italy and above Indonesia. Fitch cites President Rodrigo Duterte's administration's economic expansion, tax reforms, and foreign investment initiatives as reasons for the improved credit score. As one of the three major credit rating companies that produce data for regulatory purposes, Fitch ratings measure a country's willingness and ability to pay off debt. On the Philippines, the rating agency states, "There is no evidence so far that incidents of violence associated with the administration's campaign against the illegal drug trade have undermined investor confidence" (Leyco 2017). Duterte's administration took it as a vote of confidence. Here, the debtor becomes intertwined with the drug addict and both disappear at the promising horizon of Filipino global capital. It is another articulation of what Sarita Echavez See describes in her work on the subprime debtor as the continuous violent "occlusion" of Filipinos as the "external other to the internal contradictions of the imperial, racist state" (2012, 500). Following See's argument that the debtor is the "literalization of the logic of debt that structures capital," the Fitch rating can be seen as representing a divestment of the Filipino addict from capitalist and livable structures (496). This divestment, in the form of extrajudicial murder and record incarceration rates, is rendered an unpleasant yet tolerable condition for foreign investment.

The "law and order" rhetoric and punitive approach to drug addiction in the Duterte administration is reminiscent of and shares in the legacies of the U.S. drug wars starting in the 1970s, now well established by researchers, scholars, and policy makers as an ineffectual and harmful approach to addiction. Though the Trump administration's approach to opioid addiction has differentiated itself from the warring antidrug rhetoric of his Republican presidential predecessors, notably Nixon and Reagan, the racial capitalism of addiction remains intact. In her reflections on the current administration and the opioid crisis at the 2017 International Drug Policy Reform Conference, Michelle Alexander challenges seeing the passing of progressive drug policy as a total victory, especially in its coinciding with Trump's election. She asserts, "Whiteness makes the difference," which explains the "newfound tolerance and compassion of white users and abusers" that make up the majority of deaths in this unprecedented drug crisis in America (Alexander 2017). Alexander argues the legacy of antiblack racism in the drug wars still forms the contemporary structural lack of efficient rehabilitation and immediate medical care, even among white users.

Applying Alexander's critique of whiteness to the U.S.-Pacific, I would suggest that whiteness also functions as an exceptional crisis, as amenable U.S. capital flows into the promising Philippines, compounding racist and classist logics of U.S. drug war policy. However, beyond a black/white racial binary, I argue that understanding the racial capitalism of addiction in the U.S.-Pacific requires a cultural analysis long overdue and surprisingly scant in Asian Americanist critique. This neglect of addiction in Asian Americanist critique is a result of what Dylan Rodríguez (2005) has described as one of the oversights in Asian American studies, that is the historical convergence of what we know as the identity and civic formations of "Asian American" during the consolidation of the punitive neoliberal state and the crack epidemic. In other words, the issue of addiction points to how Asian Americanist thought must continuously redefine the conditions of transnationalism and diaspora to create renewed theory and conditions of possibility for ethnic studies and global coalition. Following Rodríguez, racial narratives of addiction, as lived experience in connectivity mobilized by "diasporic dirt," challenge the classed myopia of what constitutes valorized Asian American literature, narratives, criticism, and coalitional politics. "Diasporic dirt" as a conceptualized relationality centered in addiction and illness may point to the contradictory gestures in Asian Americanist critique that unknowingly obfuscate or overlook the predatory transnational relations that drive and market "diaspora."

The examination of addiction in Asian American critique has long been held in the curricular life of exclusion-era history as stereotype, the Opium Wars, or bounded in social science studies as a liminal fluctuation between Asian and American, or the model minority and rebel. Within the North American context, the crisis of addiction has been configured by discourses of racial exclusion, particularly Asian exclusion in its initial emergence. "Addiction" is a term that came into prominent usage among medical professionals in the U.S. by the turn of the century emerging from the well-established image repertoire of Chinese opium users threatening the white national imaginary. From this period spanning Reconstruction, the Chinese Exclusion Act of 1882, and the Progressive Era, "addiction" and its reform, as many drug policy historians point out, were unevenly applied, ascertaining bodies of color as more punishable than rehabilitative.

Mun's novel provides an opportunity to contextualize the Asian addict in literary and historical discourses, which is seldom examined in Asian American critique and literary production. Such an endeavor requires first an examination of the memoir genre. Though the author prefers to call the process of her work "fiction" in interviews and reviews, those interviews often note the many parallels between Mun's own life and that of her character, Joon (Gilmer 2009; Schutz 2009). Such a juxtaposition of the genres of memoir and the "semiautobiographical" becomes a significant context to read this novel and its marketing, also amid much scandal surrounding Mun's publisher, Riverhead Books.

Addiction and Memoir's "Dirt"

Although her character's story parallels Mun's own life (who also is a second-generation immigrant to the Bronx from South Korea and a runaway who shared some of the short-lived jobs Joon takes on to survive—from Avon lady to a nursing home activities coordinator), Mun firmly contests any autobiographical intent in her novel. Overall, Mun's favorable reviews generally fix the novel as brushing the genre of runaway and addiction memoir, an unsentimental story of survival on the streets, a coming-of-age story. However, I would speculate that Mun's choice to see her work as pure fiction may be influenced by the fact that her publisher, Riverhead, dealt with a well-publicized scandal regarding a drug addiction "memoir" not long before Mun's own publication.

The confessional or memoir form has long undergirded Western fascination with the figure of the drug addict. Scholars have pointed to Thomas De Quincey's *Confessions of an English Opium-Eater*, first published in 1821, as the first literary prototype to inaugurate the popular genre of what contemporary Western markets label as the addiction memoir. Like many nineteenth-century Western imaginings of the East, literary scholars and historians note the crude orientalism in De Quincey's writings in its polarized castings of China as both nightmare and mystique (Poetzsch 2015). Such castings shared transnational appeal, following representations of Chinese laborers into the United States. De Quincey's writings and the legacies of the Opium Wars are generally neglected in Anglo-American cultural memory and yet have been absolutely central in China's understanding of its history (Chandler 2016). I would suggest that in Asian American cultural criticism, addiction is similarly displaced as an apparition of nineteenth-century Orient writ large rather than as a materiality of precarious life that continues to endure during advanced capitalism. Why is there a difficulty in locating the Asian addict in global capitalism, particularly in the U.S. framework? Such obfuscation of the Asian addict is arguably due to narratives of diasporic uplift attached to accumulations of transpacific capital and the increasingly flexible and healthy migrant. Yet, have such narratives limited Asian Americanist critique to the promise of the rehabilitative body?

By the 1870s after the Civil War, as described by medical historian Timothy A. Hickman (2004), the increase in opiate usage (particularly morphine, cocaine, and heroin) alarmed medical and popular writers. This provoked more scientific studies linking addiction to race, specifically as an "Oriental" condition that encroached the purity of the white body politic—despite the fact that earlier usage in the U.S. prevailed among the prescribed habits of middle- and upper-class white women before spreading to working-class, urban men. In his essay on Orientalism and addiction,

Hickman examines turn-of-the-century medical literature on addiction and observes that the anti-Asian racism embedded in this discourse mobilized the "addict" "away from the description of practices and moved it instead toward the investigation of essences" (2000, 72). Whereas Chinese immigrants in the nineteenth century were portrayed and feared as opium smokers, by 1900 cocaine use caused panic in the South as a stimulant that could spur rebellious black-on-white violence (Musto 1973). From the exclusion era to the crack epidemic, the correlation of racialized others and addiction is arguably one of the defining paradigms of twentieth-century U.S. modernity.

The Orientalist fascination with whiteness and the opioid addiction memoir continues to pique interest in the literary market today. From the nineteenth century into the twenty-first, the memoir or life narrative has an extensive history in U.S. popular culture. In her study of the memoir market during the 1990s and 2000s, Leigh Gilmore (2010) coins the "American neoconfessional" as a genre that has narrowed permissible forms of memoir in favor of the "redemption narrative." The American neoconfessional is a witnessing genre that locates pain in the individual, displacing questions and histories of violence. Echoing Lauren Berlant's thesis on "cruel optimism" (2011), Gilmore suggests that the market success of the American neoconfessional is that "truth" is not produced by the protagonist's suffering, but rather their "struggle" to achieve a happier-than-predicted ending (660). As a case in point on the successful "redemptive narrative," Gilmore examines the scandal surrounding writer James Frey, whose drug and alcohol addiction "memoir" *A Million Little Pieces* captivated Oprah's Book Club in 2005, then went to top the *New York Times* Best Seller list for fifteen weeks straight. However, shortly after the Oprah's Book Club announcement in 2005, it came to light that the memoir was fabricated, from his criminal record and incarceration to the suicide of his girlfriend Lily. It is now well known that Frey, wanting to change the prospects of his manuscript after rejections as a novel, pitched it as memoir. In a televised broadcast on Oprah's show, the defamed Frey admitted to lying to Oprah, who felt "really duped" by the book. In spite of the controversy, Frey enjoyed continued success with book sales, and his second novel, a continuation of *A Million Little Pieces*, published by Riverhead Books the same year of Oprah's spotlight, also became a best seller. Although profiting from the controversy, Riverhead nervously pulled out of an agreement to publish his next two books. Gilmore sees Frey's success in spite of scandal as indicative of the market popularity of the "redemption narrative," one that "stand[s] fully in the social and psychic space of white privilege" (2010, 665). Even Frey's lies became the materiality of redemption he struggled through on Oprah's couch and in the national media.

Here, addiction is a narrative medium in which the writer, with varying commitments to truth-telling, reconstitutes a racial logic on addiction that has long captured the national imagination: the therapeutic impulse that lines the repeating concern of crisis in white drug addiction. As Michelle Alexander put it in her speech on the U.S. opioid crisis during the Trump administration, "Whiteness makes the difference" (2017). Therefore, if the labor of white redemption is a nation-building project, unifying what Berlant calls an intimate public sphere through individual acts, how can one read the addict of color within this sphere? Reading the addict of color through this prism of the addiction memoir market serves to show that representations since the nineteenth century have not altered much. When considering how labor and capital have shaped and defined race in the U.S., representations of the Filipino addict in Duterte's violent campaign are followed by the legacies of exploitable Filipino labor—ones that continue to stir no ethical deterrent in the flowing of foreign investment capital into the Philippines. At stake in the literary representation and discourse of the Asian addict is therefore its rehabilitation. From a market standpoint, the redemptive narrative and rehabilitative body share congruence toward the horizon of accumulation.

In *Race and Resistance*, literary scholar Viet Thanh Nguyen describes the "body project" as one that seeks to organize an "Asian American movement around a rehabilitated body" that for some "panethnic entrepreneurs" becomes a labor of resignifying the history of anti-Asian racism, thereby transforming the abject body into one more "marketable in the arena of multiethnic identification and consumption" (2002, 18). Nguyen's visualization of mobilizing around the "rehabilitated body" in Asian American studies is helpful in articulating a critical maneuver in the field that needs to be rethought. Such critique hand in hand with the literary market establishes an elitism that can stagnate political conceptions of the field, through limited, often binary representations. Instead, racialized pain as a "body project," borrowing from Nguyen, must be approached as more ideologically ambivalent and unpredictable, and cannot be appraised by neat categories of accommodation or resistance. If the rehabilitated body indexes the whole and healed consumer/producer, how does the Asian addict exist in this teleology of late capitalism?

Narratives of rehabilitation and redemption share a similar trajectory in its valorization of "whole" subjectivities. As discussed above, such narratives in the form of memoir or life narrative enact a feeling of belonging within the realm of U.S. citizenship. This feeling of belonging not only reaffirms individualized acts and identities, but also constitutes a nation-at-work. Addict subjectivity and addiction narratives, while impacting Asian/American families and communities in painful ways, are seldom discussed in dominant narratives. As Mari Matsuda states in her speech "We Will Not Be Used," "Suggestions that some segments of the Asian American community need special help [like drug abuse] are greeted with suspicion or disbelief" (1997, 152). When Chinese Canadian Evelyn Lau published her best-selling autobiography, *Runaway: Diary of a Street Kid* in 1989, dealing with her experiences of homelessness, sex work, and drug addiction, literary scholar erin Khuê Ninh points out that it was not well received by the Chinese Canadian community for its supposedly villainous depiction of the authoritarian Chinese family. Ninh argues that Lau's experiences of drug addiction, sex work, and suicide reflect the psychological costs incurred in failing to become the "model minority," which is tied into the capitalist ideals sustained by the Asian immigrant family/home. In *Ingratitude,* Ninh approaches narratives of illness and addiction in second-generation Asian American daughter subject formation, as racialized suffering tied to the material impacts of model minority discipline maintained by the familial, domestic space. Her writing illuminates the suffering of second-generation Asian American daughters by affixing a truth-value to the conditions or aims of the immigrant family that enforces professional-managerial class mobility. And yet, her analyses are unable to maneuver out of the bind of such representations. She admits that her readings, however unpopular or risky they may be, articulate what is often understated, that the "child-as-capital-investment," and therefore the model minority, is one that harms. However, I am cautious about this mode of representational production in the child that is so easily fetishized within the scene of Asian racialized domestic space and intimacies. She assigns the "unprofitable pursuit of literature [for the disobedient Asian daughter] . . . as an interesting precursor to other forms of masochistic rebellion: drug addiction, suicide, and running away from home" (Ninh 2011, 17). In other words, not unlike the American neoconfessional, the narrative of addiction becomes circumscribed by Ninh, as a reader, critic, and consumer, into a deeply personalized if not convoluted form of Asian-racialized "rebellion." The model minority stereotype does indeed incur a price for Asian American subjectivity; however, to render addiction equivalent to rebellion is a misplaced gesture that displaces racist histories of addiction in the North American context.

This section has elucidated the racial histories and theories of addiction to contextualize the literary framework of interest in this article, that is, of "diasporic dirt." From the "dirt" of the addiction memoir genre and Asian American literature, to the figure of the Asian addict in Nami Mun's novel, I argue that Joon's character illuminates not only an individualized life struggle, but becomes one through which we are able to perceive the violent workings of U.S. racial capitalism. Further, the application of diasporic dirt to the recent circulation of the Asian addict between the U.S. and the Pacific offers a larger global critique, in that the figure of the Asian addict is transformed from the status of surplus or failure, to the target of violent control central to the advancement of twenty-first-century Pacific capitalism.

Moving away from this more theoretical conceptualization of diaspora and diasporic dirt, I would like to bring my concept into conversation with postcolonial histories of Korea and post-1965 U.S. immigration. Diaspora within cultural studies continues to be an important framework for organizing and understanding racial formations within the movement histories of the migrant, refugee, enslaved, and laborer. Concurrently, it is important to take into account critiques of diaspora from postcolonial and transnational studies perspectives. For instance, Aihwa Ong argues that American studies' takes on diaspora often are naive renderings of the diasporic subject, which "celebrate hybridity, 'cultural' border crossing, and the production of the different" without a deep consideration of the shifting global capital and accumulation that valorize such processes (2006, 13). "Diaspora" and "dirt," in their juxtaposition, mirror similar tensions of debate and critique in contemporary cultural analysis. Like diaspora, dirt too is debated as an ambivalent and unproductive concept where it is a "domain in which all differences are lost" (Wright 2009, 36). My essay insists on this concept of diasporic dirt as a literary framework that can hold the difficult narratives of illness and addiction, but also forms a method. I argue diasporic dirt offers a generative place of return for narrative making. Mun's novel in conversation with second-generation Korean

American women's writing invites an alternative to the route of a rehabilitative body politic. Rather than demonstrating the conventions of hybridity, assimilation, fragmentation, and other diasporic methods, Mun's novel asks us to consider decomposition.

Turning Diasporic Uplift to Dirt

Upon learning of her mother's passing, Joon imagines her mother's nose "filled with dirt" (Mun 2009, 212). The reader confronts the organic permeability of Joon's mother's body. This scene invites an imagining of decomposition as a way of connecting Joon to her mother. Since mother and homeland are predominant themes studied and debated in Asian American women's literature and criticism (Kim 1982), Joon's mother lying in the dirt also functions as an allegory to country and border, in this case the 1945 division of Korea into North and South. As Wendy Ho notes, the mother-daughter narrative structure holds a privileged place in Asian American women's literature since the publication of successful works such as Maxine Hong Kingston's 1976 novel *The Woman Warrior* and Amy Tan's 1989 *The Joy Luck Club*. The mother-daughter relationship as imagined by these writers, Ho describes, is "an ambiguous, permeable, and precarious territory to work" (1999, 118). Further, it is the site of multiple crossings and convergences of geopolitical spaces that the daughter must negotiate in order to access her mother's stories. However, there is a consistent theme of unfeeling diaspora that follows Joon's narration, one discharged of longing, of imagining and turning the home/land (Korea), and therefore her mother, into dirt.

The novel begins in a transient space, the homeless shelter, with Joon looking for Knowledge, a black queer teen runaway who she befriends, and later leaves the shelter with. Joon was in the shelter for two weeks after running away from her mother's fire. Joon finds shelter life to consist of nothing but lying in her cot, waiting for counseling circles and therapy appointments, and talking to Knowledge and her other friend, Wink, a white, queer boy sex worker. In a dialogue between Joon and Knowledge at the cafeteria, Knowledge points out Joon's narrative particularity:

> "I didn't even know chinks ran away from home."
>
> "We can do a lot of neat things," I said, swallowing. I liked hearing her laugh. And I didn't care that she'd called me a Chink, though I wanted to

> say Chinks were for Chinese and Koreans had their own special name. But that was another subject, and I liked the way we were talking right then. (2009, 7)

Here, Knowledge's expression of surprise at a "chink" running away from home brings up larger considerations of the racialized runaway as tied to logics mediated by the institution of citizenship. The implied impossibility of Joon's narrative mobilized by the racist slur, "chink," which Joon registers as a misfire, reveals an orientalism at play that necessitates deeper contextualization. On one hand, Knowledge's surprise at Joon cites a statistical reality where in the U.S. homeless and runaway youth are disproportionately made up of black and queer-identified youth. Both of Joon's closest friends, Knowledge and Wink, reflect these identities. On the other hand, Knowledge's statement reflects a tension shaped by discourses of U.S. citizenship, which Helen Jun would describe as a kind of "Black orientalism" that is not simply anti-Asian or prejudicial, but refers to the strategies demanded by the institution of citizenship aligned with the logics of American Orientalism and Chinese exclusion since the nineteenth century (Jun 2011). Concurrently, what Jun describes as "Asian uplift" is not only antiblack, but encompasses how the Asian American national subject is mediated by processes of black racialization, particularly of pathology and criminality. I would extend Jun's argument to conceptualize "diasporic uplift." Jun argues that black and Asian antagonisms are maintained by neoliberal logics through the rubric of citizenship. Mun's novel stretches the comparative framework Jun offers, by situating the runaway within and relational to the intersections of gender, class, race, and sexuality. The puncture of "chink" as it entails a violent and exclusionary history of the immigrant, foreigner, coolie, and model minority thus resonates alongside Knowledge's own runaway racialization as a black, queer girl, coded as criminal, disposable, sexually deviant. "Chink" is to be interpreted literally and figuratively, as Joon is positioned as trespasser of and in her own story, especially in her confrontations with custodial figures of the state. Here, between Joon and Knowledge, the racializations of criminality are brought to the fore, pressed upon each other in friendship, yet not denuded of their systemic function as apparatuses of control and death over queer black bodies. Knowledge, as we learn later, becomes a counselor, but is shot and killed by a youth she was supporting at a homeless shelter.

Joon learns quickly living in the shelter that therapy circles, or rap sessions, are performances of untruth. She learns this lesson at Wink's expense, when in his first rap, inspired by the runaway stories of his circle, he reveals his story, only to be cornered, called "faggot," and beat up by the boys afterward who had all made up their sob stories. From the start, Mun sets up a narrative structure that is deeply embedded in a refusal, if not suspicion, of what the state can do for her. To tell the truth, like Wink did, Joon learns, is not worth it, only to circulate among an endless stream of both true and counterfeit suffering that is all the same to "them," the custodial agents of the state. After leaving the shelter, Joon continues to navigate various spaces of storytelling and confession, from an addiction support group to the unemployment office, and masters the art of untruth, which for her is silence. She holds onto this strategy when later, incarcerated for stealing, she is forced to attend a counseling group facilitated by an outreach program for those who appear to have a "chance." Still reeling from the news of her mother's death, Joon is handcuffed in a circle of girls, and she describes, "Some of them talked. I knew better." The correctional officer who escorted Joon and disapproved of her silent refusal to participate confronts her afterward:

> Listen, he whispered, and scanned the hallway. "A lot of those women, in your cell, they're supposed to be there. They grew up in shit holes worse than anything we got here. I understand that. I get it. They don't know any better. But you . . ." His voice trailed off. "Where you from?"
>
> "The Bronx," I said.
>
> "No. I'm asking you, what are you?"
>
> I knew where this was going but I told him anyway. "I'm Korean."
>
> "Korea. That's what I thought," he said. "Do you know what percentage of prisoners are Korean?"
>
> "A hundred percent," I said. "In Korea."
>
> "Forget it." He pushed me to start walking. "I'd like to see you be so funny when they drop you at Rikers."
>
> "I know what you're doing," I told him. (2009, 226)

In this scene, the correctional officer projects a racial hierarchy of citizenship that betrays his management of racialized others. Governance, as Michel Foucault discusses, implies interiority, and the promise of therapy, as facilitated by the correctional officer and the larger state, is to heal one's way to rehabilitation and full citizenship (Foucault 2009). However, as demonstrated by the correctional officer's whispering, this model emerges from serving the interests of a white liberal interiority, and admittedly, cannot benefit everyone, like her jail mates who "do not know any better." To further underscore the racist and colonial benevolence inherent in the officer's intervention, Joon notices a small medallion next to his badge with the years 1950–1953 being visible, the dates of the Korean War.

It is at the site of incarceration, handcuffed, where we first see Joon invoking Korea as a kind of home/land, albeit facetiously, to generate an ironic return, an origin of sorts, for Joon's presumed, unfit criminality. Joon disorients the officer's attempt to bind her subjectivity with the U.S. racial state's logic that decriminalizes Asian American subject formation while simultaneously essentializing the criminal and carceral character of black/brown subjects. She does so by tipping diaspora over. By spilling the contents of longing and origin, and accentuating its receptacle, Joon brings into shape geopolitics itself. She further exasperates the officer by swiftly outlining the borders that implicate his racist logics and its entailing American exceptionalism that make incarceration natural for "those" people over others. In this jail scene, Joon counters U.S. neoliberal logics of Asian American subject formation by self-fashioning a narrative of "diasporic dirt" that can elucidate the multiple displacements or nowhere, at work, as Korean, American, immigrant, runaway, teenage girl, and jail ward. "Diasporic dirt" refers to the dirt that haunts Joon's memories of her mother's illness and later, her passing, but moreover, I propose that dirt, in its material, theoretical, and conceptual considerations can generate productive questions on the limitations of diasporic framing—thus, their juxtaposition. It is this shared tension in theories of dirt and diaspora, generated across multiple fields, that, considered together, can illuminate the wayward routings of home/land, of mother/daughter. Returning to the jail scene, when Joon shoots back, "I know what you're doing," she throws dirt at the officer's geopolitical imaginings, his desires for her, disappointing his romances of Asian immigration and upward mobility, the American dream, fettered to the white patriarchal state's management; she refuses to align with this logic of possibility for the feminized Asian subject in and against racialized and gendered others.

Illness is a place of return for Joon. At the end of the novel, she returns to the home she ran away from, boarded up after her mother's passing. She runs into an old neighbor, Mr. McCommon who updates Joon on his ex-wife's cancer-related passing. He says, "I even miss seeing her sick," and Joon relates to this as a "truth I could hold on to about my mother, a place to begin" (286). For Joon, dirt is the stuff that upon hearing of her mother's passing she imagines filled her mother; it is her inheritance. Dirt is an organic substrate that eludes the capture of nation and country, and yet it is the very foundation of colony, state, and city. Dirt cannot express itself as territory or border, but is a necessary surface for its demarcation. Dirt, one can say, is psychotic.

When her mother wakes from one of her "playing dead" sessions in the garden, Joon watches as she comes into the house, and observes that not once does she attempt to dust the dirt off from her body, her hair, and her clothes. She remembers her mother's words, "I know what you did to me," as she passed her, which returned to her in echoes when Joon was told of her death (209). What does it mean to transmit dirt in the mother-daughter narrative? What do we seek in the narratives of immigrant mothers? And what are the shapes of their stories, the violent contortions demanded by certain rubrics of telling? This article briefly considers "diasporic dirt" as allowing another imaginative attachment to difference, of nation, generation, race, gender, immigration, as toggling between the psychotic or nowhere, and the contextual or everywhere, and one that rails against the rehabilitative impetus of the good, whole, or restorative. Instead, Joon imagines her mother's illness as a place to return, to miss, to begin feeling the historical weight of dirt, of her own dirt, her addiction, her mother's sickness: "That was all she had and she did her best" (224).

Peggy Lee is a doctoral candidate of American Culture at the University of Michigan–Ann Arbor. Her dissertation is titled "Politics of Composure: Performing Asian/American Femininities." She has work published and forthcoming in *The Asian American Literary Review* and *Frontiers: A Journal in Women Studies*. She can be reached at lepeggy@umich.edu.

Works Cited

Alexander, Michelle. 2017. "Michelle Alexander's Keynote Speech from the 2017 International Drug Policy Reform Conference." Drug Policy Alliance. YouTube video, 31:08, October 23, 2017. www.youtube.com/watch?v=E8yGRFNlYqM.

Berlant, Lauren. 2011. *Cruel Optimism*. Durham, NC: Duke University Press.

Chandler, James. 2016. "The Opium Connection: Thomas De Quincey, Charles Dickens, and D. W. Griffith." *SEL Studies in English Literature 1500–1900* 56, no. 4: 895–924.

Douglas, Mary. 1966. *Purity and Danger: An Analysis of Concepts of Pollution and Taboo*. New York: Praeger.

Foucault, Michel. 2009. *Security, Territory, Population: Lectures at the Collège de France 1977–1978*. New York: Palgrave Macmillan.

Gilmer, Marcus. 2009. "Interview: Nami Mun." *Chicagoist*, January 8, 2009.

Gilmore, Leigh. 2010. "American Neoconfessional: Memoir, Self-Help, and Redemption on Oprah's Couch." *University of Hawaii Press: Biography* 33, no. 4: 657–79.

Hickman, Timothy A. 2000. "Drugs and Race in American Culture: Orientalism in the Turn-of-the-Century Discourse of Narcotic Addiction." *American Studies* 41, no. 1: 71–91.

———. 2004. "'Mania Americana': Narcotic Addiction and Modernity in the United States, 1870–1920." *Journal of American History* 90, no. 4: 1269–94.

Ho, Wendy. 1999. *In Her Mother's House: The Politics of Asian American Mother-Daughter Writing*. Lanham, MD: Rowman & Littlefield.

Jun, Helen Heran. 2011. *Race for Citizenship: Black Orientalism and Asian Uplift from Pre-Emancipation to Neoliberal America*. New York: NYU Press.

Kang, Laura Hyun Yi. 2002. *Compositional Subjects: Enfiguring Asian/American Women*. Durham, NC: Duke University Press.

Kim, Elaine H. 1982. *Asian American Literature: An Introduction to the Writings and Their Social Context*. Philadelphia: Temple University Press.

Leyco, Chino S. 2017. "Fitch Upgrades PH Credit Rating; Drug-Related Killings Have Not Affected Investors So Far." *Manila Bulletin*, December 11, 2017. https://business.mb.com.ph/2017/12/11/fitch-upgrades-ph-credit-rating-drug-related-killings-have-not-affected-investors-so-far/.

Matsuda, Mari J. 1997. *Where Is Your Body?: And Other Essays on Race, Gender, and the Law*. Boston: Beacon Press.

Mun, Nami. 2009. *Miles from Nowhere*. New York: Riverhead Books.

Musto, David F. 1973. *The American Disease Origins of Narcotic Control*. New Haven, CT: Yale University Press.

Nguyen, Viet Thanh. 2002. *Race and Resistance: Literature and Politics in Asian America*. Oxford, UK: Oxford University Press.

Ninh, erin Khuê. 2011. *Ingratitude: The Debt-Bound Daughter in Asian American Literature*. New York: NYU Press.

Ong, Aihwa. 2006. *Flexible Citizenship: The Cultural Logics of Transnationality*. Durham, NC: Duke University Press.

Pinto, Samantha. 2013. *Difficult Diasporas: The Transnational Feminist Aesthetic of the Black Atlantic*. New York: NYU Press.

Poetzsch, Markus. 2015. "Fearful Spaces: Thomas De Quincey's Sino-Angino-phobia." *ESC: English Studies in Canada* 41, no. 2–3: 27–41.

Rodríguez, Dylan. 2005. "Asian-American Studies in the Age of the Prison Industrial Complex: Departures and Re-narrations." *Review of Education, Pedagogy, and Cultural Studies* 27, no. 3: 241–63.

Schutz, Greg. 2009. "Miles from Nowhere: A Conversation with Nami Mun." *Fiction Writers Review*, November 14, 2009.

See, Sarita Echavez. 2012. "Gambling with Debt: Lessons from the Illiterate." *American Quarterly* 64, no. 3: 495–513.

Wright, Patrick. 2009. *A Journey Through Ruins: The Last Days of London*. New York: Oxford University Press.

"Write Us into Existence": An Interview with Sokunthary Svay

Anita Baksh

Abstract: Sokunthary Svay is a Cambodian American writer and activist who grew up in the Bronx, New York. Her poetry, essays, and reviews appear in such publications as *WSQ*, *Mekong Review*, and *Hyphen*. Published in 2017, *Apsara in New York* is her first poetry collection. Svay is a founding member and board president of the Cambodian American Literary Arts Association (CALAA) and has been awarded an American Opera Projects Composers & the Voice Fellowship for 2017–2019 and the 2018 Emerging Poets Fellowship at Poets House. She is emerging as an important critic of and groundbreaking voice within Asian American cultural production. Rejecting the genre of survival memoirs, Svay creates a variety of personae across gender and generation. Her choice of language—Khmer, formal English, and urban vernacular—captures the individuality and complexity of each of these perspectives. As a performer, Svay draws on music and theater to move her poems beyond the page. Anita Baksh, Associate Professor of English at LaGuardia Community College at the City University of New York, conducted this interview with Svay in spring 2018. **Keywords**: Cambodian American literature, South East Asian author, Khmer, Asian American family, intergenerational trauma, Asian Americans in New York City

Anita Baksh (AB): Thank you for generously agreeing to this interview. As an Indo-Caribbean American woman and immigrant, your work resonates with my own lived experiences and with my research of Indo-Caribbean writers and artists. I'm particularly drawn to your exploration of gender, Asian immigrant experiences, the dynamics within Asian diasporic families, and legacies of trauma. One concern of this

WSQ issue is exploring how gender intersects with the politics of belonging. Do you see these tensions playing out in your poetry?

Sokunthary Svay (SS): In the persona poems, which are written in the accented voice of a Cambodian woman—the fact that she even gets space on the page, in that voice—it was unintentionally a political act. But the more I thought about it, the more I wanted to not just include that voice, but really emphasize it and highlight it. For example, I don't use strange spellings to accentuate or hyperpronounce her words. She is allowed to exist on the page. She matters. This is a woman most people wouldn't even look at twice. She works in a hotel, she cleans rooms, she says the same few words in English every day—"Hi, how are you?" or "Have a good day"—yet she already is aware of her status, of her class, of her racial and ethnic background, and where she is in the social stratosphere of the hotel industry, working alongside Caribbean Americans and other immigrants.

There are a lot of women present in [*Apsara in New York*], and it was not something I had tried to do. I was just writing what I was thinking about at the time. I'm a feminist, but I'm not a loud feminist. I'm not a pink pussy-hat feminist. By the way, I really didn't appreciate seeing one of those hats on a statue of Buddha, which I saw recently online as though that was supposed to be revolutionary. If anything, it was representative of how a lot of work needs to be done with intersectionality in white feminism. As a woman of color, a woman who came here under duress, that's something I'm constantly exploring because it took me decades to realize I lived a different experience. The more I write, the more I can understand why I feel always a bit off wherever I go. At first I thought it was being Cambodian, and then maybe it's because I'm from the Bronx, maybe it's because I grew up in the projects, or maybe it's because I grew up in (before it was rezoned) the poorest congressional district in the country. Maybe it's because I came here as a refugee and I didn't choose to be here and we didn't have the resources. Every time I add a new label, it starts to narrow my things down more but I enjoy the specificity of naming these factors that contribute to who I am and write as.

AB: So, you're exploring intersectionality through writing.

SS: Yes! I'm more than a woman: I'm Khmer, a New Yorker, a woman from the Bronx, a refugee, a classical musician, and poet in a very white world. For me, intersectionality is something I live and breathe. I don't have to go out of my way to write about it; it's my lived experience. I like to think I fight for women of color through my writing.

AB: Let's talk about your emergence as a writer. Your essay "Hearing Voices" states that you learned about the history of Cambodian refugees through film and gained an awareness of Cambodian writers through research. Describe the impact of media and research on your writing, your sense of self and community.

SS: I had to be my own ethnographer. Twenty years ago, when I began doing this research, Khmer literature was even more limited than it is now. There were about a dozen survival memoirs that had come out. The literary landscape has changed in the quantity of books but there still remains a lack of diversity in terms of content. Survival memoirs still seem to make up much of the literature, with some new poets in the mix and some novelists. We as a diaspora and literary community are ripe for growth. This is part of what I want to research during my PhD program.

I envy people who are second-generation Cambodian. As a 1.5 generation, alongside the first generation, we've done a lot of the groundwork of laying out the stories, and the initial struggle of being new arrivals. No one was there to give it to us; we had to build it. My parents wouldn't talk about the past, which is a pretty common story among our community. So what do you do when you have those walls? I remember looking on the internet at search terms like "New York City and Cambodia" just to see if there were events and language classes. There weren't really Cambodian language programs except for the Southeast Asian Studies Summer Institute at Madison-Wisconsin and one at the University of Hawaiʻi.

I got used to the idea that anything Khmer wouldn't be available to me, so I had to either keep looking, wait, or create those opportunities for myself. My sense of self became less passive. And now, I'm in a place where I'm seen as one of the people who is making things happen. And it wasn't a goal of mine to do that. I got tired of seeing us left out of the so-called "Asian American" narrative in this country. People talk about Asian Americans who are high achieving and which means what exactly? Get a good husband, go to Yale or Harvard? That's not my story. My story is: Hey, do we got food? And hey: Are my brothers gonna join a gang or are they gonna finish high school? That was my reality. So, for me it was about creating a self, having us exist first to begin with. Write us into existence, so that we can be there for the next generation.

I think Southeast Asian Americans need to have their own separation from what is called the Asian American because we came here under a different set of circumstances. *That* affects what we write, how we view ourselves, and our sense of place, because we were taken from our place! When you were ripped from that, how do you place yourself in the U.S.? And the generations that come after you, who will most likely suffer from the same economic circumstance? So we're a very different group and we need to have literature; we need to be reflected upon.

AB: The issue of language and culture you mention also arises in your collection [*Apsara in New York*]; a line from "Trespass" reads, "Every English word is a betrayal of our past." Could you elaborate on this?

SS: That line was written in a poetry class. I was thinking about my struggle with trying to speak Khmer now, versus when I was younger. When one is spoken to in Khmer by an elder, one must respond (especially juniors). Otherwise there is an accusation of not being Cambodian. It's not an unusual thing in immigrant communities, and I know we're not the only one to have this association between heritage language and identity. But I felt that with every English word I learned, I was turning my back on my family and my heritage, my ancestors, my country, my birthright—that I haven't done right by my people because my daughter doesn't speak it. So, even as I write to try to bring attention to my people, what we've been through in our country, the fact that it's not in Khmer saddens me. Part of it is that we don't have access to learning Khmer the way you can learn Chinese. You can learn Thai and Vietnamese with Rosetta Stone. Khmer is not a commerce language; no one needs to know it to make money aside from people in Cambodia. But I said to my daughter, "Don't let anybody ever tell you you're not Khmer. You don't have to speak it in order to be Khmer; that's something that's born within you." And sometimes I wish I was as kind to myself as I am to my own daughter.

AB: How does Cambodia surface as both a real and imagined place in your writing?

SS: Up until I was twenty-one, before I went to Cambodia for the first time, it was very much an imagined place for me: something I saw in photos, in videos from my mom and dad's visits there, and whatever I could read in the library at City College. I created this world where a generation of people died and became the reason we came to this country as a community. But it was also this place that was supposed to hold so many answers around my identity as a young adult. Instead, it was a real place with real people. It wasn't this land of gods fighting with swords or goddesses flying in the air. They are (re)imagined through the outfits that Cambodian women wear, the way that they curl their hair, the way they do their makeup, the way that the dancers reimagine these nymphs. So suddenly Cambodia became much more concrete.

AB: Along with Cambodia, the Bronx is also present throughout your work. How does it influence your poems?

SS: When I think of the Bronx, I think of my childhood. It's where I was before I really had to think about all these heavier issues. I think of it as this magical time where I watched a lot of TV, like *The Wonder Years*, and was fascinated by small-town American life. But I felt like I lived in a small town, too; we got the Korean-owned pharmacy, then we got the sports bar, and all these other places, and I thought, this is my little hometown. There was a certain innocence about it. And people always wanted, and still continue, to talk down about the Bronx. The Bronx feels like one of the last places where it really feels like old New York. Or as someone recently said to me, "The Bronx is like what Brooklyn was in the nineties." Now Brooklyn is too priced out. The Bronx has a special place in my heart, and I'm trying to save these snapshots in my poems. I don't want to forget what it was like growing up in that first apartment, with all the mold, with all the roaches, because it didn't bother us to live that way as kids. We didn't know. And I liked that. Because, if I were to think about it as an adult, it would just anger me. And I don't want to look back on my childhood with anger.

AB: Poems like "Fresh Oriental" and "Make Room for Tenderness" engage with the resettlement of Cambodian American refugees in Bronx neighborhoods that were inhabited by other marginalized groups, mainly African American and Latino. Can you speak to your exploration of these interactions?

SS: It's not been easy, the interaction between certain Asian American communities with the Black and Latino communities. The Southeast Asian diaspora—the refugees who came here—were placed in the same poverty-stricken areas, and so, unlike the East Asian populations who were here and have been established here and came here for opportunity, we are pretty much in the same boat as Black and Latino communities, such as not having access to resources and education levels being very low. Add to that the cultural misunderstandings between the communities that fight for the few resources. I wanted to show some narrators who aren't perfect. I didn't want to sanitize it. I certainly could have. It could even have been a little more raw (although now I'm just getting into postpublishing regret, the way a book is never fully done in one's mind). I wanted to show that, even in the misunderstandings (the misunderstandings of the Cambodian man with the communities that he is surrounded by) in the projects, they still want the same things as parents; they want better for their children. So even if there might be the noise of bigotry and misunderstanding in the lines, it's ultimately that they are connecting in some way—even if they can't actually connect just yet.

AB: You seem to draw parallels between intergenerational trauma and mental health. Do you see these connections?

SS: A lot of first-generation Cambodian Americans—my parents' community—suffer from undiagnosed posttraumatic stress disorder. I would argue that all Khmers who came to the U.S. after surviving the Khmer Rouge suffer from PTSD. We don't really have psychotherapy in our culture, so there's no talking about it: you lock it away somewhere in the back of your mind. But how do you get past the trauma of having your family murdered by people who look like you? That autogenocide means that you can't trust your own people. What do you do with that? My parents also lost a child during the Khmer Rouge. I can't even begin to imagine how they got through that.

But there are things that I still keep with me from the way that I grew up. For example, I don't like to answer my door if someone unannounced comes because we didn't answer our door growing up. We were afraid of who would come for us. We were there legally but it felt like someone was going to question our right to be here. (Not unlike under this administration.) Even more recently, I remember people would come and try to solicit me for some service I didn't need. One man was so aggressive, I became scared. Even though it was my home and I could close the door, I didn't feel like I had a right to do that. Or even the act of crying—I prefer to cry alone. Growing up in my household, you didn't show your suffering. I think the more that we can get the first generation, who are not used to talking about pain and trauma, to open up, then perhaps we can finally move on. At the same time, I don't want to keep talking about the Khmer Rouge. How can we imagine ourselves outside of that?

Sokunthary Svay is pursuing her PhD in English at the CUNY Graduate Center with a focus on Southeast Asian American sociopoetics. Her poetry collection, *Apsara in New York*, is available from Willow Books. She is a 2018 Poets House Fellow and can be reached at sokuntharysvay@gmail.com.

Anita Baksh is associate professor of English at LaGuardia Community College at the City University of New York. Her teaching and research interests include Caribbean, African, and Asian diasporic literatures, gender studies, postcolonial theory, and composition. She can be reached at abaksh@lagcc.cuny.edu.

Narrating Against Assimilation and the Empire: Diasporic Mourning and Queer Asian Melancholia

Wen Liu

Abstract: As U.S.-led imperialism spreads in the Asia Pacific region through neoliberal trades and military occupation, how do "Asia" and "America" as both geopolitical units and embodied spaces construct and assemble diasporic Asian subjects affectively? Furthermore, as national allegiance is aggressively demanded by the surge of white nationalism in the Global North, how does an immigrant subject afford to be continuously attached to an object—"Asia"—that she must reject before becoming Asian American? Drawing on narrative study with queer Asian American activists involved in anti-imperialist organizing, this paper situates narratives of racialized queer grief in the framework of racial melancholia (Cheng 2000; Eng and Han 2000) as a form of protest against the splitting of Asian and American identity as the U.S. empire actively recruits Asian Americans into nationalist discourses. With a queer and intersectional method of narrating identity, this paper highlights how racial melancholia involves strategies of subjectivity-making against the colonial splitting of blackness and whiteness, the erasure of imperial history, and the segregation of communities. **Keywords:** queer theory, diaspora, Asian American studies, racial melancholia, affect theory

On October 9, 2016, the *New York Times* deputy Metro editor, Michael Luo, was strolling through the Upper East Side of Manhattan with his family, when a woman suddenly yelled at them, "Go back to China . . . go back to your fucking country!" Luo protested, "I was born in this country!" After this racist encounter, Luo started the Twitter hashtag #ThisIs2016 to describe this experience (Luo 2016). The hashtag soon went viral on multiple social media sites, as Asian Americans came forward to speak about similar forms of racism they faced in their everyday lives (Woo and

WSQ: Women's Studies Quarterly 47: 1 & 2 (Spring/Summer 2019)

Al-Hlou 2016). The response publicly exposed the racism Asian Americans have been experiencing regularly since the labor-migration diaspora. That it was directed toward an Asian American man with a prestigious job, which symbolizes literacy, intelligence, and the liberal values of multicultural America, and in one of the wealthiest neighborhoods in the country, makes this incident even more ironic, intolerable, and theatrical, since his social status and cultural capital do not protect him from such kinds of racialized assault that continue to frame Asian bodies as the perpetual foreigners. Yet, the social effect of the incident would have been dramatically different for someone who carries a stronger signifier of foreignness that yelling at her would no longer be intelligible as an assault. For instance, if a Chinese immigrant had encountered such an attack, she may not have even protested it. Had she really been from China, she may have lacked urgency to refute her national affiliation and thus the assault would not hold the same emotional weight for both her and the yeller.

This common experience has directed Asian American communities to claim belonging in the U.S. as expressed by the #ThisIs2016 campaign. However, as an immigrant with deep commitments in both the United States and my country of origin, I began to wonder about the limits of the dominant Asian American subjectivity that overwhelmingly emphasize the need to claim loyalty to and citizenship in the United States (Chuh 2003), which inevitably comes with separating and detaching from one's other history linked to labor migration, imperialist wars, U.S. militarism, and colonial exploitation (Lowe 1996; Parreñas and Siu 2007). In many ways, forgetting one's history is the precondition of achieving the "good Asian American life" that is inseparable from the American Dream: hard work, family values, economic advancement, and the promise of future prosperity for the next generation, where some Asian Americans are recruited for middle-class status by making racial politics secondary to their lives (Tuan 1998). The rhetoric of the good life is indeed implicitly addressed in the #ThisIs2016 hashtag campaign, demanding an end to the association with the stereotype of the unassimilable Asian American. The futurity constituted by the urgency to *move forward* and to have closure regarding the past is ingrained in Asian American subjectivity that regulates one's performance, feelings, and actions as a multicultural citizen. The foreignness that the Asian American subject embodies turns into a "wounded attachment," creating a condition of liberal identity politics that is incapable of moving beyond the nationalistic politics which it has inscribed (Brown 1993, 391).

This nationalist order does not only push the racial subject toward forgetting, but also demands the nation's sexual other to get over queer suffering and to look forward to the neoliberal promises of assimilation and inclusion, while queers of color continue to be excluded from this whitewashed homonormative citizenship (see Eng 2010; Muñoz 1999). The unattainable assimilation to white queerness creates the conditions in which queers of color are perpetually immersed in a melancholic process—their present preoccupied with feelings of ambivalence and estrangement—that makes them *stuck* in a timespace away from the present (Ahmed 2010). In this article, I aim to articulate the intersectional subject position of "queer" and "Asian American" through a diasporic framework as my participants narrate their sense of belongingness and displacement in the current political conditions. The focus on the queer Asian diaspora in this project, firstly, invokes the centuries of colonial and racialized wars, labor migration, capitalist expansion, and transpacific political relations that have created the contested contemporary formations of Asianness and, secondly, queers the heterosexual genealogy of national origin implicit in diasporic discourse (Gopinath 2005; Eng 2010). The framework of queer temporality destabilizes the boundaries of the past and the present, as well as critically interrogates the hegemonic future (Halberstam 2005). Refusing to be always uprooted from home or ever grateful to the host country, submitting to color-blind queer liberalism, I demonstrate how queerness may serve as a strategy of holding historical pain but also building new affiliations against the process of assimilation.

To examine how the affective spaces of "Asia" and "America" are constructed and performed, I turn to the narratives of queer Asian American activists in the context of anti-imperialist organizing in New York City. These activists' political consciousness has widened their lens on how imperialism in the Asia Pacific region is intimately connected to their everyday lives as Asian American subjects in the United States through the forms of neoliberal trade, military occupation, cultural neocolonialism, and white supremacy. Karen Shimakawa (2002) has theorized how the Asian American body serves as an abjection to U.S. nationalism, as their difference is dramatized to signify non-Westernness, particularly through its gendered and sexualized parts. Whereas the dominant Asian American paradigm centers on U.S. national belonging, the narratives of queer

Asian Americans involved in solidarity activist work in the Asia Pacific region shows a heightened ambivalence toward both the United States and their nations of origin that situates them in a perpetual diasporic state of rejecting citizenship in the United States and simultaneously refusing to be attached to a homeland based on unreflexive forms of nostalgia. Their diasporic subjectivity illustrates what Rhacel Parreñas and Lok Siu (2007) address as the concurrent processes of alienation from and attachment to both the U.S. and Asia and a sense of collective consciousness with others who share similar histories of colonialism and racialization.

On Racial Loss and Melancholia

The Asian American process of racialization is inevitably intertwined with a loss of place, a lack of origin. In *The Melancholy of Race*, Anne Anlin Cheng depicts the unique racialized subjectivity of Asian Americanness as a "ghostly position" in which one is forcibly attached to the fantasy of the "East" yet constantly under pressure to pass as American and nonblack in order to sustain life (2000, 23). Lisa Lowe articulates that this persistent tension between racial inclusion and racial erasure in the project of U.S. nation-making "requires the orientalist construction of cultures and geographies from which Asian immigrants come as fundamentally 'foreign' origins anti-pathetic to the modern American society that 'discovers,' 'welcomes,' and 'domesticates' them" (1996, 5). The uprooting of Asian origins must be understood as an intentional process of effacing the history of exploitation and colonial conquer. The subjectification of Asian Americans is therefore wrapped up with narratives of loss and mourning linked to histories of dispersal as well as a yearning for belonging. Cheng coins this racial identity construction attached to the lost object as "racial melancholia," a process of becoming consumed by one's loss, "swallowing" the object, and turning into a subject defined by the possession of loss. The melancholic racial formation of Asian Americanness is constructed by its perpetual grief for the loss of place. Once consumed by her own melancholia, the Asian American subject is defined by her own grief and cannot afford an imagined or real return to the lost place.

This melancholic state is widely demonstrated in the psychological literature on the bicultural trauma and acculturative stress of second-generation Asian Americans (LaFromboise, Coleman, and Gerton 1993; Romero and Roberts 2003), who have supposedly lost their place of origin and are defined by the perpetual ghostly emptiness of racial positionality. The failure to resolve colonial trauma results in the ways that violence and terror linger in the present and continue to haunt Asian American subjects despite the relative high rates of assimilation and economic advancements (Cho 2008). Bicultural Asian Americans have reported higher levels of acculturative stress and depressive symptoms than white Americans due to the pressure to adopt both majority and minority cultures (Benet-Martinez et al. 2002; Romero et al. 2007; Romero and Roberts 2003; Wei et al. 2010). The hyphenated subject is constantly haunted by the sense of being neither Asian nor American *enough*. Thus, the bicultural is perpetually tied to a sense of not fitting in to either the host society or the "home country"—which is now a lost object, "Asia," that becomes melancholically devoured and internalized.

In seeking the political and creative possibilities of loss, David Eng and David Kazanjian propose a depathologized understanding of the melancholic attachments to loss that might generate a more productive conceptualization of temporality, where "melancholia's persistent struggle with its lost objects is not simply a 'grasping' and 'holding' on to a fixed notion of the past but rather a continuous engagement with loss and its remains" (2003, 4). By holding on to the object, the melancholic subject may have more capacity and flexibility to represent history and the various forms of loss—of a beloved person, or "an abstraction which has taken the place of the person, such as fatherland, freedom, an ideal, and so on" (Freud 2005, 203). As dwelling in the past may offer the mourner a different sense of time and space, melancholia—the attachment to the object of loss—can provide a more nuanced and productive conceptualization of Asian American subjectivity beyond the binary of assimilation and opposition and the bicultural blues of inadequate becoming. For subjects who desire to uncover erased histories, the state of melancholia should not be considered as uniformly psychologically damaging.

Certainly, the risks of being stuck in the past or dwelling on losses are not equal for all subjects, who as a consequence might be seen as permanent outcasts or utterly irrelevant. In her book on the "backward turn" of queer theory, Heather Love indicates, "For those marked as temporally backward, the stakes of being identified as modern or non-modern were extremely high" (2009, 6). Its association with psychic immaturity and the perversity represented by the AIDS crisis have marked queerness as particularly backward and melancholic, where the losses and memories of the past haunt the present. With the growing legal measures to include lesbians and gays in state protection, the queer future has become more foreseeable. However, queers of color are often excluded from homonormative citizenship and become the *racialized remains* of white queer futurity (Halberstam 2005; Puar 2006). Specifically, queer Asian Americans' multiplicity of identities is often constructed as a site of irrecoverable and unresolved losses, where queerness is viewed as a Western construct and not fitting for Asian ethnic cultures (Chung and Katayama 1998; Kimmel and Yi 2004, 145; Szymanski and Sung 2010). The present racist and heterosexist structures are thought to segregate and foreclose spaces instead of producing alternative possibilities of belonging. However, these losses are only intelligible when queer space and racial space are considered mutually exclusive and inherently incompatible in the first place. Instead of regarding the negative affects of melancholia and grief as quantifiable damages or inconsolable wounds, I am curious whether it may be more productive to read melancholia as a refusal to "feel better" under the current condition of neoliberal hegemony within which happiness is narrowly defined (Ahmed 2010; Love 2007). The "unhappy queers" and "melancholic migrants" hold on to the negative affects that interrupt the presumed route of assimilation, allowing the body encounter another kind of desire that "may even queer our aspirations" (Ahmed 2010, 120).

Methods: Queer Diasporic Attachments

If the intersection of queer and Asian subjectivity creates the conditions of melancholia and ambivalent attachments to both the host society and homeland, how does one begin to mourn? As Cheng asks, "How does an individual go from being a subject of grief to being a subject of grievance?" (2001, 3). These questions of queer melancholia arose from my larger ethnographic research on Asian American political participation in anti-imperialist solidarity activism in New York City. Although queerness was not the political focus of the Asian American activists involved in the movement, it was the social and material bond that brought us together as the API People's Solidarity, a coalition of approximately fifteen anti-imperialist activists working to connect issues of militarism and neoliberal trades abroad to racialized violence in the U.S.[1] The emergence of a more solidified queer Asian American subjectivity can be contributed to the increasing politicization of this intersection through the efforts of local and national queer Asian American organizations such as the National Queer Asian Pacific Islander Alliance in the past decade. The Asian American activists in the coalition all have personal and political ties to their countries of origin, including South Korea, Japan, Taiwan, China, and the Philippines. Since becoming involved in the coalition in 2013, I have been curious about its members' capacity to forge transpacific political alliances and psychological bonds flexibly across the U.S. border and carry a sense of obligation to defy the U.S. nation-state and imperialist apparatus as individuals who have the privilege to reside within the U.S. borders.

Nevertheless, the activists' relationships with their countries of origin, for both first-generation and second-generation immigrants, were infused with different forms of negative affects. Particularly, as queer Asians in the United States, they must negotiate with processes of both racialization and sexualization while intersectional and inclusive spaces are not always readily accessible. I became curious about how they could afford to be continually attached to Asia, the object infused with trauma and pain, yet at the same time generate the capacity to actively resist dominant narratives of assimilation and orientalization. To understand how queer Asian subjects negotiate these multiple spaces of loss and grief, I interviewed six Asian American activists who identified as queer (out of the total fifteen coalition members in which the majority consisted of women and queer leadership) on their migration history, political development, and social identity and how these dimensions of their lives intersect with their queerness.[2] The six participants were queer women of Chinese, Korean, Japanese, and Taiwanese ethnicities whose ages ranged from early twenties to late forties. Starting with their motives behind migration, the interviews gradually built on the *critical events* in participants' lives that highlighted a central struggle or dilemma around their identities that did not easily fit into normative categories of race, gender, sexuality, or nationality.

Although I did not probe regarding trauma and loss initially, these subjects related to imperialist and racialized violence emerged as primary narrative themes that cut across participants' articulations of identities. Traumatic events of imperialist violence, racism, sexism, and heterosexism, whether experienced directly or indirectly, could be particularly memorable and elicit powerful affects that moved subjects' stories across time and space, rescuing the objects of loss—the nation of origin, family, or ideal self. Through critical narrative analysis (Langdrige 2007), I examined how their narratives organized their multiple identities across different events of trauma and loss, but also sites of transformation and healing as the participants connect the events to structural forces outside and beyond their body. I am especially interested in the narrative functions of queerness across the participants—how the introduction of their queer narrative deepens and widens their conversations on migration to complicated webs of violence and power across personal and political spaces of nationhood, family, and intimate partnership. For some, queerness helped them reach out to political projects and affiliations beyond one's identity groups; and for others, queerness served as an armor that helped them resist the white male gaze on their bodies. In my analysis, I depart from the conceptualization of queerness as a sexual identity and instead examine queerness as a narrative structure that makes the multiplicity of participants' identities intelligible, and in a sense, *grievable* for others (Butler 2004, 30). That is, deviating from the hegemonic narrative of assimilation in which the subject must lose the nation of origin in becoming Asian American, queerness has a capacity to divert and transform this sense of loss.

Narrating Melancholia

My entry into the queer Asian American activists' narratives began with their migration motives; some came due to the political instability of their countries of origin and some came as an adoptee or were born into immigrant families. Across the participants, migration stories overlapped with an urgency to reclaim national history to make sense of the shattered myth of "the better life" in the American immigrant narrative and a trajectory of intergenerational trauma linked to histories of imperial conquer, state violence, or patriarchal family conflicts. The capacity of reencountering the colonial relations often neglected by mainstream Asian American politics allows the emergence of the "queer regeneration" sites for developing radical politics beyond assimilation (Haritaworn 2015, 143). The melancholic affect that arises from the process creates a diasporic timespace in between being home and away, damaged and agentive. Here, I highlight two narratives, one from a second-generation Korean American woman and another from a first-generation Japanese woman, that express these participants' melancholic attachment to the nation and colonial history as sites not of self-orientalization but rather of a deep examination and critical analysis of their process of racialization.

Gia's Racial Losses.

Gia, a second-generation Korean American queer woman, articulated her reencountering of the colonial past in the context of sex and intimacy. The experience was racially troubling yet simultaneously helped her make sense of the ambivalence she feels in intimate relationships and how her own body is tied to a historical and structural relationship:

> I think as Korean women, the relationship that we have with white American men in this country is unbelievably fucked up. I understand the first huge wave of Korean immigrants in this country being military brats, camp town sex work. That kind of stuff colors everything that I feel and see in the city. . . . If I'm at a bar, sitting alone, and some white dude is coming on to me, trying to talk to me, there's this really intense, a colonial relationship that's understood popularly. (Gia, pers. comm., April 30, 2015)

What Gia articulated is the militarized history to which she is melancholically attached, a reinvestment in the unspoken past in her family that has haunted her, even after moving away from her family home. The haunting effect of the militarized relationship is particularly built on the national erasure and seemingly consensual silence around the Korean War (Cho 2008). The "ghosts" transported across time and space have neither bodily nor national borders, and live through the psyche of the diasporic subjects such as Gia, who may have not been through the war personally yet feels it and carries it as part of her identity. In a sense, her baggage around being an Asian woman took on a new shape as she became aware of the Korean-American colonial relationship. Her racial trauma in her teens around the narratives of Asian stereotypes, such as "Asian eyes" or being perceived as not capable of speaking English, was no longer an untouchable and unintelligible sense of being haunted, but rather became something deeply historical, structural, and tangible, though much harder to escape from. This newly formed affective relationship with her past has congealed as a distinct frame and experience of time and space which she said "colors everything" she feels and sees. This intensity of racialization reaches beyond the appearance and the contour of her body toward a collective colonial history.

Akiko's National Losses.

This narrative pattern of reencountering colonial relationships is consistent across all interviewees' experiences of racialization and sexualization in the United States, particularly around discussions of home and national origin. Akiko, a first-generation Japanese queer activist who used to work in the American military base in Okinawa, noticed the familiar yet exacerbated sexualized racialization she faced when she immigrated to the United States. Eager to leave an abusive marriage, Akiko left the country hoping to find a new sense of identity away from the patriarchal expectation for her to endure the shame of domestic violence. However, migration did not bring the freedom from gendered expectations she had hoped for, and instead, the burden of being a "good Japanese woman" at home became much more public and sexualized as her race turned her body into an exploitable subject in the United States. When I asked her about the changes in gender dynamics since her migration, she said, "I was asked many times by white men if I want to have sex with them to make money. . . . At the beginning I really thought, Do I really look something like that, something they can buy?" (Akiko, pers. comm., December 18, 2015). The intensified racialization process that Akiko encountered after coming to the United States initially made her question her worth as a person—whether it existed only as "something they can buy." Yet through recalling the violence she faced back in Japan, she started to question how the sexualized encounters with men stretched across spatial borders and were not resolvable simply through the process of migration.

Akiko seeks to get rid of her gender, which is attached to the traumatic intimate relationship she experienced in Japan, as well as her identification with Japan. The sexualized and racialized violence in the United States does not strengthen her national identity. On the contrary, surrounding herself in the queer Asian diasporic activist group helps her recognize Japan's own complicity with imperialism and militarism. Her narratives about being a racialized Asian woman and being Japanese equally demonstrate a deep sense of ambivalence that is filled with the desire of both rejection and reclamation: "I feel detached from [my Japanese nationality] now. . . . Japanese people should be uncomfortable and ashamed when they hear about the country's imperialist issues, like what it did to other Asian countries and the use of comfort women" (Akiko, pers. comm., December 18, 2015). What she is melancholily attached to here, again, is the history of Japanese imperialism instead of Japanese national identity. Yet rather than seeing this violent history as a barrier to politics, Akiko has formed alternative affiliations through connecting this racialized and sexualized violence to other gendered subjects at a broader scale. What both these narratives have highlighted is the new homeland's racialized violence enabled through rearranging the gendered and sexualized colonial relationship. Gia's and Akiko's struggles to negotiate their identities indicate not a passive adoption of the American racial position but a deep reflection on violence as reencountering historical and structural power relations.

Mobilizing Queer Negative Attachments

Whereas under the framework of assimilation, the negative attachment to home and nation must be overcome through identification with the new love-object of the U.S. nation-state that promises multiculturalism, dwelling in the diasporic space of lost history allows the marginalized subject to adopt an empowering strategy of *disidentification* (Muñoz 1999)—recirculating the encoded meanings of race and moving the stereotypical image from the self to a public structure. Across Gia's and Akiko's narratives, I found that queerness supports the possibility of mourning and reentering these lost spaces filled with violence and trauma and filling them with new kinds of identification.

Queerness initially did not alleviate Gia from the racial trauma, as she struggled with the queer people of color spaces in which she found herself: "I find it very frustrating when young queer people act as if queerness is the end of the line, that this is the final 'frontier.' Some of them actually use the word 'frontier,' which is like, 'Do you know where that word comes from?'" (pers. comm., April 30, 2015). Although queerness was her first site of exile from the restrictive gender expectations she encountered in her Korean immigrant home, she recognized its limits regarding transcending colonial relationships. What dominated Gia's narratives was the theme of bodily traumas, from the stereotyping of Asian features to fetishization and abuse in intimate relationships. Yet she spoke about these events with a high level of self-awareness as well as ceaseless self-analysis. I began to understand Gia's politics of dealing with the different layers of violence she encountered as aimed not toward finding a "resolution" but toward being in the constant tensions and forming ambivalent attachments with the various identity spaces in which she exists. Queerness does not serve as a permanent escape from trauma, but instead helps her to reengage and reexamine her experiences and her body. The disidentifying subject does not simply assimilate or reject the dominant ideology, but rather seeks a third strategy of reworking the available cultural resources (Muñoz 1999).

For the queer Asian activists, queerness helps them reenter the racialized communities that they may have previously rejected or been excluded from. For Gia, her practice of "queer kink" has helped her make sense of the violence in her life and reshape her understanding of intimacy:

> I'm coming from a space where my intimate relations with my family were all structured around silence, where "I love you" being something very awkward to say and physical contact being very minimal. And to be practicing queer kink in my relationships is forcing myself to relearn how to be vulnerable with people. (pers. comm., April 30, 2015)

The silence mentioned by Gia is common for the second-generation participants when they describe their childhood experiences in family. The silence is not just about family history, but also part of their experiences of racialization and queerness. The push toward assimilation has traditionally made Asian American subjects to be complicit with historical erasure of imperialist trauma and to assimilate to a depoliticized, diluted version of U.S. multiculturalism. Despite the lack of resources for Gia to understand her racial formation when she was younger, coming to terms with her queerness becomes a way for her to reconnect with her racialized body. Her troubles in intimate relationships and intensely racialized encounters have made her realize that the way to move beyond trauma is not to exile from her race as defined by the U.S. nation-state or her familial past of imperialist pain, but to reinvest in her troubling attachments to racial pain with new forms of queer intimacy. In other words, queerness enables both an exile and a reentering of her racialized body. Queerness contests the roots of bodily trauma and silence, and provides her with a path toward reengaging with an alternative form of affiliation with queers of color.

Similarly, Akiko's narrative started to shift toward a possibility of escape as she spoke about her desire to be with women, not only politically but intimately. She said, "I've never had a female partner. But since I experienced a lot of crazy stuff with men, I'm more inclined to be close to women." The questioning of her desire was the only hint of a possibility of escape from the cycle of patriarchal and racial violence she has encountered across space and time, as she articulated, "In my experience, [white men] tend to think of me through stereotypes in their own imagination. And now I think men in general do that too, whether they are white, Asian, or black" (Akiko, pers. comm., December 18, 2015). For Akiko, queerness is mobilized as a possibility to counter the racialized sexualization she has encountered with men. Queerness to her is not yet a solidified identity but, in her questions around and search for her sexuality, it provides an imaginative capacity of what could be, without the burden of being that "good Japanese woman," to feel less like an object or commodity. What is significant in Akiko's narrative is that her home country was a symbol of patriarchy to which she did not want to return, yet it continues to act as a reference point in her life in the United States. The racialization and sexualization she has faced in the United States made her realize how patriarchy travels across national and racial lines, and thus in neither of these national identifications has she found relief from her traumas. It was only through disidentifying with both places that policed her into the racialized-gendered body, and through the potential of forming an alternative kind of intimate affiliation, that is, through queerness, that she found an escape and the possibility of a new self.

Conclusions: Mourning Against Assimilation

In *Mourning and Melancholia*, Freud (2005) defines melancholia as a state of loss in which the subject is unable to choose a new love-object to invest in. Sometimes it is difficult to even identify *what* exactly the subject has lost; it is only through the process of mourning that the loss of an object surfaces in the subject's consciousness and, in a sense, becomes grievable. For all of the participants, home—as home country, biological family, or the idea of national belonging—is a lost object with which they have formed ambivalent attachments. Their love and hatred for this lost object becomes part of their immigrant subjectivity. Whereas the dominant immigration paradigm of model minority prohibits the racialized subject's mourning and coerces them to simply accept the new love-object of the American nation-state, these queer Asian Americans have resisted to comply with this subjugation and sought new forms of belonging. The perspective of reencountering historical and structural trauma through the participants' narratives rejects the common framework of queer immigrants' lives as a movement from repression to freedom, where queer migrants become agentive sexual subjects in the (Western) host society away from the burdens of (non-Western) traditional values (Luibhéid and Cantú Jr. 2005; Manalansan 2006). Migration, to queer people of color, is not a splitting between violent and nonviolent spaces but a continuation of racist and heteropatriarchal oppression. The participants' narrative strategies of coping and resisting violence through queerness are thus not simply about leaving, but about embodying queerness as a strategy of mourning against the colonial splitting of spaces and subjects, the erasure of history, and the segregation of communities.

The notion of "Asia" for the Asian American subject is a complicated site of identification and belonging. For the participants, it is often a site of judgment—to be a "good Asian woman" or a "grateful immigrant"—but through their politics of disidentifying, the diasporic space becomes not merely the basis of identity escape, but an oppositional figure with which they battle. It is an object they continue to hold on to as a basis of remembrance of what not to be. Whereas this idea of home country is commonly associated with a patriarchal figure that they have rejected, they carried it over across migration journeys and generations for ongoing reinvestment in the traumatic pasts of these places to find alternative identification with them away from judgment. For Gia and Akiko, particularly, their persistence of negative attachment to Korea and Japan allows them to critically evaluate the racial and gendered encounters they experienced across contexts and recognize the similar dynamics of regulation and control in the new place, instead of finding the West or the whitening queer space to be their savior from traumatic experiences.

Despite the nationalist pressure to assimilate and to "move on" as highlighted in the #ThisIs2016 campaign, what I present here with the narratives of queer Asian American activists is the opposite of simply moving on and is, rather, a process of *dwelling in* a lost place and to feel intimately attached to the history and presence of colonial relations. It is through such ambivalent attachments to nations and a permanent state in the diaspora that the activists conceptualize their loss not as something immediately resolvable through identifying with a new love-object, but rather as a process of mourning against assimilation and the empire. These activists illustrate alternative forms of subjective agency to live and resist in the colonized society beyond the binary of identification and negation. Therefore, rather than prescribing how the public in general should "get over" the fact that colonial and imperial histories are part of what constitutes Asian Americanness—to simply celebrate the multicultural ideal of #ThisIs2016—the attachment to losses and the unresolved tensions of their multiple identities can indeed be sites of regeneration, uncovering how the past is a fertile ground that sustains the present mechanisms of racialized and gendered subject regulation.

Wen Liu is an assistant professor of women's, gender, and sexuality studies at the University at Albany, State University of New York. As an interdisciplinary scholar, her research focuses on the engagement between global social movements and psychological theories of racial, gender, and sexual subjectivities, particularly at the intersection of queer and diasporic Asian American experiences. She can be reached at wliu2@albany.edu.

Notes

1. The API People's Solidarity came together as a coalition in 2013 in response to the Trans-Pacific Partnership Agreement (TPPA), a neoliberal trade deal between the U.S. and twelve countries that border the Pacific Ocean initiated by the Obama administration. The cross-national and pan-Asian solidarity campaign shifted toward linking the racialized policing practices and U.S. militarism as the Black Lives Matter movements broke out in 2014.
2. I joined the API People's Solidarity initially as an activist from the anti-imperialist Taiwanese milieu in New York City to work against the U.S. government's aggressive push for Taiwan to join the TPPA as well as to create new dialogues around anti-imperialist politics in the Taiwanese American circles that have traditionally endorsed any U.S. military and economic interventions in Taiwan. As a queer-identified person, I was socially affiliated with many of the activists in the coalition through other queer API organizing spaces in NYC. The queer activist connection was certainly key for me to become part of the close-knit circle of radical queer API activists as well as gain access and trust to the participants.

Works Cited

Ahmed, Sara. 2010. *The Promise of Happiness*. Durham, NC: Duke University Press.

Benet-Martínez, Verónica, Janxin Leu, Fiona Lee, and Michael W. Morris. 2002. "Negotiating Biculturalism: Cultural Frame Switching in Biculturals with Oppositional Versus Compatible Cultural Identities." *Journal of Cross-cultural Psychology* 33, no. 5: 492–516.

Brown, Wendy. 1993. "Wounded Attachments." *Political Theory* 21, no. 3: 390–410.

Butler, Judith. 2004. *Undoing Gender*. New York: Routledge.
Cheng, Anne Anlin. 2000. *The Melancholy of Race: Psychoanalysis, Assimilation, and Hidden Grief*. New York: Oxford University Press.
Cho, Grace M. 2008. *Haunting the Korean Diaspora: Shame, Secrecy, and the Forgotten War*. Minneapolis: University of Minnesota Press.
Chuh, Kandice. 2003. *Imagine Otherwise: On Asian Americanist Critique*. Durham, NC: Duke University Press.
Chung, Y. Barry, and Motoni Katayama. 1998. "Ethnic and Sexual Identity Development of Asian-American Lesbian and Gay Adolescents." *Professional School Counseling* 1, no. 3: 21–25.
Eng, David L. 2010. *The Feeling of Kinship: Queer Liberalism and the Racialization of Intimacy*. Durham, NC: Duke University Press.
Eng, David L., and Shinhee Han. 2000. "A Dialogue on Racial Melancholia." *Psychoanalytic Dialogues* 10, no. 4: 667–700.
Eng, David. L., and David Kazanjian. 2003. *Loss: The Politics of Mourning*. Berkeley: University of California Press.
Freud, Sigmund. 2005. *On Murder, Mourning and Melancholia*. London: Penguin Books.
Gopinath, Gayatri. 2005. *Impossible Desires: Queer Diasporas and South Asian Public Cultures*. Durham, NC: Duke University Press.
Halberstam, J. Jack. 2005. *In a Queer Time and Place: Transgender Bodies, Subcultural Lives*. New York: NYU Press.
Haritaworn, Jin. 2015. *Queer Lovers and Hateful Others: Regenerating Violent Times and Places*. London: Pluto Press.
Kimmel, Douglas C., and Huso Yi. 2004. "Characteristics of Gay, Lesbian, and Bisexual Asians, Asian Americans, and Immigrants from Asia to the USA." *Journal of Homosexuality* 47, no. 2: 143–72.
LaFromboise, Teresa, Hardin L. K. Coleman, and Jennifer Gerton. 1993. "Psychological Impact of Biculturalism: Evidence and Theory." *Psychological Bulletin* 114, no. 3: 395–412.
Langdridge, Darren. 2007. *Phenomenological Psychology: Theory, Research and Method*. London: Pearson Education.
Love, Heather. 2009. *Feeling Backward: Loss and the Politics of Queer History*. Cambridge, MA: Harvard University Press.
Lowe, Lisa. 1996. *Immigrant Acts: On Asian American Cultural Politics*. Durham, NC: Duke University Press.
Luibhéid, Eithne, and Lionel Cantú Jr. 2005. *Queer Migrations: Sexuality, U.S. Citizenship, and Border Crossings*. Minneapolis: University of Minnesota Press.
Luo, Michael. 2016. "An Open Letter to the Woman Who Told My Family to Go

Back to China." *New York Times*, October 9, 2016. https://www.nytimes.com/2016/10/10/nyregion/to-the-woman-who-told-my-family-to-go-back-to-china.html.

Manalansan, Martin F. 2006. "Queer Intersections: Sexuality and Gender in Migration Studies." *International Migration Review* 40, no. 1: 224–49.

Muñoz, José Esteban. 1999. *Disidentifications: Queers of Color and the Performance of Politics*. Minneapolis: University of Minnesota Press.

Parreñas, Rhacel, and Lok C. D. Siu. 2007. *Asian Diasporas: New Formations, New Conceptions*. Stanford, CA: Stanford University Press.

Puar, Jasbir K. 2006. "Mapping US Homonormativities." *Gender, Place & Culture* 13, no. 1, 67–88.

Romero, Andrea J., and Robert E. Roberts. 2003. "Stress within a Bicultural Context for Adolescents of Mexican Descent." *Cultural Diversity and Ethnic Minority Psychology* 9, no. 2: 171–84.

Romero, Andrea J., Scott C. Carvajal, Fabian Valle, and Michele Orduña. 2007. "Adolescent Bicultural Stress and Its Impact on Mental Well-Being among Latinos, Asian Americans, and European Americans." *Journal of Community Psychology* 35, no. 4: 519–34.

Shimakawa, Karen. 2002. *National Abjection: The Asian American Body Onstage*. Durham, NC: Duke University Press.

Szymanski, Dawn M., and Sung, Mi Ra. 2010. "Minority Stress and Psychological Distress among Asian American Sexual Minority Persons." *Counseling Psychologist* 38, no. 6: 848–72.

Tuan, Mia. 1998. *Forever Foreigners or Honorary Whites?: The Asian Ethnic Experience Today*. New Brunswick, NJ: Rutgers University Press.

Wei, Meifen, Kelly Yu-Hsin Liao, Ruth Chu-Lien Chao, Brent Mallinckrodt, Pei-Chun Tsai, and Raquel Botello-Zamarron. 2010. "Minority Stress, Perceived Bicultural Competence, and Depressive Symptoms among Ethnic Minority College Students." *Journal of Counseling Psychology* 57, no. 4: 411–22.

Woo, John, and Yousur Al-Hlou. 2016. "#thisis2016: Asian-Americans Response." *New York Times*, October 16, 2016. http://www.nytimes.com/video/us/100000004706646/thisis2016-asian-americans-respond.html.

"It was Akiko 41; it was me": Queer Kinships in Nora Okja Keller's Mother-Daughter Narrative

S. Moon Cassinelli

Abstract: Nora Okja Keller's *Comfort Woman* (1997) prioritizes the point of view of women to discuss the aftermath of war. The novel is centered on a mother-daughter relationship and scholars of Asian American literary studies often interpret the daughter's story line as a gendered legacy in which she inevitably inherits her mother's history of sexual traumas. In this article, I consider the role of queerness threaded throughout the novel's representations of World War II military outposts and Korean "comfort women," to argue that Korean American intergenerational models contain multiple sexualities as a result of Japanese colonialism and U.S. militarization. **Keywords:** mother-daughter narratives, "comfort women," queer kinships, reproduction, Korean diaspora

> *Indeed, the barely submerged histories of colonialism and racism erupt into the present at the very moment when queer sexuality is being articulated. Queer desire does not transcend or remain peripheral to these histories but instead it becomes central to their telling and remembering: there is no queer desire without these histories, nor can these histories be told or remembered without simultaneously revealing the erotics of power.*
>
> —*Gayatri Gopinath,* Impossible Desires

> *So I begin the search for the female figure that haunts the Korean diaspora, tracing her back through the body of the comfort woman to the body of the home-coming woman, displaced and thereafter always homeless.*
>
> —*Grace M. Cho,* Haunting the Korean Diaspora

Nora Okja Keller's 1997 novel, *Comfort Woman,* is notable as one of the first Asian American novels to feature a Korean "comfort woman"

WSQ: Women's Studies Quarterly **47: 1 & 2 (Spring/Summer 2019)**

character. Akiko, one of the novel's narrators, is an immigrant Korean mother and former comfort woman, living in Hawai'i with her American daughter, Beccah. Akiko's story is a fictional representation of the estimated sixty thousand to two hundred thousand women and girls (mostly Korean, but also including those from Taiwan, China, the Philippines, and Indonesia) coerced into sexual conscription for the Japanese Imperial Army during World War II. Although the mother's history is introduced early in the narrative to the reader, this information remains unknown to her daughter for the majority of the novel. This narrative strategy parallels the actual history of comfort women, which scholars of gender and sexuality studies within Asian and Asian American studies have characterized as largely erased within the national histories and official positions put forth by Japan and South Korea, following World War II. As discussed by Elaine H. Kim and Chungmoo Choi, since the 1990s, the effort to make Korean comfort women a part of public discussions about sexual violence and war crimes is the result of Korean women's activism that demanded the South Korean government acknowledge its traumatic past and called for a national apology from Japan (1998, 2–4).[1]

Given its year of publication in relation to public discussions on comfort women issues, Keller's novel was likely the first time American readers had been introduced to Korean comfort woman as a historical occurrence and a global women's issue. According to a 1997 book review in the *New York Times,* Keller's novel is praised for "juxtaposing Akiko's story with that of her American daughter, Beccah, [turning] her tragic history into a familial saga of love and pain and resentment" (Kakutani 1997, B8). Likewise, a 1998 book review in the *Missouri Review* suggests that the "conflict between Asian-born mothers and their American-born daughters has been a reoccurring theme for a number of Asian American women writers" and that "Keller also mines this rich territory, but . . . she introduces issues previously unexplored: the Japanese occupation of Korea and the duplicity of Christian missionaries in Asia" (Lee 1998, 184). Both book reviews frame the familiar mother-daughter story line within Asian American women's writing as helpful in orienting American readers to unfamiliar material.

My discussion of *Comfort Woman* is interested in literary interpretations of mother-daughter narratives within Asian American studies and the feminist scholarship on Keller's novel, situated in public discussions on Korean comfort women. I mobilize analyses of Asian American literature, the Korean diaspora, and Korean American immigrant family formations, all which directly examine the effects of World War II and the U.S. Cold War era on Korean and Korean American subject formations. Through a queer reading of Keller's novel, my analysis includes existing feminist and anti-colonial interpretations, but also considers how sexual desire and kinship are, as Gayatri Gopinath asserts, "central to [the] telling and remembering" of Korean comfort women histories and legacies (2005, 2). Scholars of Asian diasporas within Asian American studies have argued that "it is impossible to discuss the formation of Asian diasporas without addressing their relationship to labor, colonialism, and globalization" (Parreñas and Siu 2007, 20). The figure of the Korean comfort woman within the novel's Korean American family foregrounds how Korean and U.S. nation-states have disciplined Korean women's sexuality through national cultures of silence and family-based immigration policies during the second half of the twentieth century. For sociologist Grace M. Cho, an analysis of the female figure who "haunts the Korean diaspora" is as much a critical reflection on genealogy and collective histories as it is a study of the *yanggongju,* a term that "refers to a Korean woman who has sexual relations with Americans" (2008, 3). I contend that once Korean American mother-daughter narratives are unburdened by reading practices that perpetuate heteronormativity and procreative logics, alternative kinships come to the fore of Keller's novel, revealing how queer and normative intimacies inextricably structure the Korean diaspora.

Mother-Daughter Generational Models and the Geopolitics of the Korean Diaspora

Keller's *Comfort Woman* is a multivoiced, intergenerational narrative about the complexities of love and affective labor between a mother and daughter. After escaping the Japanese military "comfort" camps at the age of fourteen, Akiko marries a U.S. missionary, which results in her emigration to America and later, the birth of Beccah. The novel's narrative structure places the mother and daughter's experiences and perspectives alongside one another; the individual sections are labeled, either *Beccah* or *Akiko,* according to whose voice pushes the narration forward. When Beccah is a child, after the death of her father, Akiko attempts for the two of them to return to Korea but is unable to afford the entire journey. Consequently, the mother and daughter live with little money and in relative isolation in Honolulu during the 1970s and 1980s. Although beyond the scope of this article, it is important to recognize the role of Hawai'i as the novel's setting. Scholarship invested in questions of belonging within Asian diasporas involving the U.S. cannot overlook how displaced individuals who live in America become settlers on indigenous lands.[2]

The novel's dual narration, voiced in equal parts by Akiko and Beccah, does not flow easily from mother to daughter in a linear or progressive manner. This narrative structure prevents the sections from being read as a single-family narrative because they don't share specific events, stem from the same origin story, or retell the same interactions from different perspectives. Instead, each woman narrates various stories through a series of flashbacks and recovered memories that lead readers to understand the mother and daughter's lives as proximal and codependent, but also separate. Although the figures within the novel, an immigrant Asian mother and an American daughter, might signal to readers to interpret Akiko and Beccah's interactions through the familiar theme of intergenerational conflict, I caution that such reading practices frame the miscommunications between the pair as representative of inevitable culture loss due to U.S. assimilation.[3] I contend, instead, that the novel's dual narration helps establish the spatial and temporal conditions of the Korean diaspora, which cannot be strictly contained within the national borders of either the United States or Korea.

The formation of the Korean American family reflects the geopolitical conditions of the Korean diaspora, which includes Japanese colonialism and World War II, and later, U.S. militarization and the Korean War. Korean American narratives, such as *Comfort Woman*, that feature Korean American immigrant families whose genealogies and histories of migration are the result of mid-twentieth-century warfare, undermine the "sociological literature on immigration [that] often classifies Koreans as a part of the post-1965 demographic trend that diversified the ethnic and national makeup of immigrants in the United States" (Cho 2008, 12). Keller's novel, for instance, opens in Hawai'i with the recent passing of Akiko when Beccah is thirty years old; but through Akiko's narration, the text's timeline extends beyond World War II and includes the Korean March First Movement of 1919. In her discussion of Korean American contemporary literature, Kandice Chuh insists that Asian American studies scholars be attentive to "the material effectivity of multiply located histories and chronologies . . . [which] means recognizing the limitations of knowledge produced by distancing 'America' from 'Asia' as limitations that do ideological work" (2003b, 111). As such, the dual narratives within *Comfort Woman* enable the story to travel between Korea and the United States and between events that include most of the twentieth century.

At the center of *Comfort Woman*'s constellation of historical touchstones are Akiko's experiences as a Korean comfort woman. Keller's treatment of the sexual violence within the context of a mother-daughter relationship has a commanding effect on how the novel is interpreted and the perceived narrative function of Akiko's history. That the reader is made aware of Akiko's past from the onset, but that the daughter's discovery serves as a climatic, late-novel reveal, solidifies Akiko's sexual trauma as a major plot device. The fictional mother-daughter relationship must subsequently bear the burden of translating the Korean comfort woman history to the reader, which leads to the question of history and its role within the novel. For many scholars of Asian American literary studies, *Comfort Woman* is best interpreted as a bildungsroman, or at the very least, a novel preoccupied with knowledge production. The publication and reception of Keller's novel is contextualized within its contemporaneous public discourse on Korean comfort women. For example, many critics cite Keller's own edifying moment in 1993 regarding the history of Korean comfort women as her motivation for writing Akiko's story and thus, that the author intended the narrative to be interpreted as a fictional testimony.[4]

When read against the political activism on behalf of and by surviving Korean comfort women during the 1980s and 1990s to "break the silence," it *is* likely that Keller imagined Akiko's voice and narrative sections would represent the systemic silencing of the victims by, and as counter-narrative to, national histories. Following World War II, Chungmoo Choi asserts, the Korean women who survived were forced to "live for a half a century carefully guarding their past" while their "existence had been completely erased even in the most fervent anti-colonial, nationalist narrative in Korea" (1998, 13). Given the postcolonial political and social climates that shamed surviving Korean comfort women into silence, scholars of Asian American studies characterize Akiko's escape from the military recreation campus and later, her refusal to be saved by her husband and his Christianity, as testaments to the character's strength and resilience. On one hand, these aspects of her narrative are easy to champion; Keller seemingly has created an ideal version of a Korean comfort woman who has sidestepped the trappings of perpetual victimhood. But on the other hand, requiring Akiko and her narrative to be both empowering *and* educational creates tension when the novel also supposedly functions as Beccah's bildungsroman.

The mother-daughter relationship helps structure the diasporic spatial logics of the novel, moving the story (and its reader) between Korea and the United States, even as our interpretive practices must contend with the limits of the bildungsroman which, to echo Chuh's caution, positions Akiko's "Asianness" as significantly distinct from—and sometimes at odds with—her "Asian American" daughter (2003a, 18–19). In her article "Haunting History," Jodi Kim argues that "through the 'voice' of Akiko's wounds [from sexual trauma], Keller gives us access to a historical truth that has been otherwise occluded and obscured by nationalist patriarchal discourses of Japan, Korea, and the U.S." (1999, 63). Recognizing that Akiko is asked to be an ideal comfort woman while also educational, Jodi Kim examines the novel's complicated representations. For instance, Kim notes how the struggle to give voice to certain historical events is represented by Akiko, even as she "breaks the silence" on those very events. This reveals the limited and incomplete nature of nationalist narratives while offering a feminist critique against the "extent to which nation-building depends on institutional sexual violence" to uphold its patriarchal and colonial agendas (Kim 1999, 73–75). Kandice Chuh, also interested in Akiko's body, claims that Rick, Beccah's father, "serves as a means for this novel to criticize U.S. imperialism" and "in both cases [sexual servitude and marriage], [her] body functions as but a vessel for the desires of a gendered empire" (2003a, 18). Chuh ultimately believes that *Comfort Woman* is unable to provide radical interventions, and that "despite its invocations of histories and stories that are arguably unfamiliar to many U.S. readers, the novel may be seen to operate on well-trodden, even clichéd grounds. [. . .] The critiques *Comfort Woman* offers are circumscribed by its formal properties such as the importance of the retrieval of this history as ascribed to the desire for happiness for the next (U.S.) generation" (2003a, 19). The immigrant mother's narrative, Chuh contends, ultimately takes a secondary position to allow the Americanized daughter's chance at one day achieving national belonging.[5]

I concur with Jodi Kim and Kandice Chuh that Akiko and her experiences are meant to carry a critique against institutional, patriarchal, and colonial forces described in the novel; however, I argue Beccah's narrative does more than serve as a plot device that enables the novel to "break the silence" on Akiko's past sexual traumas. To frame Beccah's story lines as independent and in relation to Akiko's experiences draws our attention to the formation of the Korean American family in ways that reorient mother-daughter generational models away from easy formulations that cast the immigrant mother as "Asian" and the daughter as "American." The purposeful disconnect between mother and daughter structured by the narrative is not simply a generational conflict which Beccah must overcome so she may become self-actualized as her mother's daughter, but creates space to consider the women as individuals without minimizing one story line for the sake of another.

The Queerness of the Japanese Military Recreation Centers

To consider the significance of Beccah's story independent from Akiko's means pulling the daughter's narrative from the shadows of the mother's narrative. My intent is not for readers to disregard the fact that Akiko and Beccah are mother and daughter, but to release the impulse to read kinship and desire within generational models as exclusively heteronormative. And while the novel's narrative structure enables readers to reorient their thinking about mother-daughter storylines by reading their experiences contiguously, it's the queer relationship between Akiko and Induk—a fellow comfort woman at the Japanese military recreation camps—that make possible multiple channels of female desire within Akiko and Beccah's genealogies. I am suggesting that because Akiko's relationship with Induk originates at the military recreation camp, their queer bond is built from shared gendered experiences of nationalism and sexual trauma characteristic of the Korean diaspora. In the context of South Asian diasporas Gayatri Gopinath explains her refusal to position queerness as oppositional to feminism, arguing that "by making female subjectivity central to a queer diasporic project, it begins [. . .] to conceptualize diaspora in ways that do not invariably replicate heteronormative or patriarchal structures of kinship and community" (2005, 6).

Induk's comfort woman name is Akiko 40; she is Akiko's namesake ("she was the Akiko before me"). In the novel, when Japanese soldiers murder Induk/Akiko 40, a young Akiko must serve soldiers in her place, becoming Akiko 41. Induk and young Akiko are a part of a queer genealogy that plays on different forms of reproduction: their relationship is matrilineal but also uses the language of replication. On Akiko's "first night as the new Akiko," she is given Akiko 40's old clothes: a brutal symbolism that the young girl has inherited the responsibilities previously forced onto Akiko 40 (Keller 1997, 21). Through Akiko 40's death, Akiko 41 is born, which is both symbolic and incredibly accurate to the conditions of the recreation camp. Additionally, Akiko 40's death enables the return of her former personhood, Induk. As a spirit, Induk continually visits Akiko for the remainder of the novel.

Akiko 40's death is simultaneously horrific and mundane, which makes Akiko 41's incarnation devastating for the young girl (and by extension, for the American reader), but unexceptional with regard to the recreational camp. On one hand, the repetition of names and succession of numbers suggest that Akiko 41 is a mere duplicate of Akiko 40, meant to emphasize how institutional sexual violence denies the comfort women their personhood. But a queer reading also suggests that the novel depicts an alternative form of reproduction between the two women. When Akiko explains that "the corpse the soldiers brought back from the woods wasn't Induk. It was Akiko 41; it was me" (Keller 1997, 21), she articulates how the intricate relationship between herself and Induk is formed through multiple iterations of Akiko 40 birthing Akiko 41; Akiko 41 as always already Akiko 40; and Akiko and Induk as one and the same. Threaded throughout the iterations are the conditions of state-sanctioned sexual violence.

The novel's representation of relations between the Korean comfort women presents the Japanese recreation camps to be a queer space. Keller uses gender as a tool of resistance, specifically female solidarity and reclaimed womanhood, to redefine Korean nationalism, within the space of the camp. When Akiko first arrived at the Japanese recreation camp at twelve years old, she is not immediately placed in sexual servitude but instead tasked with caring for the other comfort women. As an errand girl, Akiko describes her duties with relative innocence: "I was kept to serve the women in the camps. Around women all my life, I felt almost like I was coming home when I first realized there were women at the camps" (Keller 1997, 19). The women Akiko initially references, those she had been "around [. . .] all my life," are her sisters and mother. The repeated use of the word *women*, without any qualifiers, draws connections between her family members (those to whom she is bound by blood and duty) and the comfort women (those to whom she is bound by institutional violence). Keller does not seem to prioritize biological relations over nonbiological relations and indeed, the mere presence of women and the caretaking service required of Akiko initially shields her from the violent realities of the recreation camp. But given the extreme patriarchal and colonial conditions of the camp, this female solidarity is a response to the nation-state's use of gender as a tool for violence, as opposed to an essential understanding of comfort women, Korean women, or Asian women more generally.

The youngest daughter in her family, Akiko's caretaking in the camps resembles her relationship with her Korean mother. On the night that her mother passes away, in a demonstration of filial love, Akiko lets her mother's hair down from its bun and rubs the older woman's temples (Keller 1997, 18). The novel creates a parallel when, for the comfort women, Akiko's labor is also characterized with domestic qualities: she "kept their clothes and bedding clean, combed and braided their hair, served them their meals" (Keller 1997, 20). The similarities between the different caretaking experiences and Akiko's initial feelings of "coming home" create a familial-inspired kinship amongst the Korean women in the novel. According to Silvia Schultermandl, examples of maternalism are powerful critiques because "Keller inscribes into the mother-daughter relationship [here referencing Akiko and Beccah] aspects of corporeality that articulate women's struggles for survival and agency" (2007, 93). Rather than focus on the body, I contend that Akiko's affective, domestic, and filial labor is meant to minimize imagined incompatibilities between the space of the home and the space of a military recreation camp, characterizing the Korean diaspora through gender and sexuality, as opposed to ethnic groups and nationality. And by presenting the camp and the women through a child's perspective (which parallels Beccah's sections that recount her own childhood), Keller can more easily present the camp as a space where feminist caretaking and affiliation are not only possible, but crucial for survival. This is not to say that Keller has fabricated the possibilities of care within a violent space; indeed, archival and ethnographic research on the politics of caretaking within Japanese military campus could speak more to this. But Keller uses the love between a mother and daughter to make legible the humanity of the comfort women, even as the kinship extends beyond the familial.

As a mechanism of violence and control, Akiko recalls how the women of the Japanese recreation camps were not allowed to speak, either to the soldiers or one another. It is a clear act of rebellion, then, when Induk uses her actual voice to reclaim her personhood through her Korean identity. She "denounced the soldiers, yelling at them to stop their invasion of her country and her body. Even as they mounted her, she shouted: I am

Korean, I am a woman, I am alive" (Keller 1997, 20). Induk's condemnations forge a defense on behalf of her body and her nation; her declarations establish agency for herself and in turn, for Korea. She uses her voice to turn herself into a political weapon against Japanese occupation, while fighting against the sexual violence that deems her to be disposable. Shamed by her words and unable to force her back into silent submission, the Japanese soldiers brutally murder Induk as a lesson to the remaining comfort women.

This narrative moment also parallels the history of Korean women's liberation, specifically how "during the Japanese occupation (1910–1945), Korean feminism was entwined with the cause of national liberation" (Kim and Choi 1998, 2). Thus, in reclaiming her body, Induk constructs a feminist nationalism by reminding the soldiers of her Koreanness: "All through the night she talked, reclaiming her Korean name, reciting her family genealogy, even chanting the recipes her mother had passed on to her" (Keller 1997, 20). As long as Induk has a voice, her Koreanness returns to her body. Her sense of nationalism is then affirmed by the familial and its promise of continuance through generational relations. Here, I interpret the novel as redefining patriarchal nationalism through the gendered worth and reproductive capabilities of Korean comfort women from within the space of the recreation camps. Induk's verbal assault is a refusal to be identified and defined by sexual trauma, and by extension, Japanese imperialism. But a queer diasporic reading also reveals the degree to which Induk/Akiko 40 "remains unimaginable and unthinkable . . . within dominant nationalist and diasporic discourses" (Gopinath 2005, 19). As such, this moment also speaks to the promotion of cultural silence through post–World War II Korean nationalism that demanded Korean women, including surviving comfort women, uphold the fictions of female purity and heteronormativity. Gopinath's queer "impossibility," then, is a generative theory to discuss the history of comfort women and their legacies of sexual violence in ways that prevent the reification of the Korean woman as either constant victim or the embodiment of shame. Both Japanese colonialism and Korean postwar nationalism produced the conditions for queerness, and especially for the queer female desire that characterizes Induk and Akiko's relationship following Akiko's escape from the camp.

One of the first times that Induk appears as Induk (as her ghost self, not Akiko 40) within the novel is when Beccah is born. Akiko's experience giving birth is made difficult when the Western doctors misunderstand her fear and vulnerability. The men are described as clumsy and dismissive, handling Akiko's body in ways that cause her "mind [to] slip back into the camps" (Keller 1997, 35). When Induk appears, she is the lone woman's voice in a room of men, taking on the corporeal form of the one of the male doctors to let Akiko know she is there. As with every visit by Induk, Akiko experiences her physically and completely: "She comes in singing, entering with full voice, filling me so that there is no me except for her, Induk" (1997, 36). While giving birth to her daughter under traumatic circumstances reminiscent of the Japanese military camps, Akiko and Induk's queer relationship blurs the boundaries where one woman begins and the other ends.

Their relationship is sensual and based in survival and as such, sometimes needy, desperate, and tinged with jealousy. Akiko reveres Induk: the mother prays to her and sets food aside as sacrifice, eventually teaching Beccah to do the same (Keller 1997, 95–6). It is Induk who helps adult Akiko experience sexual pleasure, as opposed to her American husband, Rick, and it is Induk who is instrumental in Beccah's conception. With Induk as her lover, Akiko's sexual experiences are as much spiritual as physical:

> I open myself to her and move in rhythm to the tug of her lips and fingers and heat of her between my thighs. The steady buzzing that began at my fingertips shoots through my body, concentrates at the pulse point between my legs, then without warning explodes through the top of my head. . . . My body sings in silence until emptied, and there is only her left, Induk. (1997, 145).

One evening, Rick encounters his wife while she is experiencing Induk and proceeds to have sex with Akiko. Although to him it appears that his wife is alone, seemingly masturbating, Induk is not chased away by Rick's participation. To the contrary, Akiko observes, "It was as if Induk was still there, between us, inside him and inside me. The buzzing that I felt with her unfurled within me, gaining strength until I could not contain it. As it burst over me, I cried out against my husband's shoulder and was answered by his own shout of pleasure" (Keller 1997, 146). Beccah is the result of that encounter. For Jodi Kim, who describes the sexual event as Akiko "physically substituting her husband's body with that of Induk," this is Akiko's refusal to be "contained by Western Christianity and the heterosexual economy" (1999, 67).[6] But a queer reading would suggest that Akiko is not "substituting" her husband's body with the idea of Induk, as if Induk's involvement occurred in Akiko's imagination. The sex between Akiko, Induk, and Rick involves each equally and physically: "inside him and inside me." And arguably, it is Induk who makes the encounter possible, because when Rick enters Akiko, she is "slick, made ready by Induk's endless caresses" (Keller 1997, 145), objectifying Rick as a mere carrier of semen. As Gopinath argues, "Interestingly, it is often in moments of what appears to be extreme gender conformity, in spaces that seem particularly fortified against queer incursions . . . that queer female desire emerges in ways that are most disruptive to dominant masculinist scripts of community and nation" (2005, 25). Indeed, Beccah's conception and genealogy are constructed from queer—as well as biological—reproductive practices.

The mother-daughter and queer genealogies come together one last time at the conclusion of *Comfort Woman*. Beccah has put her mother to rest by scattering her ashes in the river near the house where they both lived. That night, Beccah dreams of swimming through water and sky, until her vantage point allows her to look down at her physical self to "where I lay sleeping in bed, coiled right around a small seed planted by my mother, waiting to be born" (Keller 1997, 213). The novel seems to return to where it began, leaving its readers with the mother and daughter and the suggestion that all Beccah will ever need has already been provided by Akiko. But this final pairing of mother and daughter, I am suggesting, is firmly situated within a queer diaspora that includes the kinship cultivated at the Japanese military recreation centers and the queer conception that not only included, but required Induk's participation. Literary scholars, in contrast, have assessed the ending as a suggestion for what's to come for Beccah and how this reflects on the novel as an edifying narrative. If we, as readers, can learn just as Beccah has, what then might be the horizon of possibility for justice for Akiko and others like her? Kandice Chuh, for example, describes this moment as "insemination by mother," noting the absence of a male participant and Beccah's enlightenment confirmed by the rhetoric of her own (re)birth (2003a, 19). For Akiko, the ability to inseminate broadens her reproductive and procreative capabilities, certainly, but I resist interpreting Akiko as an exceptional mother with concerns that the construction of remarkable mothers requires the categorization of bad, unfit mothers.[7]

And rather than consider Beccah as about to be born again, potentially dismissing her childhood experiences because they were produced in ignorance, I argue that this moment is a purposeful backward look to Beccah's moment of conception and the queer kinships that helped make it possible. As feminist scholars rightfully champion feminist rewritings of genealogies within the Korean diaspora, a queer reading of Keller's *Comfort Woman* reminds us that histories of sexuality are built through interwoven queer and biological practices. Furthermore, I posit that tracing the queer relations within the sexual histories of the Korean diaspora constitute another type of feminist genealogy. And with an understanding that genealogies in the Korean diaspora are primarily constructed through gendered responses to conditions of militarization and colonialism, I have been arguing that analyses of queer figures and desire provide new insights to the study of the family formation and generational models within contemporary Korean American narratives by recontextualizing diasporic political intimacies through gender and sexuality. As such, rather than try to forecast what is about to unfold for Beccah, her dream about a seed "waiting to be born" might be reminding us to continue to look backward as a way of moving forward.

S. Moon Cassinelli is a Presidential Pathways Postdoctoral Fellow in the Department of English and the Women's and Gender Studies program at Virginia Tech. His current project analyzes queerness and kinship within contemporary Korean American narratives. He can be reached at smooncass@vt.edu.

Notes

1. On December 6, 1991, three former Korean "comfort women" filed suit against the Japanese government, in the Tokyo District Court, using legal channels to control the narrative and lay direct responsibility at the national level (Choi 1998, 13). In December 2015, as reported by Steven Borowiec for *Al Jazeera*, Japan and the Republic of Korea reached a formal agreement about comfort women that involved degrees of public accountability. Japan issued an apology and agreed to pay $8.8 million to help support surviving comfort women; and in return, Korea agreed to refrain from criticizing Japan for its war crimes and forced sexual conscription. Additionally, Korea resolved to work toward having the comfort woman statue removed. The bronze statue, an expression of commemoration and protest, was installed in 2011 by local Seoul artists and activists and features a young girl who sits facing the Japanese embassy in Seoul. A 2017 proposed resolution, cosponsored

by twenty-one scholars of the Association for Asian American Studies, represents the ongoing discussions and academic activism around the comfort woman issue. According to the cosponsors, there remains a continued fight to "confront the Japanese government's denial and coercion of hundreds and thousands of women and girls into the largest known sexual slavery system of the 20th-century. We stand together to resist historical denialism" (Proposed Resolution).

2. The growing discussions of Asian settler colonialism by scholars in Asian American studies and American Indian studies strive to address how Asian American communities uphold settler ideologies and practices through claims of national belonging. In the context of Hawai'i, Native Hawaiian scholar Haunani-Kay Trask has argued that when Asian American communities refer to themselves as "local," they are trying to ideologically and politically position themselves outside the American colonial system (2008, 46). But Asian immigrants' settlement in the U.S. does not exist within, as Candace Fujikane criticizes, a "third space that exempts [settlers of color] from colonial responsibilities" (2008, 10). Asian immigrant and refugee groups' experiences, including being colonized in their countries of origin and struggles against anti-Asian racism in the U.S., do not negate their complicity in the ongoing U.S. colonization of indigenous peoples.
3. Within twentieth-century Asian American literary studies, two prominent genres have received considerable attention within discussions about representations of the Asian American experience, especially with regard to immigration and assimilation. The bildungsroman and mother-daughter narratives are distinct genres, and yet, scholarship on both has similarly focused on the narrative's knowledge production and self-realization.
4. The 1997 Penguin Books edition of the novel features an "Author Questions" section, in which Keller explains her introduction to the Korean comfort woman history: "I first heard of 'comfort women' in 1993. Keum Ju Hwang, a woman who survived the comfort camps of World War II, was speaking at several American universities in order to 'bear witness,' to bring to light this chapter in history" (1997, 5).
5. With similar implications, Samina Najmi argues that when Akiko's past is framed through the mother-daughter narrative, the gendered familial roles and dynamics encourage interpretations where the focus is ultimately on Beccah and her sense of self (2005, 219). Attaining knowledge about Akiko's past as a former comfort woman, Najmi argues, enables Beccah to achieve a sense of wholeness and closure because she can now access her Koreanness. The daughter's delayed discovery ultimately ensures the proper transmission of knowledge and history through biological and procreative logics: from

parent to child and through successive generations. In this sense, Akiko's comfort woman history is Beccah's birthright; but as Tina Chen argues, this inheritance is only fully comprehensible when the daughter learned how to listen to her mother, a task not possible initially because of Beccah's Americanness (2005, 147).

6. Silvia Schultermandl's article discusses Induk at length alongside Akiko and Beccah but frames Induk's narrative presence as resistant to patriarchy and nationalism (when alive) and as an element of Akiko's Korean folklore and shamanism (when dead). Schultermandl analyzes sexuality in reference to Korean comfort women and violence, but not desire or pleasure.
7. Within the context of the Korean diaspora which includes transnational Korean adoption and Korean birth mothers, I am cognizant how the narrative about the "unfit" Korean mother is based on ideas of sexual deviance, including prostitution, sexual promiscuity, or being working class and lower. Hosu Kim and Grace Cho argue that "at the heart of societal beliefs about 'unfit' motherhood lies the unregulated sexuality of the birthmother" and that "the notion of excessive and immoral female sexuality, epitomized by the figure of the prostitute, extends to all birthmothers who fall outside the patriarchal family order" (2014, 45).

Works Cited

Borowiec, Steven. 2017. "The Debate over South Korea's 'comfort women.'" *Al Jazeera*, January 29, 2017. http://www.aljazeera.com/indepth/features/2017/01/debate-south-korea-comfort-women-170127120244979.html.

Chen, Tina. 2005. *Double Agency: Acts of Impersonation in Asian American Literature and Culture.* Stanford, CA: Stanford University Press.

Cho, Grace M. 2008. *Haunting the Korean Diaspora: Shame, Secrecy, and the Forgotten War.* Minneapolis: University of Minnesota Press.

Choi, Chungmoo. 1998. "Nationalism and Construction of Gender in Korea." In *Dangerous Women: Gender and Korean Nationalism*, edited by Elaine H. Kim and Chungmoo Choi, 9–31. New York: Routledge Press.

Chuh, Kandice. 2003a. "Discomforting Knowledge, Or, Korean 'Comfort Women' and Asian Americanist Critical Practice." *Journal of Asian American Studies* 6, no. 1: 5–23.

———. 2003b. *Imagine Otherwise: On Asian Americanist Critique.* Durham, NC: Duke University Press.

Fujikane, Candace. 2008. "Introduction: Asian Settler Colonialism in the U.S. Colony of Hawai'i." In *Asian Settler Colonialism: From Local Governance to the Habits of Everyday Life in Hawai'i*, edited by Candace Fujikane and Jonathan Y. Okamura, 1–42. Honolulu: University of Hawai'i Press.

Gopinath, Gayatri. 2005. *Impossible Desires: Queer Diasporas and South Asian Public Cultures*. Durham, NC: Duke University Press.

Kakutani, Michiko. 1997. "Repairing Lives Torn by the Past." *New York Times*, March 25, 1997.

Keller, Nora Okja. 1997. *Comfort Woman*. New York: Penguin Books.

Kim, Elaine H., and Chungmoo Choi. 1998. "Introduction." In *Dangerous Women: Gender and Korean Nationalism*, edited by Elaine H. Kim and Chungmoo Choi, 1–8. New York: Routledge Press.

Kim, Hosu, and Grace M. Cho. 2014. "The Kinship of Violence." In *Mothering in East Asian Communities: Politics and Practice*, edited by Patti Duncan and Gina Wong, 31–52. Bradford, ON: Demeter Press.

Kim, Jodi. 1999. "Haunting History: Violence, Trauma, and the Politics of Memory in Nora Okja Keller's *Comfort Woman*." *Hitting Critical Mass: A Journal of Asian American Cultural Criticism* 6, no. 1: 61–78.

Lee, Kathy. 1998. "*Comfort Woman* (review)." *Missouri Review* 21, no. 1: 184–85.

Najmi, Samina. 2005. "Decolonizing the Bildungsroman: Narratives of War and Womanhood in Nora Okja Keller's *Comfort Woman*." In *Form and Transformation in Asian American Literature*, edited by Xiaojing Zhou and Samina Najmi, 209–30. Seattle: University of Washington Press.

Parreñas, Rhacel Salazar, and Lok C. D. Siu. 2007. "Introduction: Asian Diasporas—New Conceptions, New Frameworks." In *Asian Diasporas: New formations, New Conceptions*, edited by Rhacel S. Parreñas and Lok C. D. Siu, 1–27. Stanford, CA: Stanford University Press.

Proposed Resolution. 2017. "Supporting Remembrance of 'Comfort Women' and Their Endangered History." Proposed 2017 Association for Asian American Studies Resolution, February 13, 2017.

Schultermandl, Silvia. 2007. "Writing Rape, Trauma, and Transnationality onto the Female Body: Matrilineal Em-body-ment in Nora Okja Keller's *Comfort Woman*." *Meridians: feminism, race, transnationalism* 7, no. 2: 71–100.

Trask, Haunani-Kay. 2008. "Settlers of Color and 'Immigrant' Hegemony." In *Asian Settler Colonialism: From Local Governance to the Habits of Everyday Life in Hawai'i*, edited by Candace Fujikane and Jonathan Y. Okamura, 45–65. Honolulu: University of Hawai'i Press.

The Sphinx Experiment

Heather H. Yeung

We all know the story.

A man, on the road toward the city that is his birthright and his doomed future, comes to the intersection of three roads and encounters a strange thing: a creature not-quite a woman not-quite a lion not-quite an eagle.

The creature, guilty of ruining the agricultural produce of the distant city and terrorizing those who pass outside the city bounds, aggressively poses a riddle to the man. Should he fail to solve it he will never reach the city limits and will become one with the pile of bones of other travelers over which she presides.

But he solves the riddle, passes, fulfills the second stage of a prophecy, and rules, for a while, the city that he is moving toward.

Defeated, the creature leaps from a cliff and plummets to her death.

*

PROPOSITION

To be like the sphinx is the basic condition of the nonnormative person at any border zone.

In encounters with self-nominated protectors of the border, she becomes a being-made-thing. She lacks the appropriate bearing. She can't—or won't—appear wholly "acceptable." The viewer/interlocutor tries to classify the nonnormative person, and in the process is somehow permitted to throw away their handbook of personal ethics.

The sphinx baffles us on multiple levels: its age, its appearance, its manner of being, its language. So we must test it on all these levels.

WSQ: Women's Studies Quarterly **47: 1 & 2 (Spring/Summer 2019)**

RESEARCH QUESTIONS

- Is it always the case that anything appearing to be both within and outside the norm will give us pause, will trouble our thoughts?
- In an encounter with this enigmatic *thing*, what makes us interrogate it, force it to produce its credentials and answer any questions we feel like posing?

FIRST EXPERIMENTAL PHASE

A colleague has invited me to chair a panel at a conference on the influence of Mary Wollstonecraft. I'm delighted to do so; the panel intersects with some of the concerns of a book I am trying to amass out of a series of articles I have already written.

Before the session, I introduce myself to one of the panelists. Hands are shaken.

And then the question, enunciated with ponderous clarity:

So are you a student here, dear?

I clarify that in fact I am a faculty member, an assistant professor in the English literature department.

So have you always been interested in philosophy?

I gently mention that my next book—about female intellectual identity at the limits—deals with concerns similar to those of the conference.

During this conversation, my interlocutor continues to look a little puzzled.

Your English is very good. Where did you learn it? (school in England)

But where are you from? (Scotland)

No, where are you actually from? (I'm British)

You don't look it, with dark hair and . . . are you from . . . ? (it may help you to know that one of my parents is from Hong Kong)

Ah! that's it, I knew there was something exotic about you. You could almost be a Turkish girl; you look like one of my students.

(a pause)

Did you come here with your husband? (silence, as I wonder, —?)

A moment of delight:

You will be happy to hear that in my talk I'm going to defend your type. I'm going to argue that Wollstonecraft actually liked literature. (I respond, Will the talk therefore, given it is going to look at Wollstonecraft from a

Kantian-cum-Aristotelian perspective, pay some attention to Wollstonecraft as a novelist of Reason? Her Mary? Maria?)

I give voice to my questions. Conversation tails off with an expression, still, of moderate incomprehension, a shrug. The discussion is not renewed.

REFLECTION

Human enough to speak to, human enough to question, but not human enough to be declared as such or incorporated within the realms of the growing polis, the sphinx is *not quite*: not quite human enough in appearance, not quite occupying a human space, and not quite operating on the same temporal or linguistic level to be tamed. Not quite anything enough, she cannot be fully accepted.

She confounds, in multiple ways, her interlocutor. Uncivilized in human terms—corrupted by her nonhuman existence in time, space, appearance, and language—she is defeated by Oedipus's declaration of the age of the Anthropocene, in which there is narrative space only for man's own monstrosities. The exclusion of those outside the norm of humanity's physical appearance is celebrated in sculpture and myth; the process of its extinction, forgotten.

This is a cautionary tale.

Whatever is a recognizable other to the dominant nature of the ever-encroaching polis must be policed, normalized, or eradicated; its monstrosity made a symbol and thus placed outside the bounds of normative treatment.

The sphinx, with the head of a woman and the twisting riddling speech to match, is too close for comfort: like the oracle, she can be heard and must be attended to, although her wings and her lion's body mean that she is a troubling thing, her different roots a cause for concern. Always, any encounter with the figure of the sphinx is interestingly, piercingly, unidirectionally, isolatedly personal.

And thus the control and expulsion of the sphinxian figure is effected, most often, on a personal level with the apparently tacit, silent acceptance of the state.

The sphinx, once holder of the crossroads, is unable to venture even that close to the city bounds. And if it is possible to venture closer, disguised in part by her part-human appearance, the sphinx, once the questioner, becomes that which is under question. No longer subject of her own laws or able to define herself in her own language, she must wait for the whimsy of another to discover whether or not her othernesses are of the currently acceptable sort. Too often she will turn away preemptively. The sphinx is a dying breed.

*

I sit in my space, without time. I do not speak in this language. This story is already a different version from my own, but who can tell . . .

In the distance, a city is built. I look on. The land around me is apportioned, and changes color and smell not according to the seasons, but according to what is planted or reared there in a given year.

Time comes to me, therefore. Foreign plants and foreign beasts are introduced. Canals for irrigation of this land are built. The city grows, the apportioning of the land spreads. The contours of the land change.

Roads connect the distant city to other places I do not see. Trade routes develop. Others populate the land closer and closer to me, roads closer and closer. There is no more wild.

I must sustain myself. I eat what I can, when I can. I protect my cwn place from those others who try to take from me the land.

I try to speak to them; we do not speak in the same tongue.

They brandish metal; I have sharp teeth, claws.

They gain speed in chariots; I rise up, winged.

We do not speak the same language, even in battle.

Increasingly these others look at me with disgust and aggression, intrude more and more. They change the land into fields whose boundaries are marked by bushes or low stone walls.

Bones pile up.

I sit between three roads; one points to the city that both repels and moves steadily toward me.

I sing and another arrives, limping toward the city. He seems troubled, yet comes toward me.

I speak.

He responds in a new version of the language that has been developing in the city. A question? A challenge? A greeting?

He looks increasingly troubled; stares for a long time at the length of my figure.

I ask a question. At first I do not comprehend, but finally the response stuns me: it leaves out all things other than himself and those who most resemble him.

Ἄνθρωπος

A violence greater than that of the pitchforks and swords of the others before is directed toward me.

I do not speak this language fully; cannot respond in kind. He does not understand that I, too, may have terms that could be brought to bear, here.

Finally, I am excluded even from the small space I have preserved in the face of the growing city.

At the limit, I sheathe my claws, fold my wings. It no longer matters that I, too, am.

The man turns away from me; walks toward the city and his people.

I turn away from the city. With no space left and silent, I jump.

*

PROPOSITION

Consider academe as a space with border controls that are operated officially (institutionally) and unofficially (personally). Now, make an analogy between this and the tale of Oedipus and the Sphinx; argue that there is a danger in monolithic, nonfluid self-identification.

RESEARCH QUESTIONS

— What is it about this thing, perhaps with deceptive comportment or elocution, that puzzles us, that resists the most obvious curation into our mental Great Exhibition of knowledge?

— Why does the encounter with this enigmatic thing still give us pause, provoke us to consider it not without undue fascination, and, subsequently, to treat it either as a lauded exception, emblematically parading its rehabilitated person as such, or as a challenge and something to be rejected outright, only to be remembered occasionally, if at all, and even then, with an expression of hazy puzzlement?

SECOND EXPERIMENTAL PHASE

On the basis of a book I have written, I am invited to give a keynote presentation at a conference whose subject, Space in Literature, is related to that of my book.

I travel to the conference with a colleague, who is giving a paper later in the day. We are greeted at the university. Or, more accurately, my colleague is greeted at the university; I introduce myself, to some puzzlement.

My colleague explains, after being asked, that I am not his student but his colleague, and that, as well as appearing to possess the same name as the conference's keynote speaker, I am indeed that person.

Confusion leads to my being congratulated on having completed a monograph so young, told I do not look like an academic and, in the same breath, that I will provide an excellent example to the female students at the conference for whom English is not their first language.

I present my paper, which concerns the manners in which (linguistically, formally) the violent incursion of nonliving systems into human spaces is written into British poetries from the Anglo-Saxon "Wanderer" poem to the present.

A question from the audience reconfigures my paper as something "very romantic," a reconfiguration that is based less on the subject of my paper and more on my gender and because the paper concerned poetry (a "feminine" pursuit).

Subsequent conversation compliments me on the fluency of my spoken English and on my bearing ("You really blossomed up there on the podium"; "I love your skirt").

Attempts to bring the conversation back to the subject of the talk or conference are deflected by a prohibitively biographical, bullish obsession with my nonwhite appearance, linguistic identity, apparent age.

REFLECTION

It is time, like the Hellenic Sphinxes who guard the modern Athenian academy, to raise a paw not in protest, but as a demonstration, even celebration, of this power to provoke questioning.

There must be a way of advocating for the legitimacy of the sphinxian without violent protest or exclusion, without grandstanding or finger-pointing and exposing the weak biases particularly to/of those who possess the protective, interrogative habits of an Old Guard.

There must be a way of narrating these experiences without recourse to personal tale or long-departed mythic precursor. Without creating out of the experiences a certain kind of objectification akin to that which has provoked their telling in the first place.

Or, is it finally time for the academy—or the individuals whom the academy comprises—to take a personal as well as institutional or disciplinary stance for difference, for many sorts of speech, appearance, comportment, and value systems, for nonexclusion, nonfetishization, parity? It is time that we practice what its long-standing and long-defended institutions have supposedly long upheld: that the academy acknowledges and promotes all kinds of balanced critical debate, and that this debate is allowed to span the multiple possibilities of thought practiced by any interested thing; that this debate admits all interested things in its process, and that it, too, admits change.

One day the traveler may not turn his back on the riddling enigma, and rather will sit down and share stories, be open to the simultaneous existence of different appearances and methods of expression, realize that the "riddle" is not aggressive, and does not need to be responded to with aggression.

And he may feel, too, not only that the enigma is different from him, but also that, to the enigma, perhaps he too is strange in many ways. Not-quite could turn into the productive not-*quiet* of conversation and acceptance *on one's own terms*.

Perhaps then fewer of these sphinxian figures would choose to preemptively leave the interrogative border zones, rather than be made subject to such violent, personal interrogation. Perhaps then not only the comportment of the interrogative self-appointed border controllers, but also the limits of the polis of academe, with its not-quite enacted rules of inclusion, could *truly* begin to shift.

*

Another arrives, walking toward the city. I sing. He seems troubled, yet comes toward me.

I speak.

He responds in a new version of the language that has been developing in the city. Is it a question? A challenge? A greeting?

He looks interested, somewhat; stares for a long time at the space in which I move.

He moves closer, as do I.

I ask him a question. At first I do not comprehend, but finally his response stuns me: he has, in turn, asked a question, allowed for time for speech (however difficult) to occur.

Together, we develop a means to communicate: about the changes in the land, about the governance, ways of managing space, time, and appearance. He hears my terms and I his.

At the limit I sheathe my claws, he his sword. I fold my wings.

Wrapt in conversation we turn toward the city, and all around. The fields are farmed while incorporating aspects of their overtrodden wild. Old city gates are unblocked. As well as roads, the sky opens up again for travel. Others join us, survey this common ground.

Heather H. Yeung (楊希蒂) is a poet, critic, and theorist who currently teaches in the School of Humanities at the University of Dundee, Scotland. She is interested in work in literature and the wider arts which sit at the intersection of forms, media, languages, and disciplines; in the articulation of precarious and transitive states of existence. She can be reached at h.yeung@dundee.ac.uk.

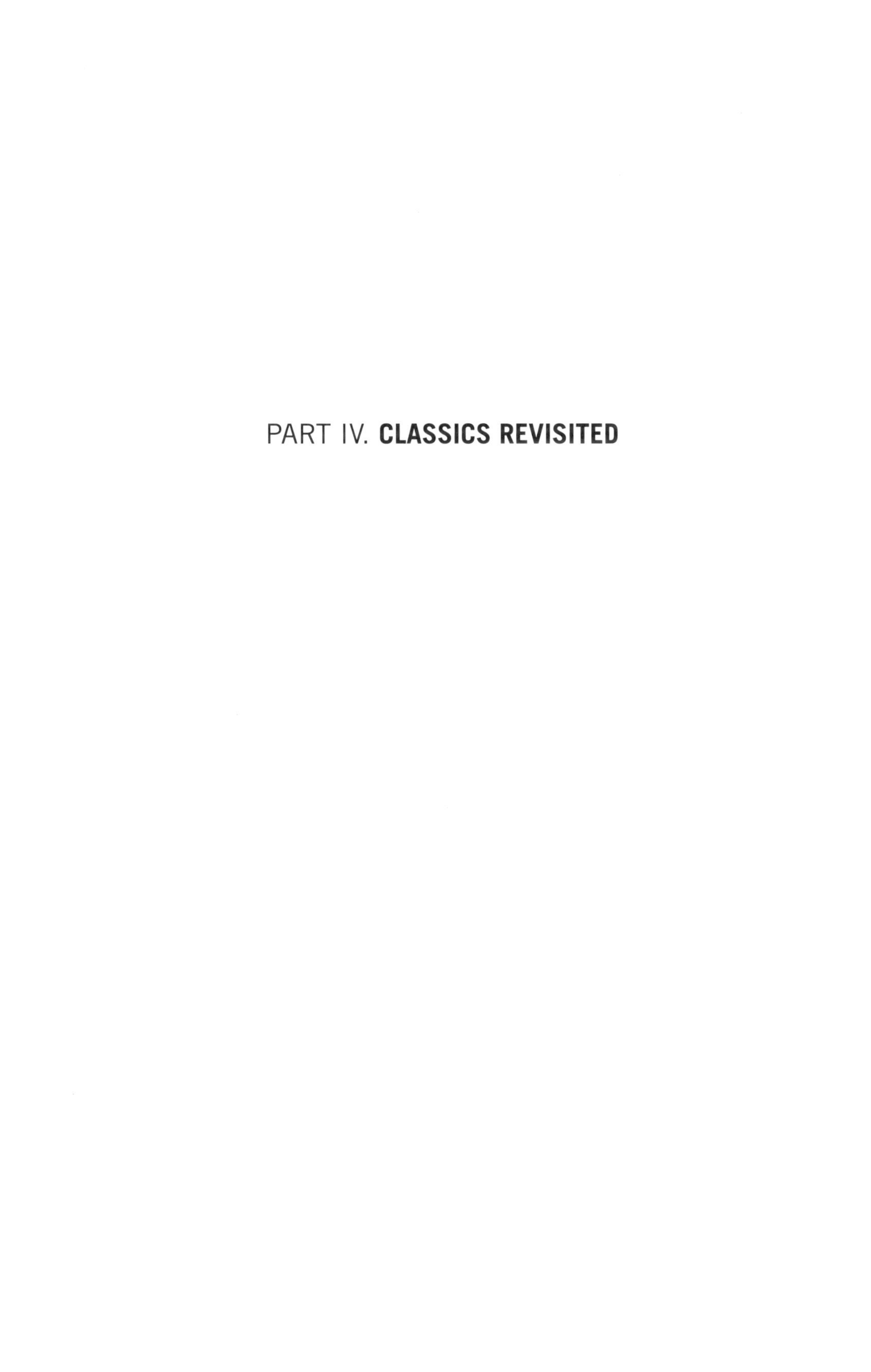

PART IV. **CLASSICS REVISITED**

Fifteen Years after *Buddha Is Hiding*: Gesturing Toward the Future in Critical Refugee Studies

Emily L. Hue

Dedicated to the memory of Daw Hlaing Hlaing

According to the United Nations Refugee Agency, as of early 2017, less than 1 percent of the world's refugees receive visas to resettle (UNHCR 2018). In the United States, recent travel bans and escalated rates of deportation of undocumented immigrants from Asia, Latin America, and the Middle East have made the distinction of citizen status increasingly unattainable. Among the underreported numbers of refugees recently deported from the United States for minor crimes or botched adoption and/or resettlement paperwork from the Cold War, include those of Cambodian, Vietnamese, and Korean descent (Yam 2018; Pearson 2018; Sang-Hun 2018). The alarming uptick of punitive anti-immigration policies highlights the price of citizenship: the discriminatory freedom implicit in the process of holding citizenship itself, in that others may fall short of it.

Anthropologist Aihwa Ong's critical ethnography, *Buddha Is Hiding: Refugees, Citizenship, the New America* (2003), elaborates on the term "refugee," pushing it beyond a static descriptor for political status for those seeking refuge from religious, ethnic, and/or political persecution. The monograph features in-depth interviews with twenty Cambodian American women who escaped the Khmer Rouge and were resettled by the U.S. federal government in Oakland and San Francisco, California.[1] Rather than build her work around a dichotomy between the dangers of postconflict Southeast Asia and the safety of resettlement, Ong's analysis reflects on the *continuum* of interviewees' experiences as they resist the legal, medical, social, and economic violences of resettlement in spaces such as refugee camps at the Cambodian-Thai border, hospitals in the U.S., and refugee processing centers along the way. Reflecting on Ong's work fifteen years after its initial publication reveals a multitude of ways in which the work remains relevant to how scholars theorize the movement of refugees and asylum seekers in relation to the fraught political landscape of migration. This essay focuses on two of the book's important contributions to scholarship on migration and refugee subjectivities: firstly, setting the stage for the multivalent notions of queerness situated between the concepts of "refugee" and "citizen"; and secondly, invoking the multiple temporalities of "freedom" that are possible for diasporic subjects under the conditions of the unending War on Terror.

Ong's ethnographic approach models a methodology that accounts for refugee life in relation to the concept of "citizen" that exceeds the legal definitions of both terms. The author reorients the fields of migration studies and Asian American studies away from their fraught investments in citizenship as an inviolable status such that

> the idea of citizenship [is] not only the idiom of rights articulated in the legal context, but also in the context of the ways in which a set of common (in this case American) values concerning family, health, social welfare, gender relations, and work and entrepreneurialism are elaborated in everyday lives. (Ong 2003, xvii)

While the figure of the refugee emerges in the U.S. consciousness after World War II, and reemerges after the Vietnam War, Ong reconciles how women refugees who fled the Khmer Rouge resist the totalizing discourse of rescue and transformation in the U.S. state's account of its own humanitarian benevolence after its role in wars in Southeast Asia.

Ong turns to the machinations of what she calls "refugee love" or a "liberal variation of humanitarian domination, as enacted by refugee workers, social workers, the police, and some health providers, who in their various capacities provide pastoral care in the broadest sense of the term to refugees" (2003, 146). Ong critiques how social workers engaged Western feminist projects that attempted to regulate economic and family relationships, or intersectional performances of gender and race, within Cambodian refugee communities. Her transnational feminist analysis of interviewees' experiences with social workers suggests that some social workers defined Cambodian refugees as not yet possessed of purportedly singularly American values such as autonomy, gender equality, and nuclear family relations in the face of social welfare's intrusions upon their lives. Ong argues that the prescribed suggestions for addressing household dynamics effectively "feminized refugees" through a "strategy of ethnic transformation" by emphasizing their lack of traditional family caregiving structures and encouraged transformation of aspects of Cambodian culture itself. According to Ong, interviewees rebuffed social workers' attempts to assimilate them into "norms" of American life that interviewees interpreted as "excessively materialist[ic] and individualist[ic]" (2003, 147).

In the years since the publication of *Buddha Is Hiding*, scholars working at the intersections between queer and migration studies have brought into focus the omissions in both fields of struggles uniquely faced by queer and trans refugees and asylum-seeking subjects who do not necessarily adhere to heteronormative family structures and gender roles. Ong's concept of "refugee love" provides a theoretical framing for the absences in the legal concept of refugee, particularly for nonheteronormative subjects. While seeking asylum may provisionally protect refugee communities in the realm of legal rights, scholars such as Audrey Yue suggest that the right not to be persecuted for gender identification and/or sexuality can be outweighed by the privileges promised through the right to marriage, such as citizenship (2012, 269). Scholars of migration and sexuality such as Martin Manalansan IV suggest that the term "refugee" is also always tempered by the interactions with various disciplinary institutions of social welfare, immigration, and medicalization, in ways that potentially "queer" the project of the nation and citizenship itself (2006, 225).

Ong also underscores how the reemergence of the refugee figure after the Vietnam War shifts the timeline of "freedom" from the violences of war, especially as she suggests that freedom is not necessarily attainable for refugee communities through the process of resettlement alone. In this way, Ong foreshadows how scholars and policymakers of migration must constantly grapple with the shifting historical context attached to the term "refugee," and the term's relevance in the era of what many scholars term permanent war following the terrorist attacks of September 11, 2001 (Rana 2016; Singh 2012). What are the roles of permanent war, perpetual policing over migration, and purportedly temporary refugee status in contemporary refugee experiences? Yen Le Espiritu (2014) has called attention to how refugees can become key figures in fueling U.S. militarism *after* they have already experienced nationalist violence in their countries of origin and seek asylum in the U.S., such as when refugees from the Vietnam War became critical in extending the afterlife of U.S. military bases in the Asia-Pacific region as these bases were transformed into refugee camps and processing centers. Mimi Nguyen (2012) has spoken to the elusive terms of freedom, and the indebtedness of refugees necessitated by the state, over forty years after resettlement in the U.S. after the wars in Southeast Asia. As Eric Tang (2015) considers "refugee temporality" with regard to Cambodian communities that resettled in the Bronx, New York, he underscores how these communities experience continuity between the power struggles they faced during war, encampment, and in resettlement; especially as they are contradictorily framed by U.S. policy makers as unable to meet the tenets of the American dream at the same time as they are framed as exceptional model survivors, suggesting that the conditions of refugee status are never "over." Given that the average amount of time that refugees spend stateless (in what the U.S. State Department calls a "protracted refugee situation") can be an average of twenty-six years, the various degrees of what being suspended in "unsettled" life means is more timely than ever (United States Department of State 2018).[2] In critical refugee studies, the concept of "refugee" demands consideration of the future of refugee lives outside of normative timelines for obtaining citizenship and dominant interpretations of the freedom of resettlement. Ong's work emphasizes the importance of attending to refugees' multiple displacements under both war and resettlement. What work remains to be done to contextualize those lives on the brink of or yet to be displaced? Throughout my research over the course of the past decade, the scope of humanitarian concern regarding Burma has shifted, alongside significant transitions within the government, reflected in the changing targets of military and paramilitary violence. These shifts bring to mind the importance of Ong's invocations to the historical contextualization of refugee experience outside a linear story of resettlement, with particular regard to the shifting contours of U.S. and international policies and practices that impact refugees' freedom of movement.

In an increasingly dire humanitarian crisis, an estimated 606,000 Rohingya Muslims have fled Burma since late 2017 to escape state-sanctioned attacks on their communities in western Rakhine State (IDMC 2017).[3] Global news reports of this recent swell of violence frequently frame it as an unforeseen circumstance, given the 2016 transition of the

Burmese government from a military to civilian regime (Human Rights Watch 2017). However, most news coverage fails to recognize that the Rohingya have been officially classified as noncitizens since 1982 when the government instituted an ethnocentric nationality law, and unofficially, as stateless people for almost two hundred years (with the exception of a brief period after Burmese independence from British colonialism) in which Rohingya communities have lived in rightless precarity, disavowed by both Burma and neighboring Bangladesh (Human Rights Watch 2017; Agence France-Presse 2017).[4] Rather, news reports focus on the endless lines of displaced Rohingya survivors waiting for humanitarian assistance, or in refugee encampments awaiting entry into Bangladesh. This reporting conveys horror through the sheer magnitude of the crisis and evokes compassion for refugees and asylum seekers. However, what more is there to examine about the political landscape asylum seekers and recent refugees are entering into?

These images at once adhere to, but also exceed, parameters of human rights legibility—emphasizing the spectacle of human rights atrocities, which are incongruous with the measure of the international community's response. Prior to the current Rohingya Muslim refugee crisis, and under the previous military junta regime in Burma, the United States admitted thousands of Rohingya, Chin, Kachin, and Karen minority ethnic groups from Burma fleeing ethnoreligious persecution (Winn 2017). As of August 2018, the current U.S. presidential administration's policies have allowed for the resettlement of only 1,114 Rohingya refugees fleeing the genocide (Gelardi 2018). Fifteen years on, Ong's call to examine various spheres in which asylum seekers and refugees are pushed to resettle, and to "focus on everyday processes of being-made and self-making in various domains of administration, welfare, church and working life," is urgent (Ong 2003, xvii). In view of daily shifts in restrictive immigration policy and the diversification of the role of the state as it interfaces with the global humanitarian industry, it is also urgent to interrogate other intersections between the state and international NGOs where refugees might seek support. Contemporary asylum-seeking communities are asked to demonstrate vulnerability in front of a diverse arena of state and nongovernmental institutions that have become increasingly key to accessing support without the promise of resettlement; especially for those doubly or thrice unsettled. Heeding Ong's call, in part, may mean continuing to apply pressure to how these spheres could be more flexible and ethical to punctuated movements of refugee and asylum-seeking communities.

Emily L. Hue is an assistant professor of ethnic studies at the University of California, Riverside. Hue can be reached at emily.hue@ucr.edu.

Notes

1. For scholarly work on the afterlife of war as it affects Cambodian diasporic communities, see Chea 2009, Schlund-Vials 2012, and Um 2015.
2. The Office of the United Nations High Commissioner for Refugees (UNHCR) defines a protracted refugee situation as one in which twenty-five thousand or more refugees from the same nationality have been in exile for five or more years in a given asylum country. People in protracted refugee situations are often deprived of freedom of movement, access to land, and legal employment.
3. These communities originally settled in Burma during the sixteenth century as migrant workers, and to varying degrees, during Burma's period of British colonialism from the late nineteenth century to the post–World War II period.
4. Today, Rohingya Muslim communities in Burma occupy the western part of the Rakhine State of Burma, a northern territory of Burma that borders Bangladesh.

Works Cited

Agence France-Presse. 2017. "Tracing History: Tension between Rohingya Muslims, Buddhists Date Back to British Rule." *Hindustan Times*, September 6, 2017. https://www.hindustantimes.com/world-news/tracing-history-tension-between-rohingya-muslims-buddhists-date-back-to-british-rule/story-9mo9eTjOaJ4JQmXGef0BHL.html.

Chea, Jolie. 2009. "Refugee Acts: Articulating Silences Through Critical Remembering and Re-membering." *Amerasia Journal* 35, no. 1: 20–43.

Espiritu, Yen Le. 2014. *Body Counts: The Vietnam War and Militarized Refuge(es)*. Oakland: University of California Press.

Gelardi, Chris. 2018. "Here's How Many Refugees the US Has Accepted in 2018." Global Citizen, April 26, 2018. https://www.globalcitizen.org/en/content/us-accepted-refugees-2018/.

Human Rights Watch. 2017. "World Report 2017: Rights Trends in Burma."

Human Rights Watch, January 12, 2017. https://www.hrw.org/world-report/2017/country-chapters/burma.

IDMC. 2017. "Expert Opinion | Internal Displacement Monitoring Centre," September 2017. http://www.internal-displacement.org/expert-opinion/how-many-internally-displaced-rohingya-are-trapped-inside-myanmar.

Manalansan IV, Martin F. 2006. "Queer Intersections: Sexuality and Gender in Migration Studies." *International Migration Review* 40, no. 1: 224–49. https://doi.org/10.1111/j.1747-7379.2006.00009.x.

Nguyen, Mimi Thi. 2012. *The Gift of Freedom: War, Debt, and Other Refugee Passages*. Durham, NC: Duke University Press.

Ong, Aihwa. 2003. *Buddha Is Hiding: Refugees, Citizenship, the New America*. Oakland: University of California Press.

Pearson, James. 2018. "U.S. Seeks to Deport Thousands of Vietnamese Protected by Treaty: Former Ambassador" Reuters, April 11, 2018. https://www.reuters.com/article/us-usa-vietnam-deportees/u-s-seeks-to-deport-thousands-of-vietnamese-protected-by-treaty-former-ambassador-idUSKBN1HJ0OU.

Rana, Junaid. 2016. "The Racial Infrastructure of the Terror-Industrial Complex." *Social Text* 34, no. 4 (129): 111–38. https://doi.org/10.1215/01642472-3680894.

Sang-Hun, Choe. 2018. "Deportation a 'Death Sentence' to Adoptees after a Lifetime in the U.S." *New York Times*, August 7, 2018. https://www.nytimes.com/2017/07/02/world/asia/south-korea-adoptions-phillip-clay-adam-crapser.html.

Schlund-Vials, Cathy J. 2012. *War, Genocide, and Justice: Cambodian American Memory Work*. Minneapolis: University of Minnesota Press.

Singh, Nikhil. 2012. "Racial Formation in an Age of Permanent War." In *Racial Formation in the Twenty-First Century*, edited by Daniel Martinez HoSang, Oneka LaBennett, and Laura Pulido, 276–01. Oakland: University of California Press.

Tang, Eric. 2015. *Unsettled: Cambodian Refugees in the New York City Hyperghetto*. Philadelphia: Temple University Press.

Um, Khatharya. 2015. *From the Land of Shadows: War, Revolution, and the Making of the Cambodian Diaspora*. New York: NYU Press.

United Nations High Commissioner for Refugees (UNHCR). 2018. "Resettlement." UNHCR. http://www.unhcr.org/resettlement.html.

United States Department of State. 2018. "Protracted Refugee Situations." https://www.state.gov/j/prm/policyissues/issues/protracted/.

Winn, Patrick. 2017. "The Biggest Group of Current Refugees in the US? Christians from Myanmar." Public Radio International, May 4, 2017. https://www.pri.org/stories/2017-05-04/biggest-group-refugees-us-christians-myanmar.

Yam, Kimberly. 2018. "The U.S. Just Quietly Deported the Largest Group of Cambodians Ever." *Huffington Post*, April 6, 2018. https://www.huffingtonpost.com/entry/cambodians-deported-trump-immigration_us_5ac77dd9e4b07a3485e3da6c.

Yue, Audrey. 2012. "Queer Asian Mobility and Homonational Modernity: Marriage Equality, Indian Students in Australia and Malaysian Transgender Refugees in the Media." *Global Media and Communication* 8, no. 3: 269–87. https://doi.org/10.1177/1742766512459122.

(In)Flexible Citizenship: An Autoethnography of an Iranian New Zealander

Mediya Rangi

In an attempt to seek better life conditions my family migrated to Aotearoa, the Land of the Long White Cloud, some fifteen years ago. The simplicity of this sentence does not even begin to capture the decade-long arduous and Kafkaesque trials we experienced before obtaining citizenship in New Zealand (NZ). When migrating to a developed democratic "first-world" country one does not expect to be subjected to measures that continue to reduce one's sense of humanity and social belonging. By way of an autoethnography, I connect Aihwa Ong's concepts of "technologies of government" as creators and regulators of a particular order, with my family's experiences as Iranian migrants, in order to introduce a new layer to the investigation of Asian diasporas and the measures of control they are often subjected to by state ideologies. By considering Iranian migrant stories, we can deterritorialize the racist categories forged by dominant forces that aim to control populations into a manageable and profitable market labor force. We need to consistently reframe our understanding of "Asian" toward a more inclusive, heterogeneous, and fragmented framework that allows the space for more diverse voices to be heard.

Analyzing the implications of such processes of control on my family's sense of belonging, quality of life, and future prospects requires a powerful framework that allows for a radical critique of the neoliberal ideology at work. Ong's significant work on key concepts of transnationalism, diasporas, and "flexible citizenship" has no doubt shaped our understandings of the complexities of today's increasingly complicated movements in a post-globalized world (1999, 2003, 2006). In *Buddha Is Hiding* (2003), Ong's interrogations of the processes through which dominant ideologies shape and reproduce particular values, such as self-reliance, individualism, and

***WSQ: Women's Studies Quarterly* 47: 1 & 2 (Spring/Summer 2019)**

freedom, assist me in understanding the ways in which neoliberal capitalist states operate to root power in shifting environments. Ong examines "citizenship [as] a cultural process of 'subjectification,' in the Foucauldian sense of self-making and being-made by power relations that produce consent through schemes of surveillance, discipline and control, and administration" (1996, 737). More specifically, on both the micro and macro levels, welfare states enforce a dependency complex upon marginalized groups, and subsequently accuse them of inferiority and weakness due to the very same condition that has been deliberately imposed on them (Ong 1996).

For over twenty-four years, my parents sought opportunities to leave Iran before finally arriving in NZ. A deputy principal and a military helicopter pilot, each with twenty-seven years of experience, did not qualify for skilled migration to NZ. As a result, we remained on temporary visas with limited rights for several years while our multiple applications for Permanent Residency (PR) were denied. The final appeal court gave us fifty-six days to pack five years' worth of life and return to "where we had come from." However, as a minority migrant, you must either know or learn the art of hustle rather quickly. Ong's work on American Cambodians' "continuous struggle to survive low-wage economy in which they cannot depend on earnings alone" demonstrates the need for minorities to "develop complex strategies for manipulating and evading rules" and "pooling" resources, to secure both economic and civic independence (1996, 743, 744). Similarly, my father refused to accept "no," mainly because they had given up everything they had in this gamble and had nothing to return to.

Through unorthodox means, we managed to get our story heard for the hundredth time in five years, and thanks to the humanity of a single individual who *decided to believe us,* we finally obtained our PR. During the next five-year interim period waiting for citizenship status, we remained bound to NZ. The Iranian passport did not hold enough credibility for traveling, not even a transit visa from Australia. We also could not travel to Iran; given the unstable regional circumstances, NZ could refuse us entry back in the country, unless we had citizenship rights. We were studying and/or working, creating a new life. Even a reunion with the *homeland* and the family we had left behind was not a risk we were willing to take. Coming from a small, close-knit family, missing significant moments in loved ones' lives was emotionally and mentally challenging while living an uncertain diasporic life. It was difficult to cope with the notion that we had voluntarily exiled ourselves for a presumed freedom that had transpired as even more restrictive, keeping us away from our kin. Throughout the years, we have maintained regular phone contact, exchanged letters and hundreds of emails. Across the fiber-optic lines, we share random medical advice, food recipes, literature and film recommendations, and family gossip. That is how we negotiate our longing for *home*.

During the initial pivotal years of migration, my mother's struggle to settle into a host society that continued to reject her family, future uncertainties, and her longing for *home* resulted in severe anxiety, stress, and depression. As we were receiving our PR, she developed thymoma, a cancerous lump in her upper chest under the breastbone. Once removed, she recovered slowly and returned to work, though the separation from her support system and the legal challenges had taken its toll. Sometime later, we applied for my aunt to visit us for the first time. She is a head surgical nurse and a university lecturer in Tehran. As the sole caretaker of my eighty-two-year-old grandmother, she provided an ample amount of evidence to prove "significant ties with the community and strong reasons to return to home country." Short of having thousands of dollars in the bank, she had a solid case. Her application, however, was denied as the case manager found her evidence *insufficient*.

While neoliberal values such as mobility and flexibility are prioritized as desirable merits of citizenship, the opportunity to exercise these principles are largely denied to migrant populations who have arrived in host lands via a diverse range of means, from varied backgrounds. If a family becomes reliant on any type of social welfare, the state has the capacity to control and limit their movements and demands regular reports of individuals' whereabouts. Their circumstances, including the reasons for traveling, are "objectively" evaluated by case managers and one may be "granted" permission to leave NZ temporarily for a limited time set by the law. While these policies are of course not limited to individuals from migrant families, they are particularly impacted by this type of disciplining surveillance and punitive control methods. Despite thousands of miles that are between most migrants and their families, given the geographical isolation of Aotearoa from the rest of the world (with the exception of the Pacific), there is a constant effort to maintain ties as closely as possible, not only to people and faces, but also to places. However, that becomes increasingly difficult when immigration policies continue to further limit visitation rights for relatives, and people's capacity of movement is simultaneously curbed by the threat of cutting off welfare services if they transgress borders "too much."

Ong's work assists in understanding how various state agencies, as domains of power, redefine modern subjects according to capitalist transnationalism, where citizen rights are only guaranteed to those who participate in the market in profitable ways defined by the neoliberal agenda. Today, though my parents now have civic stability, NZ citizenship has subjected them to new regimes of control, particularly economic, that bring about new insecurities and limited travel opportunities. Nearly at the retirement age, my parents cannot travel outside of NZ for more than twenty-eight days in any given year, if they wish to maintain access to accommodation and medical supplements they have recently begun to receive from Work and Income (WINZ), NZ's social welfare department. The recipients of any type of government assistance including Jobseeker Support, Sole Parent Support, and Supported Living Payment, must report to the authorities in advance of any scheduled travel and provide evidence of departure and return dates. The new and ever-improving passports provide real-time alerts to the relevant government agencies upon leaving and arriving *home*. WINZ reviews your "request" to leave the country by examining and evaluating your reasons for traveling against a set of predetermined criteria and assumptions. You are considered a poor (in this instance) immigrant, who surely cannot and should not be able to afford a "holiday." My parents had to prove that their daughter had paid the airfare in order for them to attend her doctoral degree graduation ceremony in Australia. They had to provide evidence to show that they are still struggling financially, that this is not a "luxury holiday," and they are still in need of government assistance. Additionally, recipients of these supplements must be "consistently trying to return to/find work." This includes those who are on a sickness supplement, which by definition indicates the *inability* to work. Therefore, assistance stops when one is traveling as the client is not physically available to search for employment. Rent and other expenses that are ongoing, even while one is away, are not considered a priority.

As members of Iranian diasporic communities of Down Under, holding New Zealand passports, world-renowned for its *flexibility in mobility*, our movement has been further limited. We are branded by a third state, whom we have no connections with, with yet another label: the "dual nationals." Most recently, the U.S. issued a travel ban on "dual nationals" of a number of countries, including Iran (Travel.State.Gov n.d.). The irony lies in the fact that even though Iran does not legally allow for dual citizenship, we are accused of, labeled as, and punished for it by an international superpower acting in its own interests. Despite being a New Zealander, my movement within the "global village" can be restricted according to ever-evolving capitalist transnationalist ideologies.

Mediya Rangi is a lecturer at Trinity College and a research assistant at the University of Melbourne, Australia. Her research focuses on repression and expressions of identity, explorations of resistance, diasporic consciousnesses, displacement, and exile. She can be reached at mediyarangi@gmail.com.

Works Cited

Ong, Aihwa. 1996. "Cultural Citizenship as Subject-Making: Immigrants Negotiate Racial and Cultural Boundaries in the United States." *Current Anthropology* 37, no. 5: 737–62.

———. 1999. *Flexible Citizenship: The Cultural Logics of Transnationality.* Durham, NC: Duke University Press.

———. 2003. *Buddha Is Hiding: Refugees, Citizenship, the New America.* Oakland: University of California Press.

———. 2006. *Neoliberalism as Exception: Mutations in Citizenships.* Durham, NC: Duke University Press.

Travel.State.Gov. n.d. "Visa Waiver Program." Accessed October 31, 2018. https://travel.state.gov/content/travel/en/us-visas/tourism-visit/visa-waiver-program.html.

Locating Asianness in the Transnational Field

Kuan-Yi Chen

Based on the first novel of a trilogy written by Kevin Kwan, the film *Crazy Rich Asians* became a box office hit in 2018, grossing more than $200 million worldwide by October that year (Rodriguez 2018). Widely touted as the first mainstream Hollywood production featuring an all-Asian cast since *The Joy Luck Club* in 1993, the film centers on Rachel Chu, a second-generation Chinese American professor, and her boyfriend Nick Young, who hails from an ultrarich, old-money Chinese family in Singapore. What drives the plotline forward is Rachel's introduction to Nick's family and friends to a mixed reception as they travel from New York City to Singapore to attend Nick's best friend's wedding. As a romantic comedy, the film's ostensible moral is a familiar one: it is about how a woman reaches for love and respect against all odds while not losing sight of who she is. However, as a cultural artifact, *Crazy Rich Asians* signifies the shifting meaning of Asianness in the ongoing reshuffling of global economic and political orders. Using Aihwa Ong's works as analytical probes, I situate *Crazy Rich Asians* within the transnational field of the Asia Pacific Rim to offer a deeper reading of the Chinese diasporic tension that threads through the film. In so doing, I wish to highlight Ong's contributions to theoretical inquiries on technologies of governing and politics of belonging.

Ong's works trace the contour of late capitalism not as a globalizing phenomenon with universal characteristics, but as a multilayered, multinodal development imbricated with global, regional, and local conjunctures and contingencies. She interrogates the relevance of the nation-states in an era defined by cross-border mobilities, and the modalities of governmentality aimed at regulating different subjectivities in motion. The analytical and methodological emphases on transnational flows and linkages

WSQ: Women's Studies Quarterly 47: 1 & 2 (Spring/Summer 2019)

enable a more dynamic look at the politics of belonging and subject-making that takes shape within a broader regional and global geopolitical and economic context. Ong's book *Flexible Citizenship* (1999), for example, focuses on the circulation of capital, labor, and cultural imageries across multiple nation-states in the Asia Pacific Rim, as the ascendancy of Asian economies in the nineties offers up alternative modernities outside the West. Her work reveals the intersecting regimes of power and human actions operating transnationally to produce different configurations of citizenship beyond merely a legal category.

In *Crazy Rich Asians,* Rachel's encounter with the Chinese Singaporean society exemplifies an exercise of diasporic subject-making, in that her membership in the Chinese diaspora is frequently called into question. From the outset, a transnational logic of hierarchy that codifies and ranks different diasporic subjects based on national origin and family repute serves to assess and locate Rachel's relative social position. In several scenes, Nick's mother Eleanor further points out that Rachel does not belong because she is too *American* to sacrifice her own happiness to benefit the family. In these vignettes, Rachel's Chinese-ness is invalidated vis-à-vis a local construction of cultural citizenship based on the notion of Chinese familism. The Youngs perhaps exemplify what Ong calls "family biopolitics," where elite Chinese families develop a set of instrumental logics and practices to ensure security and prosperity for their members (1999, 121). Through the valorization and reification of ethnic distinctions, the extended kin network of the Youngs reaches the upper echelons of different nation-states through marriage, education, business, and consumption. Based in Singapore, its members get educated in Cambridge, shop in Shanghai and New York, invest in Taipei and London, and marry into power in Hong Kong and Bangkok. The transnational network of acquaintances from the same social milieu also becomes a tool of biopolitical control. In a much-talked-about scene, it takes less than a meal's time for Eleanor to learn that her son is bringing a mysterious girl on his homecoming trip. The news first takes off when an acquaintance overhears Nick discussing the trip with Rachel at a restaurant in New York. Soon, it gets bounced across the globe through multiple insiders eager to ascertain Rachel's identity. By the time it reaches Eleanor in Singapore, a transnational gossip-as-surveillance apparatus is activated to keep Rachel from undermining the well-orchestrated family biopolitics.

It is important to note that the constructed distinction between Asian and Western values is not confined in the family but an integral part of governmentality wielded by the state. Ong observes that ascending Asian states often deploy discourses that valorize and reify ethnicity-based values such as neo-Confucianism, which "allows the state to produce disciplinary knowledges and ideologically align family and state interests along a single moral continuum" (1999, 151). While they appear to be assertions of sovereignty on the part of postcolonial states, the mobilization of such discourses in fact works to secure an alliance with capitalism that purports to be distinct from and more morally stable than the capitalism of the West. A scene in *Crazy Rich Asians* takes the audience to the bachelor's party of Nick's friend, who is set to marry a woman from another powerful Singaporean family. The success of the family regime is apparent, as conjugal ties enable the intergenerational transmission and consolidation of capitals. Yet if we consider the space in which the celebration unfolds, a different reading emerges. The party takes place onboard a container ship on international waters refitted to welcome partygoers. Since Singapore's economic rise can in no small part be attributed to the city-state's successful positioning of the Port of Singapore as a globally connected maritime hub, the container ship therefore becomes a metaphor for the state power that has shaped the seemingly unencumbered individuals onboard in pursuit of flexibility and mobility. Ong contends that the coordination between the moral economies of the state and the family is founded on a decidedly male vision. Women's domesticity is often supported by the state for their contribution to the growth of the nation (Ong 1999). In this sense, the relentless sense of American individualism Rachel expresses through her professional identity is not only not Chinese enough, but also violates the gendered logic of citizenship.

In response to the dislocation of her Chinese-ness, Rachel stands behind her upbringing as an "immigrant nobody" raised by a poor single mother who migrated to the U.S. from China with no education, yet worked her way up to become a top real estate agent in Flushing, New York. This complicates the tension derived from the Chinese-versus-American binary. That is, Rachel's Americanness is constituted through her struggle on the margin of America's ethnoracial order. What Asian American subjectivity is forged through that struggle? In the U.S., some Asian Americans' reach of socioeconomic parity with whites has helped legitimate a cultural explanation that locates their success in the hardworking ethos of the model minority. By highlighting the striking intergenerational mobility in

Rachel's family history—from the poor Chinese migrant, to the successful entrepreneur in the ethnic economy, to the cosmopolitan academic in a white-dominated institution—*Crazy Rich Asians* seems to celebrate the notion of Asian Americans as a self-made minority that stands to disprove the oppressiveness of structural racism. While the model minority stereotype has been challenged and complicated by the reality of class differentiation and diverging experiences of racialization and migration (see Nguyen 2002; Ong 1999; Tang 2015), its cultural logic continues to be appropriated by some Asian Americans and conservatives to oppose policies such as affirmative action as placing unwarranted emphasis on race (Eligon 2018). The continued deployment of the model minority stereotype to narrate Asian American experience may not only hinder the formation of cross-racial alliance, but also divert us from understanding the relation between the group's heterogeneity and the varied pathways of citizenship formations.

How do we make sense of the diasporic subjectivities in *Crazy Rich Asians*? Applying Ong's framework, we see that Chinese-ness is an unstable category that shifts its meaning within particular modalities of governmentality. Its boundary can be redrawn as regimes of power on the family, the state, and the economy operate to regulate diasporic subjects variously mobilized on the transnational field. Ong's sensitivity to governmentality and human actions in subject-making, and the robust analytical frame attuned to transnational linkages and geopolitical contexts, will remain useful tools to locate Asian diasporic subjects in the ongoing transformations of geopolitical power relations in the Asia Pacific Rim today.

Kuan-Yi Chen holds a PhD in sociology from the CUNY Graduate Center. She currently teaches sociology at the College of Staten Island and can be reached at kuanyichen@gmail.com.

Works Cited

Eligon, John. 2018. "Asian-Americans Face Multiple Fronts in Battle Over Affirmative Action." *New York Times*, August 7, 2018. https://www.nytimes.com/2018/06/16/us/affirmative-action-asian-americans.html.

Nguyen, Viet Thanh. 2002. *Race and Resistance: Literature and Politics in Asian America*. Oxford, UK: Oxford University Press.

Ong, Aihwa. 1999. *Flexible Citizenship: The Cultural Logics of Transnationality*. Durham, NC: Duke University Press.

Rodriguez, Ashley. 2018. "'Crazy Rich Asians' Is the Top-Grossing Romantic Comedy in 10 Years." *Quartz*, October 1, 2018. https://qz.com/1408252/crazy-rich-asians-is-now-the-top-grossing-rom-com-in-10-years/.
Tang, Eric. 2015. *Unsettled: Cambodian Refugees in the New York City Hyperghetto*. Philadelphia: Temple University Press.

PART V. **POETIC WORKS**

If They Come For Us

Fatimah Asghar

these are my people & I find
them on the street & shadow
through any wild all wild
my people my people
a dance of strangers in my blood
the old woman's sari dissolving to wind
bindi a new moon on her forehead
I claim her my kin & sew
the star of her to my breast
the toddler dangling from stroller
hair a fountain of dandelion seed
at the bakery I claim them too
the Sikh uncle at the airport
who apologizes for the pat
down the Muslim man who abandons
his car at the traffic light drops
to his knees at the call of the Azan
& the Muslim man who drinks
good whiskey at the start of maghrib
the lone khala at the park
pairing her kurta with crocs
my people my people I can't be lost
when I see you my compass
is brown & gold & blood
my compass a Muslim teenager

***WSQ: Women's Studies Quarterly* 47: 1 & 2 (Spring/Summer 2019)**

snapback & high-tops gracing
the subway platform
Mashallah I claim them all
my country is made
in my people's image
if they come for you they
come for me too in the dead
of winter a flock of
aunties step out on the sand
their dupattas turn to ocean
a colony of uncles grind their palms
& a thousand jasmines bell the air
my people I follow you like constellations
we hear glass smashing the street
& the nights opening dark
our names this country's wood
for the fire my people my people
the long years we've survived the long
years yet to come I see you map
my sky the light your lantern long
ahead & I follow I follow

Partition

Fatimah Asghar

you're kashmiri until they burn your home. take your orchards. stake a different flag. until no one remembers the road that brings you back. you're indian until they draw a border through punjab. until the british captains spit *paki* as they sip your chai, add so much foam you can't taste home. you're seraiki until your mouth fills with english. you're pakistani until your classmates ask what that is. then you're indian again. or *some kind of spanish.* you speak a language until you don't. until you only recognize it between your auntie's lips. your father was fluent in four languages. you're illiterate in the tongues of your father. your grandfather wrote persian poetry on glasses. maybe. you can't remember. you made it up. someone lied. you're a daughter until they bury your mother. until you're not invited to your father's funeral. you're a virgin until you get too drunk. you're muslim until you're not a virgin. you're pakistani until they start throwing acid. you're muslim until it's too dangerous. you're safe until you're alone. you're american until the towers fall. until there's a border on your back.

WSQ: Women's Studies Quarterly **47: 1 & 2 (Spring/Summer 2019)**

Boy

Fatimah Asghar

what do I do with the boy
who snuck his way inside
me on my childhood playground?

the day other kids shoved
my body into dirt & christened me
he appeared, boy, wicked

feral, swallowing my stride.
the boy who grows my beard
& slaps my face when I wax

my mustache. he was there too
the day on Ben's couch, wearing
my skirt, ranking the girls

in class. again, his legs slamming
concrete, my chest heaving
when we ran from cops

the night they busted the river party
again when I smashed the jellyfish
into the sand & grinded it down

WSQ: Women's Studies Quarterly **47: 1 & 2 (Spring/Summer 2019)**

to a pink useless pulp. together
we watched it throb, open & close
begging for wet. he was there.

I have a boy inside me & I don't know
how to tell people. like when
that man held me down & we said no.

& my boy, my lovely boy
he clawed & bit & cried just like
we were back on the dirt playground

scraped wrists & steady pounding
his eyes wide, until
he stopped making a sound.

Fatimah Asghar is the writer and creator of the Emmy-nominated web series *Brown Girls*. She is the author of *If They Come For Us* and a recipient of a 2017 Ruth Lilly and Dorothy Sargent Rosenberg Poetry Fellowship. In 2017 she was listed on *Forbes*'s 30 Under 30 list.

Anthem for Taking Back

Mai Der Vang

Even after what shrivels

on pillows

are the syllables of a dream

and our braided furies huddle

under porch light

After skyline of lashes

close over our ocular machines

and a lightlessness governs

the way we move our arms

Long from now

how every breath turns out

a copy of the air before and all air

moves through us as cotton

WSQ: Women's Studies Quarterly 47: 1 & 2 (Spring/Summer 2019)

What we heed

after a fluorescence capes

the skin of our early moon

Whatever be the scourge

thumping inside our ears

Ember our wings

out of exile it says ember loudly

all of our furious tellings

They Think Our Killed Ones Cannot Speak to Us

Mai Der Vang

As if to adjourn all
oxygen from the neck

is how they try to take
the voice   As if attempts

to render us pale, ripped
lungless from woke into

wild ash   As if ashes
cannot blink howl testify

with the pulse of their own
tatters   As if hymn and

whistle, hail and pour
We've seen how they

shame the light, stripped
hollow, tearing out

filigrees of stars from
protocols of dust to make

drink a bouquet of venom
sprayed down a constellation's

WSQ: Women's Studies Quarterly 47: 1 & 2 (Spring/Summer 2019)

throat They must be so
earless, as if we've no legs

to kneel We are each
other's memory of the

future forty years from
here arriving at ourselves

by way of the dead
History will not beget

powder will not beget
myth will not make us

into marginalia As ever
possessed by what we

have lost There are no
language barriers in the

afterlife A toxin is a toxin
is a toxin is the manmade

truth is the dead who
leave everything behind

Mai Der Vang is the author of *Afterland*, winner of the 2016 Walt Whitman Award of the Academy of American Poets. The recipient of a Lannan Literary Fellowship, her poetry has appeared in *Poetry*, *Tin House*, and the *American Poetry Review*, among other journals and anthologies.

new world literature, or we'll be together in the end

Minal Hajratwala

my friend paced lower brooklyn all night desperate for a gun.
your lover hooked the gas mask to her chair, inhaled.
hundreds leapt from the red bridge, 1 last swim
before ∞. what pushes us

faster than the speed of life
into the icy breach? the poet told me
everything takes longer than you think
before she slit her toddler's throat, her own.

every celebration: an elegy. every anonymous:
someone's labor squall. machines get numbers,
gods 1,008 epithets. but we, like ghosts or fungi,
deflate, nameless at the end.

Minal Hajratwala is the author of several award-winning books including a poetry collection, *Bountiful Instructions for Enlightenment.* The poem that appears here is part of their manuscript in progress, "Wound Theory." They can be reached at minal@minalhajratwala.com.

WSQ: Women's Studies Quarterly **47: 1 & 2 (Spring/Summer 2019)**

The Cost of Breath

Tanya Ko Hong

Talk about the wood
stacked high in the living room
what it costs
to breathe in my home—
raw wood, oak
so long and thick—
a dead elephant stretched wall to wall

He said to acclimate takes time
and more money—heartwood
slow to open, to breathe—
one week
            became a month
                        became a year

I couldn't breathe
A pile of planks
unusable, forlorn
it had to go.

I want to speak my mind
instead of smile.
Nice girls don't speak
their minds or
question men—

How dear it is
to breathe.

WSQ: Women's Studies Quarterly 47: 1 & 2 (Spring/Summer 2019)

Confronting My Father's Mistress

Tanya Ko Hong

1
Ten years after he died
I phone her.
I could finally call him
bastard
in English.

2
Yeo bo say yo? she said (in Korean).

Can we talk? I asked (in English).

Ung, she said. *I have no customers*
now.

I swallowed.
How did you meet
my father?

I hear the train passing—

Through a friend, she said.

Liar. I heard:
You were engaged.
Your fiancé was in army.
You were hairdresser in

WSQ: Women's Studies Quarterly 47: 1 & 2 (Spring/Summer 2019)

our hometown.
You knew.
My father was married man
rode bicycle baby girl in the basket.
You met my father
at night club.

After that someone sent milk and
bread to my beauty shop every
morning.

You came to our house, I said.
I was only seven.

3
It was children's day in May,
my father's mistress,
dressed in strawberry with
vanilla hat.
My mom served her
tea, in my Dad's old socks
gently tucked my father's ashtray
next to his folded pajamas.
Only the smell of his
Benson & Hedges
remained.

The neighbors watched
excited to see
blood
play their roles.

Your mother invited me—
I am his wife.
These are his children
you must stop.

You didn't, I said.
Now, I am a mother.
A wife.
A woman too.

You told my mother
she makes love to emptiness.

How can I forget my mother losing
her mind. A crazy
moaning animal.
I was fourteen.

Our daughter was born,
she needed her father beside her,
she said.

4
My Father robbed my older sister's
first name, *Jung*
Gave it to *her*
child.
Half of my name
cut off
for her
child.
It felt
(I can't say it).

5
My daughter will be alone
when I die.

6

You stole my dad.
You stole my name.
You stole my childhood.

7

Too much silence
I hear the howls of my Mother's
mothers their buried sorrows
And their thousands of years
han.

I hang up the phone.

Tanya (Hyonhye) Ko Hong, poet, translator and cultural curator, is the author of four books, most recently, *Mother to Myself: A Collection of Poems in Korean*. Her work has appeared in *Rattle, Beloit Poetry Journal, Cultural Weekly, great weather for MEDIA, Korea Central Daily News, The Aeolian Harp Series Anthology*, and more. Her poem "Comfort Woman" received honorable mention in the 2015 Women's National Book Association. Tanya can be reached at tanyakohong@gmail.com.

My father cut my tongue to say . . . (six estranged sonnets)

JinJin Xu

一 / *yi*

The English language spoken in a slight
translation is made foreign to itself—
My professor asked me about the plight
of my birth language, the secret welt
on my tongue, no longer of my mother,
its anchor swallowed whole by a white whale
and dragged toward stories of a creator
who taught me the meaning of betrayal.
I look for familiarity in poetry,
images and sounds written in strange lilts,
the space in between louder, more gravity
than these words built dead on stolen-gold stilts
above an ocean salted with sunken tongues,
concealing the echo of mermaid songs.

二 / *er*

My father took scissors and cut
the flesh that anchored my tongue to the floor
of my mouth, just so I could flip
the slight lilts, say *er* instead of *ah,*
gege instead of *dede,* regurgitate the moons,
geese, wars, loves of dead poets—
Did he know this cut would allow me to say sir
instead of see, here, twenty years after?
Every three years, my tongue grew back,

***WSQ: Women's Studies Quarterly* 47: 1 & 2 (Spring/Summer 2019)**

stubborn, stronger, red like Guan Gong's anger—
and when my words began to slip and slur,
he held my head back with one hand, cut- cut - cut -
This third and final time, I remembered the taste,
a rootedness untethered, gone.

三 / *san*
My friend tells me that diasporic poets writing
away from home are inevitably chained to words
like tongue, land, mother, un-making themselves into
worn tales of homecoming, exile, strangers,
selling themselves for blue-eyed recognition,
building a traitorous home from stolen metaphors,
accents, voices, that echo a no-belonging,
a no-trespassing until the body is left behind.
I am told bilingual children are smarter—
learning at birth to carry two languages,
the first of home, the second of exile,
tucking beneath the tongue, the self.
In between one / *yi* and two / *er*—infinity screeches
silent, beyond the tip of arrival.

四 / *si*
There are words I dare not speak in daylight,
conjuring grammar books, English teachers,
restless in death, waking to seek delight
in my teething grapple of lie vs. lay vs. lain.
Past perfect, they whisper, is beyond the present,
un-grounding me from time, crossing over
tomorrow into yesterday into
what has been and what never will be—
sweeping memories into reversal,
burying mispronunciations inside termite nests,
un-naming the collapse of my existence
until I gingerly misspeak my own name.
Plagued by its aftertaste, I lick
the stomach of an opened honeybee.

五 / *wu*
The lure of the English language
is its alphabetic certainty.
The orderly curve of each letter
contained within the weight of its own breath,
tied by cursive so thin I feel the pull
of an umbilical cord pre-separation,
untangling without law, linking myself
to an ancientness whose life announces
my own—returning me to that first
inkling of sound, a persisting hotness
wrapped like skin, uniting throat with foot,
crying with kicking, sound with being—
I hear the murmur of voices that never become—
syllabic breaths gush half in—half out—

六 / *liu*
To un-erase the number of Death,
I slither *si* between the crevices—wait
for the gods to turn against me with each
tabooed count of *sì* / four and *sĭ* / death,
the fateful rhyme slapped out of my girlhood
lips, so I learned the dead cannot be called
into homes, banished outside the doorway
of language, from the words of the living.
Yet, words un-spoken do not forget—
within the repetition of four, I count to
the slow dying of my namesake,
a poem, Ming Dynasty, un-inherited by English—
JinJin sings TodayToday—a shadow
side by side with itself, my own ringing echo.

JinJin Xu is a writer from Shanghai. Her work moves in between language and memory, poetry and documentary, and has been shown in Berlin, Hanoi, Shanghai, and New York. A former Watson Fellow, she is currently an MFA candidate at NYU, where she received the Lillian Vernon Fellowship. She can be reached at jinjinxxu@gmail.com.

They Found the Body

Nancy Kang

Perhaps we are sojourners all—you, she, and I—
moored like thin-shelled barnacles to the backs of whales,
wreathed with myths of painful creation
and conjugation with animal spirits. There are no miracles
in these cold northern rivers where teens have flicked
their spent smokes.
Our River Jordans are lineups in Times Square,
the sweat of girls at Studio Sutra bowing down
in their hundred-dollar yoga gear and tossing
their arms and ears to shake the gold-plated
elephant and hamsa trinkets. If not adrift,
we are more or less frozen, but there are tadpoles
and sturgeon with secret eyes
moving in the warmth beneath.
Only waterstriders walk on water, buoyed by beds
of soft molecules, but this is in spring.
We are not yet there.
These transparent chains, vibrating, almost sentient,
slide so easily down the throat or up a flower's stem.
Death by water has lost its poetry this time.
Requiescat in pace, friend.
May you calculate the contours of heaven,
which are really just imaginary numbers
and indivisible, like that rind of honeydew that you ate
for the first time at the campus diner and texted me,
This shit is sweet.

***WSQ: Women's Studies Quarterly* 47: 1 & 2 (Spring/Summer 2019)**

Stem and Root

Nancy Kang

Mah ate garlic raw, the peels whispering down his trousers
acrid petals blooming at their night camps
it pinched his nose, punched it like a thief
the brothers called him
stinkbreath,
bulbhead,
medicine mouth,
green stems
and would not sleep
face-to-face as they leaned on stumps
in the northern Sierra Nevada forests,
darkness so pubic-thatch thick that
among the trees they felt like
minnows thrashing in a dry sock net.

Remembering the smooth cool angles of
women left behind (or so they imagined)
one-night, one-week, one-month wives
(mothers, perhaps, now)
in the smoking darkness, lost names;
each star a letter, a joint that aches
in a cosmos of bones and steel ribs, each city a pelvis
where fortune turns amniotic, or rolls in dice, spots like eyes
or flecks of pepper stirred in someone else's
clear hot broth.

***WSQ: Women's Studies Quarterly* 47: 1 & 2 (Spring/Summer 2019)**

He never complained about hands that
couldn't unfurl from a hammer grip, or a
back that quivered during the arching stream
of hot morning water, steaming up
an orange-mossed stone.

He lived one day short of ninety-nine
riding a train aloft in the sky
racing through Vancouver, saltwater city
with a small sack, almost scrotal, red plastic
loaded with good garlic bulbs, fifty cents each,
fastened to his belt with a hiker's shiny hook, as if he were still
scaling mountains, laying
dust tracks, fresh tracks, lost treks
and they still waited for him beyond the gray sea frothed with frost,
seeking again the green stems of youth,
the dependably stubborn
root-stink of life.

North Atlantic

Nancy Kang

And who quenched your thirst
with black sweat turned warm amber
a colder continent's sugar-tit tantrums?
Who beat the cream and bent them over
to bear the sick-churned sweetness
for their clotted cream and beige milk tea?
Whose bare backs were baked brown, stripped red,
made porkish lean n salty for so, so little?
You stand tall, stand down, sit up, crouch,
that we could wear each other's shirts
your skin, my sweat, twisted into
a maple syrup, cane sugar supplication, wrung out, steeped,
swallowed with a tart, spunky lemon rind
waxy sheen, fringed with a burnt-mouth
bitter feeling, suckling a stone pacifier
anchored to the frozen ocean
being reeled in, tasting
gold hooks.

Nancy Kang is Canada Research Chair in Transnational Feminisms and Gender-Based Violence, Tier II, at the University of Manitoba. She coauthored *The Once and Future Muse: The Poetry and Poetics of Rhina P. Espaillat* with Silvio Torres-Saillant, and can be reached at prof.nancykang@gmail.com.

***WSQ: Women's Studies Quarterly* 47: 1 & 2 (Spring/Summer 2019)**

HBO

David Mura

HBO wants to film *Mogadishu, Minnesota* in the towering high-rise
I've lived near for forty years (except my year *Turning Japanese*);

also near the Starbucks I visit daily where Somali men gather
and photos of African coffee fields greet the customers,

and as I write this, Nikko rambles in with Yasmine
who's flying to Qatar to visit relatives and then Mogadishu

and she's never been to Somalia, and I wonder if a film
could catch what goes on between these two,

while in the kitchen Nikko boils water for tea and the TV's on
Cartoon Network and Yasmine glances at *Squidbillies*

and then at me as I shuffle in, disheveled, in sweats,
a middle-aged Sansei who recalls when

my parents headlined a nation's fear and squint-eyed
bucktoothed caricatures cartooned editorials,

and I found no films in childhood about my parents
or Little Tokyo, though I cheered John Wayne mowing down

Japs at Iwo Jima and no, I can't make sense of any of it,
Squidbillies, Mogadishu, Minidoka, HBO.

***WSQ: Women's Studies Quarterly* 47: 1 & 2 (Spring/Summer 2019)**

Appendix: Questions on "A Yellow Ghost"

David Mura

> *Justice is possible only where it is never asked, in the refuge of bad debt, in the fugitive of public strangers not communities, of undercommons not neighborhoods, among those who have been there all along from somewhere. To seek justice through restoration is to return debt to the balance sheet and the balance sheet never balances.*
>
> —*Stefano Harney and Fred Moten,* The Undercommons: Fugitive Planning & Black Study

1. Is the ghost "yellow" because he's Asian or afraid or because white people have declared him "yellow"?

2. Why did the poet delete from an earlier draft the ethnicity and race of the boys?

3. When Kendrick sings "we gonna be all right" are these boys "gonna be all right"?

4. Are they already "all right"? How?

5. What is the problem with writing a poem about boys of color—if these are boys of color—potentially committing a crime?

6. Is there a crime? What is it?

7. What if these boys are not of color?

***WSQ: Women's Studies Quarterly* 47: 1 & 2 (Spring/Summer 2019)**

8. Is the ghost truly dead and haunting the living? Is he haunted by himself? By the boys?

9. Why is he a ghost?

10. How does bad debt enter all this?

11. Who is seeking justice here?

12. Define justice.

Nisei

David Mura

An LA summer. 1940.
My father is forgetting Japanese.
My mother
plays a girl in Seattle taking the hand

of her sister as they board
a streetcar to trolley to the beach
and my father's mowing
the lawn of a Hollywood star

and the days are umber
and burnt orange
and soon rains will overcast Lake
Washington's skies, Santa Ana winds

dust and grit the air
and they're still a decade
from meeting
not as children but freed

prisoners who will step
into a gymnasium in Hyde Park
to a tune by Glen Miller
and spy each other across

WSQ: Women's Studies Quarterly 47: 1 & 2 (Spring/Summer 2019)

the dance floor: And that
is where I enter
—as this glimmer, a shadow,
the teller of their tale.

David Mura's most recent book is *A Stranger's Journey: Race, Identity, and Narrative Craft in Writing*. His four books of poetry are *After We Lost Our Way*, *The Colors of Desire*, *Angels for the Burning*, and *The Last Incantations*. His memoirs are *Turning Japanese* and *Where the Body Meets Memory*; his novel, *Famous Suicides of the Japanese Empire*. He can be reached at davsus@aol.com.

PART VI. **BOOKS IN REVIEW**

Diasporas, Identity, and Agency in Transnational, Migratory, and Arranged Marriages

Marian Aguiar's *Arranging Marriage: Conjugal Agency in the South Asian Diaspora*, Minneapolis: University of Minnesota Press, 2018

Sari K. Ishii's, ed., *Marriage Migration in Asia: Emerging Minorities at the Frontiers of Nation-States*, Singapore: National University of Singapore Press, 2016

Gordon Alley-Young

In their respective works, Marian Aguiar (2018) and Sari K. Ishii (2016) actively complicate the stereotype of the passive, nonconsenting, transnational South Asian bride that dominates the popular Western imagination. Readers of both books are introduced to a diversity of marriage actors, not all of whom are passive, female, or heterosexual. Readers also encounter subjects who use transnational marriage as an economic survival strategy, to perpetrate fraud, to escape prior marital obligations, to satisfy community needs, as well as to pursue love and desire.

With such orientation, Aguiar's monograph and Ishii's edited volume explore agential power within the diasporic marital subjectivities of arranged marriages. In *Arranging Marriage*, Aguiar explores how popular discourses reduce arranged marriage to coercion and conflate agency with individual consent and self-chosen love marriages. Aguiar argues that consent can be a collective experience for South Asian diasporas. Similarly, Caroline Grillot's chapter "Lives in Limbo: Unsuccessful Marriages in Sino-Vietnamese Borderlands" in *Marriage Migration in Asia* presents transnational Vietnamese brides not as victims but as women claiming social identities who "exercise their agency during various acts of resistance" (Ishii, 162). Aguiar and Ishii avoid simplistic constructions of the passive, naive, border-crossing Asian bride by presenting subjects who arrange marriages to ascend social hierarchies, work transnationally, perpetuate tradition, and/or exploit their partners.

Western media depict arranged marriages according to an exploitation narrative and the result is damaging rather than protective. The exploitation

***WSQ: Women's Studies Quarterly* 47: 1 & 2 (Spring/Summer 2019)**

narrative prompts governments to act as benevolent patriarchs as *Marriage Migration in Asia* contributor Ikuya Tokoro describes in "Centre/Periphery Flow Reversed?: Twenty Years of Cross-border Marriages between Philippine Women and Japanese Men" when a Japanese government crackdown on work visas made Filipina entertainers more susceptible to exploitative marriages. Aguiar cites how negative views on arranged marriage in the West have shaped social agencies' and governments' responses to individuals in dysfunctional arranged marriages seeking help. Aguiar argues that social agencies/governments overemphasize the exit strategy (i.e., leaving the marriage) for arranged marriages even though this severs economic and community relationships and overlooks mediation for nonviolent conflicts. Aguiar cites recent UK marriage/immigration laws (e.g., 2007's Forced Marriage [Civil Protection] Act) that heightens the state's patriarchal authority to decide who is allowed to marry or divorce based on its own marriage validity standards. Aguiar notes, "Exit from a marriage often means exit from a family and even from a local community" (131). Marriage exit thus could trap some South Asian women within a foreign low-wage economic system without appropriate social supports. Alternately Aguiar notes community organizations like Southhall Black Sisters who fight government policies that unfairly target South Asian women while supporting vulnerable South Asian women in their homes and in the community.

Scholars Aguiar and Ishii complicate arranged marriage by contextualizing marriage narratives as intersected by community, national, and global socioeconomic forces. Aguiar uses literary studies methods to highlight the narrative construction of meaning. This allows Aguiar to foreground ever-changing meanings of South Asian cultures against attempts to fix the meanings of these cultures/traditions as static across time/space. Including film and literature in her analyses allows Aguiar to highlight how traditional diasporic marriage narratives are both reinforced (e.g., Crespo and Schaefer's 2007 film *Arranged*) and challenged (e.g., Patel and Patel's 2014 film *Meet the Patels*). Aguiar highlights how hidden national and global socioeconomic forces underlie the frequent references made to tradition in popular filmic, literary, and legal discourses of arranged marriage. Aguiar brings the different discourses into conversation, recognizing that they inform each other, and delineates the differing understandings and representations by those both inside of and outside of the South Asian diasporic communities.

These books present women (and men) of the Asian diasporas as active subjects constructing their own identities while resisting erasure both locally and globally. Aguiar's book guides readers "to look at the affective, social, and material forces that weigh on the consenting sexual subject as well as at the decision-making moment" in arranged marriages within South Asian diasporas (228). Aguiar's critical discourse study considers performative and symbolic discourses within fictional and lived experiences of arranged marriage to locate central narratives despite varying historical, gender, class, and global/national contexts. The chapters in Ishii's edited volume of studies cite various contextual factors as enacting multiple-marginalization and erasure on marriage subjects, leading contributor Linda A. Lumayag to argue in "Marriage 'During' Work Migration: Lived Experiences of Filipino Marriage Migrants in Malaysia" that "international marriage as an area of concern may be too narrow given the complex issues and challenges surrounding marital relationships" (98).

The studies in Ishii's book consider conjugal, socioeconomic, and legal questions within studies of culturally diverse lived experiences of marriage, but not filmic or literary texts as Aguiar does. Ishii's ten edited chapters represent a multiplicity of experiences that popular cultural discourses fail to capture. Ishii's volume reminds us that a nation's socioeconomic health is no guarantee that a marriage migrant will avoid marginalization. Marginalization can result from marriage migrations from north to south and vice versa. Even transnational marriages occurring in developed and affluent nations in Asia cannot guarantee individuals the rights to legally marry and start a family. These are rights that *Marriage Migration in Asia* contributor Chatchai Chetsumon, in "Legal Problems of Marriage between Irregular Workers from Myanmar and Thai Nationals in Thailand," points to in the UN Universal Declaration of Human Rights that are routinely denied to so-called "stateless" ethnic minorities in Asia (e.g., the Rohingya in Myanmar). Ishii also gives more visibility to Muslim subjects and the unique factors that Muslim marriages might bring in certain contexts (e.g., provisions allowing for multiple legal marriages or divorces). Critical readers will, however, want more information from both authors on how the post-9/11 climate made transnational, migratory, and arranged marriages more difficult for Muslim subjects.

Because it analyzes texts including popular films and novels, Aguiar's study could be dismissed by some critics as a superficial treatment of the topic of transnational arranged marriage. However, such a critique would risk discounting how heavily people rely on the popular imagination when negotiating their relationships to other sociocultural groups. Aguiar notes that Western courts (e.g., in the UK) rely on popular cultural assumptions of South Asian cultures when ruling on the legitimacy of arranged marriage. For instance, a British judge cited "ancient eastern established cultural and religious ethics" clashing with "what these days passes as [twenty-first-century Western] culture" in his ruling on a petition to end an arranged marriage (Aguiar 78). Aguiar notes that the judge in this example might understand South Asian culture via media discourses that present South Asian culture as static, unchanged over centuries, rather than as a cultural insider who might recognize how such traditions can and do change over time.

Aguiar asserts that she is not opposed to arranged marriage but acknowledges that it is used to curtail choice and perpetuate domestic violence. Aguiar avoids prescribing solutions, noting that change will come from activists already working within diasporic communities. Aguiar avoids cultural relativism by taking different perspectives and by focusing analysis on different factors depending on whether a text being analyzed comes from within or outside of the South Asian communities it represents. For instance, when Aguiar critiques how Western cultures promote sensationalized arranged-marriage memoirs to situate violence and misogyny as specifically indicative of South Asian cultures, she is widening our lens for us to see how larger forces such as globalization and transnational economics, and thus Western cultures, are also implicated in creating these social problems. Similarly, when she critically reads "ladki-lit" (i.e., South Asian women's marriage fiction), she notes that while the books offer a positive view of arranged marriage that blends South Asian and Western romance genres, they also tend to construct protagonists as being transnational, upwardly mobile, and becoming culturally authentic (i.e., specifically through the practice of arranged marriage). Aguiar thus critiques both Western and Eastern literatures for cultural reductionism by making arranged marriage either emblematic of domestic violence or indicative of cultural authenticity, respectively.

The studies that make up Ishii's work employ various methodological approaches including surveys, interviews (structured and unstructured, often with snowball sampling), case studies, and/or fieldwork. Ishii's edited volume benefits from drawing upon the perspectives of different researchers who study diasporic populations from across Asia (i.e., not just migrations of South Asians to the west or northern Asia). However, critics could question the dated nature of some of the sample data given the volume's 2016 publication date. For example, one chapter uses data collected from 1998 to 2001 while another chapter does not specify data collection dates. Some might take this to imply that subjects and cultural meanings remain fixed across time periods for these researchers of Asia, as this is a key criticism Aguiar makes of Western discourses on South Asian cultures and diasporas. Alternately several works in Ishii's volume explore migratory and transnational marriage from perspectives that recognize the family as an interconnected system (Aguiar does this as well), and this is particularly effective for discussing cultures and diasporas that emphasize collectivism and community. For instance, *Marriage Migration in Asia* contributor Caesar Dealwis's research in "Assimilation of the Descendants of Caucasian Muslims in Sarawak, Malaysia" and Hien Ahn Le's research in "Lives of Mixed Vietnamese-Korean Children in Vietnam" examine how the children produced of transnational and migratory marriages reproduce, magnify, transform, and/or reinscribe the cultural privilege and/or marginalization passed down to them through the primary marriage relationship in unexpected ways. These researchers also consider how community members then receive children's resulting new social identities.

As an queer scholar, one of my key foci when reviewing these works was making queer Asian experiences of migratory, diasporic, and arranged marriage visible. Aguiar gives more attention to LGBTQIA+ relationships in her analysis of South Asian popular culture in her inclusion of texts like British-Pakistani playwright Ayub Khan-Din's play *East Is East* and Indo-Canadian filmmaker Deepa Mehta's controversial film *Fire* to make the point that homosexual relationships are often, but not always (i.e., she cites the emergence of same-sex marriage ads on Indian marriage websites), positioned as antithetical to marriage in South Asian diasporic marriage texts. Aguiar argues, "Sita and Radha (the protagonists of *Fire*) could have never themselves had an arranged marriage, not just because they are the same sex but because their relationship, as Mehta presents it, is premised on a fulfillment of individual desire rather than being a part of this intricate social network" (161). Aguiar's comment underscores, as many contributors in Ishii's edited volume contend, that these books are not simply studying transnational/diasporic marriages but also the innumerable and multifaceted socioeconomic and relational contracts that come along with these marriages.

In Ishii's collection I carefully read between the lines to find LGBTQIA+ subjectivity when reading about subjects who married transnationally to secure employment or a better position but had little or no conjugal involvement. Do some of these subjects have other physical outlets for their (possibly queer) desire? I started asking this question when reading *Marriage Migration in Asia* contributor Linda A. Lumayag's "Marriage 'During' Work Migration: Lived Experiences of Filipino Marriage Migrants in Malaysia" about how subjects maintain both love and convenience marriages to manage personal and familial needs (e.g., Maricel and Asuncion leave husbands and children behind in the Philippines while pursuing work and new marriages in Malaysia). Lumayag notes, "Maricel was a very enterprising woman," as she is able to balance the economic responsibilities and relationships of two households, and observes how Asuncion supported her common-law husband even in death as she covered all of his funeral expenses (88). These examples captured my attention as a reader looking for LGBTQIA+ subjects because they speak to the intricacies of negotiating marriage for the heterosexual cultural majority, leaving me to believe that the reality for queer subjects is just as, and likely more, complex. When heterosexual subjects in *Marriage Migration in Asia* contributor chapters give voice to fraudulent and illegal marriage experiences but queer voices are silent, then it reifies the greater marginalization faced by these subjectivities.

In reflecting on these two books I am reminded again of the argument made by *Marriage Migration in Asia* contributor Lumayag, contending that "international marriage as an area of concern may be too narrow given the complex issues and challenges surrounding marital relationships" (98). This argument is reflected in both the books discussed in this essay. In discussing the challenges that subjects face, both books consistently speak to greater structures at work behind the static image of the married couple. In several cases analyzed in both works, the marriage is not what is marginalizing the individual(s). Instead the barrier may be posed by immigration policies that are xenophobic and/or sexist in wanting to limit their identities in their new countries to being housewives but not workers, workers but not brides, or as people who are not recognized as workers or spouses by either their home or adopted nations. This focus on xenophobic laws as a barrier does not deny the violence and lack of agency that can accompany transnational, migratory, and arranged marriages for women of the Asian diasporas. However, Aguiar reminds us that even violence and lack of agency are representative of more extensive historical (i.e., colonial legacies of the economic and sexual exploitation of Asian women) and social forces (i.e., lack of culturally responsive social supports for transnational marriages in the West). Both books speak to critically minded scholars approaching future studies of transnational, migratory, and arranged marriage with perspectives informed by systematic thinking. These are scholars who engage in cross-disciplinary approaches while examining the symbolic and the statistical and the theoretical along with the experiential to understand this ever-evolving sociocultural phenomenon.

Gordon Alley-Young is a professor of speech communication at Kingsborough Community College, City University of New York. He received a PhD in speech communication from Southern Illinois University. He is currently working on a critical cultural study of animated superhero *The Burqa Avenger* to be published in an edited volume in 2019. He can be reached at gordon.young@kbcc.cuny.edu.

PART VII. **ALERTS AND PROVOCATIONS**

Remembering Meena Alexander

Michelle Yasmine Valladares

> *Whether they spring from memory, history, that which lives in the world, or that which lives chiefly in the imagination, the poems . . . lead us into the presence of stark, unmitigated, uncontestable beauty—a beauty capable of swallowing us whole.*
>
> —*Tracy K. Smith, review of* Birthplace with Buried Stones *by Meena Alexander*

1.

In March 2017 I had the privilege to read with Meena Alexander and other CUNY (City University of New York) poets for "Women's Words: Solidarity in Struggle," an event organized by our faculty union PSC-CUNY. Meena, Kimiko Hahn, and I shared a table on one side of the podium. Before we began, Meena spilled her cup of coffee and I jumped to find paper towels to wipe the spill. She thanked me and whispered that she was not herself since the chemo. I would not have suspected she was ill. In that golden, afternoon light, she was radiant like her poems. We exchanged a few emails following the reading, to make plans to meet and discuss the intersections in our lives.

I reminded her that we met twenty years ago for tea at her apartment. I was invited by her niece, the artist Ayisha Abraham. I was a thirtysomething, independent filmmaker, and thrilled to meet an Indian woman poet, scholar, and literature professor. Years later, I would switch from producing films to writing and teaching. Years later, I find myself, an Indian, immigrant, woman poet, indebted to Alexander. Her art and scholarship

WSQ: Women's Studies Quarterly **47: 1 & 2 (Spring/Summer 2019)**

on dislocation/migration/postcolonial aesthetics and identity flowed into the stream of discourse on voices from the South Asian diaspora. Alexander's experience spoke to me of a sisterhood of the tongues we shared, since I made a similar journey in childhood from being born in India, raised in Kuwait, and later immigrating to the U.S., surrounded by Arabic, Hindi, and English.

It was a shock to discover that she died this past November at sixty-seven, because my strongest impression of Meena Alexander in the handful of times I met her or heard her speak at conferences and readings was her keen appetite, ambition, and curiosity. And I naively believed these traits would keep her with us for many more years.

2.

> *The poems are a sustained elegy for homelessness, for the displacement at the heart of human life.*
>
> —*Eavan Boland, review of* Quickly Changing River *by Meena Alexander*

In my class Reading/Writing the Asian American Diaspora, I teach several essays from *Fault Lines*, Alexander's memoir published in 1993. These essays document the details of Alexander's exterior journey but not in a linear narrative. Instead they are woven into meditations on spatiality, geography, and temporality created by the experience of dislocation and migration. The intriguing outline of her exterior journey—born in Allahabad, India; moved with her family at age five to Khartoum, Sudan; studied at the University of Khartoum; earned a PhD at the University of Nottingham in England; returned to India to work until she met her future husband, historian David Lelyveld; immigrated to the U.S., settled in New York City, and raised two children—are linked together by the lyrical interiority of memory, landscape, and loss. Her first and one of the more important losses alluded to is the childhood home in Tiruvalla, a small town in Kerala on the west coast of India. Here the beloved grandfather, relatives, servants, land, and trees are the anchors of memory. Here is the home of the Mar Thoma Syrian Church, in which Alexander's family plays a prominent role. When she arrived in New York City, she writes in "Mirror of Ink,"

> My two worlds, present and past, were torn apart, and I was the fault line, the crack that marked the dislocation. (Alexander 1993, 15)

This is Alexander's invention and contribution to the way in which loss of home and country split the migrant/immigrant. Fault lines mark dislocation, but also warn of greater impending disasters.

In the same essay, Alexander reinvented herself:

> I wanted to be more than a tympanum, a pale, vibrating thing that marked out the boundaries between worlds. More than a mere line in the dry earth. I wanted to give voice to my flesh, to learn to live as a woman. To do that, I had to spit out the stones that were in my mouth. I had to become a ghost, enter my own flesh. (Alexander 1993, 16)

This is the destination of the writer/seer reborn in her metaphors to recontextualize experience. The weight of the expectations of women in her family and culture, and of South Asian women of a certain generation, was marked. A line drawn that Alexander deliberately stepped over and in doing so invented a new kind of womanhood and poetic voice. For the immigrant, artist of color who is invisible—a ghost in America—Alexander proposed reentry in a new identity. Poetry with its transmutation and transformation of images and ideas was her perfect vehicle:

> Sometimes I think of the English language as the pale skin that has covered my flesh, the broken parts of my world. In order to free my face, in order to appear, I have had to use my teeth and nails, I have had to tear that fine skin, to speak out my discrepant otherness. (Alexander 1993, 73)

Despite her fluency in several languages and her love for her mother tongue, Malayalam, she established herself as a writer in English due to circumstance and colonization in both India and Sudan. At fifteen she changed her name to Meena from her baptized name of Mary Elizabeth. In Khartoum while at university, her first published poems written in English were published in Arabic. Despite writing in the colonizer's tongue, Alexander came to treasure the nuances of the languages of her childhood, Malayalam and Arabic:

> I maintained an immediacy of sound and sense in those two great languages of my childhood years that enabled me to dissolve and dissipate, if only in a partial paradoxical fashion, the canonical burden of British English. And so a curious species of linguistic decolonization took place for me, in which my own, often unspoken sense of femaleness played a great part. I set the hierarchies, the scripts aside, and let the treasured orality flow over me. (Alexander 1993, 119)

She encountered resistance to this reinvention of experience in English from the academy, as an Asian American writer, feminist, and poet of color. In the essay "Crossing Borders" she tells the story of a poetry reading she organized in 1990 for the Fourth International Interdisciplinary Congress of Women at Hunter College. She invited the poets Kamala Das from India, Claribel Alegría from Nicaragua, and Audre Lorde from the U.S., and discovered that in one of the printed programs the three names were missing. Audre Lorde responded, "They cannot bear us, Meena . . . those women of color who talk out" (Alexander 1993, 74).

In "Real Places or How Sense Fragments: Thoughts on Ethnicity and the Writing of Poetry," Alexander acknowledged/named the experience of the minority, immigrant writer in America. And it is here that she related her strategies of survival as a writer.

> Everything that comes to me is hyphenated. A woman poet, a women poet of color, a South Indian woman poet, who makes up lines in English, a postcolonial language, as she waits for the red light to change on Broadway. A Third World woman poet who takes as her right the inner city of Manhattan, making up poems about the hellhole of the subway line, the burnt-out blocks so close to home on the Upper West Side, finding there, news of the world. (Alexander 1993, 193)

Alexander, who was tutored to speak and write perfectly in British English by a Scottish teacher in Khartoum, distinguished the subtle differences between two types of colonization:

> There is a violence in the very language, American English, that we have to face, even as we work to make it ours, decolonize it so that it will express the truth of bodies beaten and banned. After all, for such as we are the territories are not free. The world is not open. That endless space, the

> emptiness of the American sublime is worse than a lie. It does ceaseless damage to the imagination. (Alexander 1993, 199)

In a sequence of paragraphs at the end of the essay Alexander dismantled what we perceive as ethnicity and the work of the "ethnic poet." These are kaleidoscopic insights and revelations:

> My ethnicity as an Indian American or, in broader terms, an Asian American, the gateway it seems to me now to a life in letters, depends upon, indeed requires, a resolute fracturing of sense. (Alexander 1993, 201)
>
> Ethnicity for such as I am comes into being as a pressure, a violence from within that resists such fracturing. It is and it is not fictive. It rests on the unknown that seizes you from behind as darkness. (Alexander 1993, 202)
>
> The bigger hunk of what needs to be told . . . comes with rage, with the overt acknowledgement of the nature of injustice. The struggle for social justice, for human dignity, is for each of us. Like ethnicity, like the labor of poetry, it is larger than any single person or any single voice. . . . It is shaped by forces that well up out of us, chaotic, immensely powerful forces that disorder the brittle boundary lines we create, turn us towards a light, a truth, whose immensity, far from being mystical . . . casts all our actions into relief, etches our lines into art. (Alexander 1993, 203)

3.

> *Meena Alexander sings of countries, foreign and familiar, places where the heart and spirit live, and places for which one needs a passport and visas. Her voice guides us faraway and back home.*
>
> —*Maxine Hong Kingston, review of* Raw Silk by *Meena Alexander*

While Alexander was prolific and published numerous volumes of poetry, two novels, a memoir, and many essays, she will be remembered as a poet. Her poems are lyrical and elegiac, and weave her travels, Rumi, Lorca, Gandhi, conversations, myths, and goddesses into lines that draw us into the poet's fierce gaze of the world. The reader travels in an Alexander poem, whether by boat, plane, or bike, or by memory, a child's dream, or a cry.

Amma calls through the monsoon wind—
Come, Meena, pick up your sari hem
The snails mustn't catch in it,
If you go too slow into the next world
You'll stumble over a brawl of fireflies,
(Alexander 2008, 9)

In her address to the Yale Political Union in 2013, Alexander attempted to answer the question "What Use Is Poetry?":

> I think of the invisible archive that each of us bears within, a deeply personal ingathering of sights and sounds and scents and bits of the sometimes ruined materiality that memory allots—and perhaps this is another way of thinking about the coruscating flow of the inner life that gives meaning to our existence, all that comes up when we dare to say "I." And surely this is the province of poetry.

Using incantation, the poet investigated questions of being and the power of language. Her poems discover the "I" and ultimately this search leads the reader away from the ego to a larger sense of self which includes each woman's potential as Goddess.

A firefly threads my eye
Who am I?
(Alexander 2004, 28)

I am Sita and Iphigenia, Demeter and Draupadi
I am not fit for burning.
(Alexander 2004, 6)

Tracy K. Smith, the twenty-second Poet Laureate of the United States, writes about the poems in Alexander's *Birthplace with Buried Stones* (2013):

> . . . they also prove something unsettling about the prevalence and necessity of all that is not beauty: the violent evidence of history, the inescapable reality of death.

Poetry answers the questions we are not prepared for. The shadow of death is prevalent in Alexander's poems whether in the conversation she extended to poets living and dead, but also in her acknowledgement of life's cruelty. In this second stanza from "Cantata for a Riderless Horse," included her last book, *Birthplace with Buried Stones,* the poet was prescient.

> We like to think of the inner life
> As the cause of things.
>
> One might as well say that the happiness
> Of Sanskrit is the cause of speech
>
> As Novalis did when he was very young.
> Was he watching death round the corner,
>
> Past the broken barn on the mountainside
> With the tangle of blue flowers no one else noticed?
>
> Death in the shape of an old horse
> Tied to a laurel tree,
>
> (Alexander 2013, 35)

During her life, Meena Alexander appeared as poetic mentor, heroine, and activist doing important work on the frontlines of the literary world by delineating the "fault lines" and creating a precious archive of her own imaginings. She mapped the territory that I would venture into, hoping for a chance encounter to continue the conversation initiated by her poems and essays. For me, she was the first writer to peel the layers of the invisible archive that we inherit as women writers of color. We who occupy the space of dislocation beautifully rendered in Meena Alexander's writing owe her a great debt. She made my existence meaningful and my work possible. From our diaspora, she remains one of the pioneers to journey as the "hyphenated poet" and earn her place in American letters. She will be missed.

Michelle Yasmine Valladares is director of the MFA Program in Creative Writing at the City College of New York, CUNY. Her writing and research include poetry, the Asian American diaspora, and Native American film. In her previous life, she was an independent film producer. She can be reached at mvalladares@ccny.cuny.edu.

Works Cited

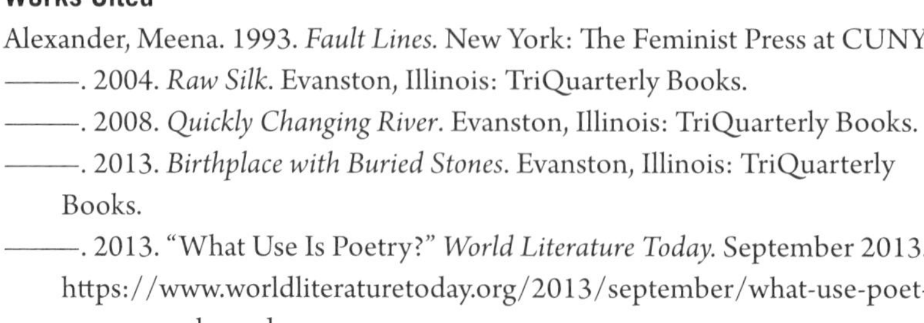

Alexander, Meena. 1993. *Fault Lines.* New York: The Feminist Press at CUNY.

———. 2004. *Raw Silk.* Evanston, Illinois: TriQuarterly Books.

———. 2008. *Quickly Changing River.* Evanston, Illinois: TriQuarterly Books.

———. 2013. *Birthplace with Buried Stones.* Evanston, Illinois: TriQuarterly Books.

———. 2013. "What Use Is Poetry?" *World Literature Today.* September 2013. https://www.worldliteraturetoday.org/2013/september/what-use-poetry-meena-alexander.